Musical Understandings

Musical Understandings and Other Essays on the Philosophy of Music

Stephen Davies

OXFORD
UNIVERSITY PRESS

Great Clarendon Street, Oxford OX2 6DP

Oxford University Press is a department of the University of Oxford.
It furthers the University's objective of excellence in research, scholarship,
and education by publishing worldwide in

Oxford New York

Auckland Cape Town Dar es Salaam Hong Kong Karachi
Kuala Lumpur Madrid Melbourne Mexico City Nairobi
New Delhi Shanghai Taipei Toronto

With offices in

Argentina Austria Brazil Chile Czech Republic France Greece
Guatemala Hungary Italy Japan Poland Portugal Singapore
South Korea Switzerland Thailand Turkey Ukraine Vietnam

Oxford is a registered trade mark of Oxford University Press
in the UK and in certain other countries

Published in the United States
by Oxford University Press Inc., New York

© in this volume Stephen Davies 2011

The moral rights of the authors have been asserted
Database right Oxford University Press (maker)

First published 2011

All rights reserved. No part of this publication may be reproduced,
stored in a retrieval system, or transmitted, in any form or by any means,
without the prior permission in writing of Oxford University Press,
or as expressly permitted by law, or under terms agreed with the appropriate
reprographics rights organization. Enquiries concerning reproduction
outside the scope of the above should be sent to the Rights Department,
Oxford University Press, at the address above

You must not circulate this book in any other binding or cover
and you must impose this same condition on any acquirer

British Library Cataloguing in Publication Data

Data available

Library of Congress Cataloging in Publication Data

Data available

Typeset by SPI Publisher Services, Pondichery, India
Printed in Great Britain
on acid-free paper by
MPG Books Group, Bodmin and King's Lynn

ISBN 978–0–19–960877–5

10 9 8 7 6 5 4 3 2 1

Contents

Introduction	1
1. Artistic Expression and the Hard Case of Pure Music	7
2. Music and Metaphor	21
3. Cross-cultural Musical Expressiveness: Theory and the Empirical Program	34
4. Emotional Contagion from Music to Listener	47
5. Once Again, This Time with Feeling	66
6. Musical Meaning in a Broader Perspective	71
7. Musical Understandings	88
8. The Experience of Music	129
9. *Così*'s Canon Quartet	140
10. Perceiving Melodies	151
11. Musical Colors and Timbral Sonicism	160
12. Versions of Musical Works and Literary Translations	177
13. Profundity in Instrumental Music	188
References	200
Index	215

Introduction

The essays in this book cover a spread of topics in the philosophy of music: the expression of emotion in music and the listener's response to this (Chapters 1 to 4), the listener's, performer's, analyst's, and composer's perception and understanding of music (Chapters 5 to 10), the ontology of musical works (Chapters 11 and 12), and musical profundity (Chapter 13). As is made apparent in the following summary, there are many connections and common issues linking these various topics.

Some of the material is new. In a number of cases, related articles have been combined and adapted, thereby allowing a more comprehensive, unified treatment of the issues. The centerpiece of the book is the long Chapter 7, the majority of which is published in English for the first time here.

★★★★

I have long been interested in the expression of emotion in music, which is the topic addressed in Chapters 1 and 2. When they think about the topic, many people start with the observation that music cannot literally express emotion, because, being insentient, it cannot experience emotion. Two conclusions are regularly thought to follow from this truism. Attributions of emotion to music—such as, 'the slow movement of Beethoven's *Eroica* is sad'—must be metaphorical. Second, if we are not to abandon the idea that music expresses emotion, we should be able to find someone who experiences the emotion that, somehow, finds expression in the music. The candidates are the composer, the performer, and the listener. Or alternatively, a currently popular position among philosophers of music is that we hypothesize a persona as existing in and controlling the music, which is then heard as expressing the persona's feelings. In Chapter 1, I argue against these attempts to explain the music's expressiveness by connecting it to emotions felt by composers, listeners, and hypothetical personas.

Moreover, I think the two conclusions just mentioned are false. My positive account of how music is expressive makes apparent why this is so. We can be interested in the outward show of emotion, what I call 'emotion characteristics in appearances,' without regard to felt emotions. For instance, I might say that someone cuts a sad figure, and in this way refer to his appearance, without believing he feels as he looks. And it is not only to sentient creatures that we attribute emotion characteristics. The bearing of a tree might be described as proud because it resembles how proud-looking people carry themselves. I think that when music is heard as expressive of emotion, this is because we experience its movement as similar to human comportments that present appearances stamped with expressive character. Because the focus is on emotions worn by appearances but not necessarily felt, there is no need to find someone who, through their connection with the music, feels the emotion the music expresses. In addition, because this use of emotion-words to describe appearances is standardly listed in dictionaries, I see no reason to regard the usage as metaphorical. Admittedly, there is an extension from the primary case, in which such words refer to affective experiences, but something close to the primary meaning is present in the new use, with which it is polysemously connected.

One feature that distinguishes metaphor and homonymy (as when a word, such as 'bank,' has more than one meaning) from polysemy (as when a word, such as 'high,' seemingly retains its meaning across many domains: height, number, temperature, salary, and musical pitch) is that the same polysemous uses tend to occur in different languages. And indeed, people of many different cultures regard music as expressive of emotion. Inevitably, this invites one to consider the extent to which musical expressiveness is cross-culturally recognizable. In Chapter 3, I first explore the theoretical background to this question and outline the kind of research program that might test it. I then review the experimental work done already by psychologists on the topic. Though their results are suggestive, I conclude that, at this stage, the empirical data are so limited and the methodologies so frequently compromised that it is not possible to settle the question.

My interest in the work of psychologists and cognitive scientists on music is not confined to Chapter 3. It is also a major theme in Chapters 4, 10, and 11. In my view, philosophers need to inform their theorizing with relevant empirical data, rather than relying exclusively on their intuitions and personal experience. At the same time, however, they need not uncritically accept all that is presented as scientific fact. In defending my views, I sometimes cite the work of psychologists, but on other occasions I also reject or question the findings they sometimes draw from their work.

Chapter 4 continues the discussion of music and emotion, considering the listener's reaction to music's expressiveness. A common response to music's expressiveness is one that mirrors it; sad music is liable to make people sad and happy music to cheer them up. One respect in which this response is philosophically interesting I argue, is that it provides a counterexample to the cognitive theory of the emotions. According to this theory, emotions are to be characterized primarily in terms of the beliefs that go with them: if I fear for myself I must believe that something threatens me or my interests; if I envy someone I must believe they have something I do not have and I must desire to possess that thing. By contrast, when I am saddened by sad music I usually do not believe of it what would normally make it a fit object for sadness: that it is unfortunate or regrettable. The mirroring response is aroused via a kind of affective contagion, I claim. In defending my view against some recent criticisms, I go on to distinguish attentional from non-attentional musical contagion. The listener focuses on the music and its expressive character in the first case, whereas in the second she might be unaware of background music and of its effects on her. Psychologists who have studied music-to-listener emotional contagion typically consider the non-attentional type. And their models of human face-to-face emotional contagion tend to reduce to stories about the causal processes involved. Attentional musical contagion cannot involve the same causal routes, but that is a reason for seeking more abstract models of the phenomenon, not for doubting that the listener's reaction to music often involves affective osmosis.

Chapter 5 turns to the performer's role in communicating what the music expresses. I am skeptical that the performer arouses the appropriate emotion within herself or simulates doing so. Rather she plays the notes as written and crafts her interpretation to sculpt the expressive potential present in those notes. We talk of the importance of the performer's feeling the music not because playing involves emotion but rather because the kind of skill that makes sensitive playing possible is often practical and inarticulable.

The wider topic of how music is to be understood is first broached in Chapter 6, which is the only chapter to have been co-authored. The primary aim is to distinguish various approaches to musical meaning adopted by the listener. We begin with formal meaning, which involves the listener's tracking the structure of the music. We oppose accounts that model this process on that of grasping linguistic or semiological meaning. The formal progress of music is best explained in terms of reasons like those that justify human actions. What we call 'experiential formal meaning' is an even more fundamental, non-discursive kind of meaning in music, experienced as the pattern of tension and release generated by the unfolding of the musical fabric. 'Meaning-for-the-subject' concerns the personal, idiosyncratic significance music can possess for the individual listener. 'Meaning-for-us' is the shared meaning music has more widely for all human beings.

The keystone for this collection is the long Chapter 7, which extends the discussion of musical understanding to take in, as well as the listener, the performer, analyst, and composer. In the first place the listener has to locate the work that is her target among all the sounds contiguous with it, including simultaneous soundings of other works. And she must hear the work as music: for instance, she hears the closure in a cadence, recognizes a melody when it is repeated, is aware of the expressive vivaciousness of an upbeat phrase. This level of comprehension is attained via cultural absorption, without formal training, but if she wishes to refine her response to music the listener is likely to take instruction, for instance, by reading about music's history. As well, she will learn to distinguish what is attributable to the work and what to the performer's interpretation of it. I argue (against Jerrold Levinson) that the listener's understanding should go beyond noting the coherence of its progress moment-to-moment to encompass a concern for its broader structure. And I reject the view (presented by Mark DeBellis) that ear training necessarily affords a kind of understanding and appreciation that is otherwise unattainable.

The skilled musician who would perform a work must begin by correctly identifying the composer's work-specifying instructions. If the work is notated, she must understand the conventions for reading the notation and for translating this into sound. These conventions have changed often over the years, so to identify the conventions relevant to playing her target work, her understanding must be historically informed. The performer then must decide what degree of authenticity to pursue. If she is self-conscious in her choice of a manner of interpreting the work, she will plan how to handle the many microstructural details and macrostructural emphases that are her prerogative. I maintain, however, that performance always results in interpretation, whether or not that interpretation is planned: the performance interpretation of a work is the overall expressive and structural vision that emerges from the work's complete performance. I reject linguistic models of performance—ones comparing the performer with someone quoting another's words, affirming what she quotes, or providing a linguistic translation of another's words—in favor of stressing the creative aspects of interpretation that are integral to works made specifically for performance. Accordingly, performance interpretations are quite distinct from the music critic's after-the-fact, descriptive interpretation of the work or performance. Though many of the musician's interpretative acts are consciously controlled, a great deal of music making is based on practical know-how some of which may be so basic as to be cognitively impenetrable.

Music analysis aims primarily to uncover (a) the basis of effects (such as unity, closure, instability, etc.) experienced in the music, (b) how the music is (or might have been) put together, and/or (c) the process of composition. One philosophically interesting debate is about the hearability of the relations analysts dig out; many theorists insist that only those relations that can be heard (by expert listeners aware of the analysis) to affect the audible musical surface can be characterized as significant. I disagree. It is not uncommon for composers to adopt compositional procedures that direct the process of composition and that cannot be heard (and are not intended to be heard). Consider, for example, the complex rhythmic and pitch series that provide the foundations for isorhythmic motets of the fourteenth century. And it might be impossible to hear the underlying musical causes of surface effects such as unity, yet be possible to detect them doing their work in other ways, perhaps via neurological or other physiological measures.

Composing may be a practical skill and as such could be practised without theoretical training. Usually, though, it involves a reflective process and a great deal of propositional background knowledge. For instance, someone who composes for an orchestra typically needs to be notationally literate and to know what is involved in playing many kinds of musical instruments. Therefore, reference to the composer's intentions is almost always useful in indicating how her work is best to be approached, how it functions, and what is in it, though her work can include effects or levels of meaning that she did not intend. Her account of her work provides an ideal introduction, if not the last word, to understanding her music. Rather than describing her piece, the composer might convey her vision of it via her performance of it. But as

I emphasized above, any sufficiently accurate performance delivers, as well as the work, an interpretation of that work. Interpretative detail exemplified in the composer's performance is recommendatory only.

Further aspects of the listener's experience, ones not previously discussed, are considered in Chapter 8. For instance, I argue there that music does not convey ineffable truths, though, like all perceptually grounded experience, that of music is indescribably rich in its specificity. I also suggest that our historical remove from music does not mean we cannot experience it in ways relevantly similar to those in which the composer's contemporaries did. Just as we make appropriate adjustments in moving from jazz to rock or from blues to reggae, we can (and should) adjust our musical expectations when we listen to Mozart or Mahler. I then ask if we are motivated to listen to music for pleasure and propose that this is the case provided we construe the pleasure involved as nearer love than enjoyment. If listening to music has become part of a person's identity and selfhood, the suggestion that she listens for the sake of enjoyment does not come near to indicating the importance of music in her life. I go on to extol the virtues of listening to many different performances of a given piece, not because by doing so we are more likely to encounter the one, ideal performance but rather because this brings out the many-faceted aspects a work can present, including ones that could not jointly be reconciled in any single rendition. We can also re-hear a given performance that has been recorded. As a result, recorded performances lend themselves to more subtly nuanced interpretations than are appropriate to the live situation.

Chapter 9 involves a change of gear: I concentrate on a particular moment in a particular work, the final act quartet in Mozart's opera buffa, *Così fan tutte*. I argue that in his late operas Mozart sets a dramatic form against the surface structure that is conventional for such works and that he draws attention to this dramatic form in special musical moments. This quartet is a case in point. Gugliemo's refusal to take the melody the others have shared leaves him irreducibly an individual within the structure. This reveals in microcosm the subject animating the opera, which sets against the inescapable autonomy of the individual the common need for mutual acceptance and recognition.

The perception of melodies is compared with the visual recognition of individuals and objects in Chapter 10, which draws on work in the psychology of perception. Observers can identify objects presented at different orientations and they can frequently identify an item as the same despite changes in its appearance, for example by ageing. I argue that these cases are paralleled in music listening. Thematic ideas can (sometimes, but not inevitably) be recognized when they are inverted or played backwards. More importantly, within music it is crucial that various musical statements, including ones that differ in their intervallic sequence, are sometimes recognized as versions of a single theme.

Chapter 11 takes the comparison with vision in a different direction. I argue that the perception and treatment of color in visual art is echoed in music by the use of instrumental timbre or 'color,' as it is called. By appealing to research on the psychology of perception, I draw out the implications of the importance of instrumental color for an appropriate ontological characterization of musical works. In many works, timbre plays a work-identifying role and what is required in the correct realization of those works is that the appropriate timbres are realized using the instruments for which the composer wrote, and not that they are electronically synthesized. Nevertheless, instrumental color became a necessary part of musical works only under particular historical conditions, including the standardization of musical instruments, their widespread availability, and so on. Earlier, when convention and the default circumstances made it impossible for composers to require what performance-means could be employed in realizing their works, instrumental color was more a feature of the performance than a constituent of the work performed.

Music ontology also features in Chapter 12 in which I discuss the awkward fact that composers sometimes return to their finished works and change them in ways that should affect their identity. For example, when established operas were taken to Paris, their composers often added a ballet to cater to the French passion for dance. The outcome, I argue, is that works sometimes exist in multiple versions. Versions are distinct from instrumental transcriptions of a work—such as Liszt's transcriptions for piano of Beethoven's symphonies—which are better regarded as new works. This leads to consideration of literary translations: are they more like work versions or transcriptions? Though there are analogies with both, I argue that translations are usually more like work versions than like new but derivative works.

The book closes with a discussion of what makes for profundity in instrumental music. I contend that music can be profound in the way that chess sometimes is: it reveals the insight, vitality, subtlety, complexity, creativity, flexibility, and analytical far-reachingness of which the human mind is capable. This is illustrated through discussion of examples from Bartók and Beethoven, the former being loosely equivalent to tactical brilliance in chess and the latter to strategic skill.

★★★★

I thank those who offered comments on the chapters of this book. They include: David Braddon-Mitchell, Malcolm Budd, Roberto Casati, Eric Clarke, Nicholas Cook, Amy Coplan, Mark DeBellis, Nicola Dibben, Catherine Elgin, John Andrew Fisher, Alf Gabrielsson, Peter Goldie, Andy Hamilton, Sherri Irvin, Andrew Kania, Justine Kingsbury, Peter Kivy, Fred Kroon, Jerrold Levinson, Paisley Livingston, Justin London, Jonathan McKeown-Green, Robin Maconie, Joe Moore, Aniruddh Patel, Elisabeth Schellekens, William Seeley, Bob Stecker, and Paul Thom. At Oxford University Press, I thank Peter Momtchiloff.

1

Artistic Expression and the Hard Case of Pure Music

In its narrative, dramatic, and representational genres, art regularly depicts contexts for human emotions and their expressions. It is not surprising, then, that these artforms are often about emotional experiences and displays, and that they are also concerned with the expression of emotion. What is more interesting is that abstract art genres may also include examples that are highly expressive of human emotion. Pure music—that is, stand-alone music played on musical instruments excluding the human voice, and without words, literary titles, or associated texts connected to it by its composer—is often characterized as the expressive art *par excellence*. Yet how could that be possible, given that such music lacks semantic or representational content? Pure music presents the hardest and most vivid philosophical challenge to any account of expressiveness in the arts, which is why it is crucial to consider the musical case for the light it sheds on the underlying principles and issues.

In this chapter I consider two accounts of expressiveness in pure music. Both regard expressiveness as an objective property of such music. I argue for the position I call *appearance emotionalism* and against the alternative, which I label *hypothetical emotionalism*. But before I get to that, there is a different mode of musical expression to be acknowledged.

Even instrumental music comes charged with associations. Some of these are private to the listener, but many are widely shared. The latter may be included in a piece by accident but are, more often, deliberately placed for their effects. For instance, when a song is quoted in an instrumental work, its title or words may be brought to mind. Certain melodies (e.g., *Ode to Joy*), styles (e.g., tarantella), idioms (e.g., fanfares), forms (e.g., minuet), modalities (e.g., church modes), and instruments (e.g., fifes and snare drums) recall particular social events, geocultural regions, historical periods, ideas, and sensibilities, and in this way can hook up with affective life-experiences.

Though it is music's associative ties that are likely to be referred to when most people are asked about music's significance, philosophers say little about them. The reason for this neglect is straightforward: the mechanisms and results of association are

First published in M. Kieran (ed.), *Contemporary Debates in Aesthetics and the Philosophy of Art*. Oxford: Blackwell (2006): 179–91.

not philosophically puzzling. There is a form of musical expressiveness, however, that is so. After taking into account the contribution to the expressiveness of pure instrumental music made by association, a significant residue remains. I observed before that the expressiveness of such music is not semantic or representational; now we can add that nor is it all associative. The crucial question remains: how can music express emotion when it is abstract and insentient?

Appearance emotionalism

Appearance emotionalism maintains that the expressiveness of a piece of music is an objective and literally possessed but response-dependent property of that piece.

By calling it response-*dependent* I mean it is the concept it is in virtue of its ability to produce a certain characteristic response in creatures of an appropriate kind under suitable conditions. We might think of response-dependent properties as powers things have to produce certain kinds of responses, including experiences. Green, as a color, is available only to those creatures that experience light-reflecting objects as colored and that are motivated to respond to color discriminations. And to turn to a typical musical example, the pitch of a note is a response-dependent property of that note; it is its causal power to generate an experience of pitchness. More generally, the relevant response in the case of musical concepts, such as ones of expressiveness or sadness in music, is a kind of experience of auditory phenomena.

Cats can hear sounds falling within the same range as humans, but they show no signs of hearing music as such; they do not hear the music in the noise it makes. So, what is the difference between experiencing music as sound and as music? People who hear music as such hear it as organized. They can recognize where a melody begins and ends and when it is repeated or varied; they can experience the difference between the music's coming to a close and its being halted or interrupted before its end; they can often predict how a phrase will continue or a chord resolve; they can frequently tell accidental mistakes from unexpected but correct continuations; and so on. These are ways they *experience* the music. Whether or not they can describe these differences in technical terms is another matter. The majority of listeners are ignorant of the technical vocabulary familiar to musicians, composers, and theorists. (For further discussion, see Chapters 6, 7, and 8.)

Even if the acoustic properties of sounds are governed by natural laws, the ways music can be organized vary from time to time and place to place, so the experience of music includes an inescapable cultural component. Most musics are based on pitch scales and all pitch scales may treat octaves as equivalents, but after that, many ways of dividing up the available scale space have been adopted. The same goes for all of music's dimensions. Musics can differ so markedly from society to society that they are transparent only to the culturally initiated, but I see no reason to think it impossible for outsiders to learn and adjust to the music of another culture. (See Chapter 3.)

When we move to the more specific case in which the listener recognizes the music's expressive qualities, another dimension of cultural difference can come into play. For many cognitively rich emotions, differences in the prevailing beliefs, desires, and attitudes affect when and how often they are elicited and how they might be displayed. And even with the most basic emotions, cultures vary as regards both the situations in which they might be engendered and the propriety of giving expression to them. If death is viewed as a time of loss and extinction, it will be an occasion for sadness, but if it marks a passage from the pain of earthly life to a more enjoyable spiritual existence, it may be greeted with happiness. So the capacities on which the appropriate response to expressiveness in music depend include ones concerned with recognizing contexts and behaviors appropriate to various emotional experiences and displays for the culture and period in which the music finds its home.

So much for the dependence, what of the response? What form does it take when what is experienced is music's expressiveness? I believe it is an experience of resemblance between the music and the realm of human emotion.

Several elements within the human sphere are candidates for that side of the resemblance relation: the phenomenological profile of inner experiences of emotion, expressive qualities of the voice, emotion-relevant facial expressions, and other bodily behaviors through which emotions are given outward expression. As examples of the first view, Langer (1942) argues that the forms of music are iconic maps of the structure of feelings, and Budd (1995) suggests that music mimics the sensational pattern of emotions. I doubt, however, that emotions can be individuated in terms of their structural or phenomenological profiles. A single emotion can present different mixes or orderings of sensation and feeling on different occasions, and contrasting emotions can often share a similar outline. Meanwhile, while we are prone to recognize human faces bearing emotionally suggestive expressions in many non-human objects, such as the facades of houses, the fronts of cars, and the faces of basset hounds, I do not think we experience music as wearing a smiling or frowning face. A crucial aspect of our experience of music is that of its temporal unfolding, whereas the expression worn on a face comes as an atemporally structured gestalt.

As for the voice, if the similarity is supposed to lie in timbre and inflection, I am skeptical. The saxophone can sound similar, and toing and froing between duetting instruments can be very like a dialogue, but in general, the whoops, whines, bawls, wails, groans, cries, shrieks, moans, grunts, screeches, and whimpers with which emotions are vocalized strike me as very unlike the sound of expressive music. More suggestive, though, are studies showing that the distinctive prosodic contours of specific emotions can be recreated musically (Juslin 2001). The voice and music are more alike in dynamic structure, articulation, pitch, intensity, and periodicity of phrase lengths and shapes than in timbre or inflection as such. It is also instructive to recall that European composers in the eighteenth century went to considerable lengths to pattern their music according to the rules and figures of vocal rhetoric (Neubauer 1986), though I suspect this process depends more on conventional stipulations than iconic similarity.

The resemblance that counts most for musical expressiveness, I believe, is that between music's temporally unfolding dynamic structure and configurations of human behavior associated with the expression of emotion (Davies 1994a). We experience movement in music—in terms of progress from high to low or fast to slow, say—but as well in the multi-stranded waxing and waning of tensions generated variously within the harmony, the mode of articulation and phrasing, subtle nuances of timing, the delay or defeat of expected continuations, and so on. Moreover, this movement is like human behavior in that it seems purposeful and goal-directed. There are expositions, developments, and recapitulations, not merely succession; there is closure, not merely stopping. As a result, we expect to be able to account for what happens subsequently in terms of what went before, even where what will happen later is not easily predicted. To put the point as pithily as possible, the course of music usually makes sense, as is also the case typically with the activities of human agents.

More particularly, I think music is expressive in recalling the gait, attitude, air, carriage, posture, and comportment of the human body. Just as someone who is stooped over, dragging, faltering, subdued, and slow in her movements cuts a sad figure, so music that is slow, quiet, with heavy or thick harmonic bass textures, with underlying patterns of unresolved tension, with dark timbres, and a recurrently downward impetus sounds sad. Just as someone who skips and leaps quickly and lightly, makes expansive gestures, and so on, has a happy bearing, so music with a similar vivacity and exuberance is happy sounding.

Critics of appearance emotionalism deny that the movement of music exactly resembles human behavior. The claim of appearance emotionalism is that they are similar in only one crucial respect, however, not that they are indistinguishable. And to the person who points out that movement within music resembles the movements of clouds as closely as it resembles human expressive behavior, so that the similarity cannot *explain* why we hear the music as expressive (Matravers 1998), there is this reply: the connection is given in the *experience* of similarity, not in some absolute measure of verisimilitude. Resemblance is a symmetrical relation, but we do not find all resemblances salient or reversible. We are likely to be struck more by the way weeping willows resemble downcast people than by the way they resemble frozen waterfalls, even if the latter similarity is closer in many elements than is the former. And we are less inclined to see people as tree-like than to see trees as presenting a human aspect, though the resemblance is equal and symmetrical between these possibilities. Our interests shape how we see the world, thereby making some resemblances more salient than others and giving them the direction they take. For our social species, openness to the minds and hearts of others is vital, so that it becomes an attitude we adopt unthinkingly toward the world at large. Accordingly, we experience many things, events, and processes as similar to aspects of human experience, thought, and behavior. So it is with music, I claim. It is expressive because we experience it as possessing a dynamic character relating it to humanly expressive behavior.

Given the emphasis on the way the music is experienced, where is the warrant for claiming that expressiveness is an *objective* property of the music? In answering this question, it is important not to mistake the subjective/objective distinction for the independent-of-human-experience/dependent-on-human-experience one. Musical expressiveness is response-dependent, I have allowed, but this does not mean it is subjective in the sense of being personal, idiosyncratic, and non-objective. To hold that expressiveness is an objective property of music is to assume that, among qualified listeners who attend to it under appropriate conditions, there is considerable agreement in the emotion-terms with which they describe the music's expressive character.

This last is an empirical claim. Is it true? How one answers may depend on the degree of expressive specificity one expects to find. At the level of fine-grained discriminations between emotions, according to which grief, sadness, despair, depression, misery, sorrow, and despondency are distinct, there appears to be only a low level of agreement, but if these are classed as falling under a single generic emotion, the level of interpersonal agreement is high (Gabrielsson 2002). My claim is that music is capable of expressing a fairly limited number of emotional types, but that it can express these objectively, so that suitably skilled and situated listeners agree highly in attributing them to the music.

Which emotional types are these and why is their number restricted? Only a limited range of emotional types can be individuated solely on the basis of observed bodily comportment (where the face cannot be seen and nothing is known about the context of action). Music is expressive because it is experienced as resembling such behaviors, and it can express only the emotion types that they do. Sadness and happiness are the leading candidates, along with timidity and anger. Swaggering arrogance, the mechanical rigidity that goes with repression and alienation from the physicality of existence, ethereal dreaminess, and sassy sexuality are further possibilities.

Still, since music is non-sentient and only sentient creatures can be literally sad or happy, in what sense does music *literally* possess its expressive properties? Human bodily attitudes have an expressive character even in those cases where the owners of those bodies do not feel as they look. When we say someone 'cuts a sad figure,' we are referring to the look of the person, not to how he or she feels. Admittedly, this secondary use of the word 'sad' is a natural extension from the primary one, because behavior that in one context produces an expressive appearance, without regard to how the person feels, in another gives direct, primary expression to the person's felt emotion. Though connected, these uses are distinct. The same secondary use applies to music when it is experienced as generating appearances of expressiveness like those presented by the carriage and deportment of the human body.

Though I have just described the predication of terms such as 'sad' to attitudes of the human body and to music as involving a secondary use, this does not entail the further claim that such attributions are metaphoric. (See Chapter 2.) Secondary uses can be literal. Live metaphors are not listed in dictionaries, but I note that the *Concise Oxford Dictionary* gives among the meanings of 'expression,' 'a person's facial appearance or intonation of voice, esp. as indicating feeling; depiction of feeling, movement, etc., in art; conveying of feeling in the performance of music.' To say of a face or body that it looks sad, independently of what its 'owner' may feel, is to use the word 'sad' literally. The same applies when we call the sound of music sad.

Let me outline some advantages of appearance emotionalism. It does not lose the connection between music's expressive character and the human world of emotional expression, whereas this is a crucial fault in theories analyzing music's expressiveness reductively in terms of technically described musical events and processes, or that characterize music's expressiveness as belonging to a distinctive genus unconnected from the realm of human experience. And it explains how music can be objectively and literally expressive, which is preferable to theories (as in Goodman 1968, Scruton 1997) purportedly analyzing musical expressiveness as metaphoric and then not explaining what this means. Given that metaphor is a figure of speech, what is to be understood by the claim that the *music* is metaphorically sad? Declining to take the analysis further amounts to a refusal to engage with the philosophical problem that is the subject of the debate.

Appearance emotionalism has the advantage also over theories that account for music's expressiveness as involving a mediated process of abstract symbolization or indirect representation; namely, it provides, as such accounts do not, for the phenomenal vivacity with which we experience expressiveness in music. We encounter music's expressiveness fully frontally. The listener's awareness of the music's expressiveness is more like a direct confrontation with, say, a sad-looking person than like an experience of reading or hearing a description of such a person. Appearance emotionalism, because it is grounded in perceptually revealed experiences of similarity, has the quality of immediate access that is so phenomenologically distinctive of the outward show of emotions in humans, other animals, and music.

Appearance emotionalism: criticisms and replies

Despite the advantages just listed, appearance emotionalism has its critics. In this section I elaborate and develop the theory by considering some objections it faces.

If an emotion is expressed only if it is shown by someone who *feels* it, then appearance emotionalism does not involve the expression of emotion (Stecker 1999) since, by its own account, the appearance stands to no feeling as its direct expression. There is the *presentation* of the *appearance* of an emotion but not the *expression* of an *occurrent* emotion. And this is embarrassing since the theory is offered as explaining the expression of emotion in music.

What is needed by way of answer is clarification of the relation between the music's expressive character and the composer's or performer's intentions and emotions. This much must be conceded at the outset: it is possible for the music to present an expressive aspect without this being intended by its composer or performer. The music's expressive appearance depends on other of its objective qualities and need not be consciously contrived or depend on the composer's or performer's feelings.

Nevertheless, the music's expressive character is usually intended by its creator, and the performer aims to deliver and refine that expressive character. Where this is so, it is appropriate to talk about the expression of emotion in the music. We commonly mean by 'expression' that a given content has been intentionally created and communicated. Moreover, this first kind of expression or communication does often connect to emotional experiences undergone by the composer or performer. For instance, composers who feel sad and who wish to express this may intentionally write music with an expressiveness that matches their own feeling. The resulting composition is not a direct or primary expression of the composer's sadness; it is unlike the tears to which composers give way under the force of their feelings. Instead, composers intentionally appropriate the music's expressive potential (which it has independently of how they feel) in order to have it correspond to their emotions. The composer is like those who show how they feel not in the usual fashion but by pointing to the mask of tragedy, or, more dramatically, by taking it up and wearing it. This manner of displaying emotion is more sophisticated than primary, direct ventings. Nevertheless, it falls easily and naturally under the notion of expression.

In brief: while appearance emotionalism is not automatically associated with acts of expression, in the musical case this connection is frequent because musical works and performances are designed to have most of their salient properties, including their emotion-resembling ones. So long as it is deliberately created, the appearance of emotion presented in the music is the result of an act of expression (in the sense of 'expression' that is synonymous with 'communication'). Moreover, when the composer or performer does match the music's expressive tone to his own feelings in order to display those feelings indirectly, the feelings are expressed in the music. Appearance emotionalism does not sever the presentation of emotional appearances from genuine expression via the acts of the composer and performer.

Another possible criticism observes that music can express only a severely restricted palette of emotions according to appearance emotionalism, whereas it is often praised for the richness and ineffable subtlety of the expressive appearances it can present.

The replies to this objection come in a number of forms. The first ones try to duck the bullet. Even if pure instrumental music is limited with respect to the range of emotions it can present, music with words and the rest can express the full gamut by linking complex contexts for feeling with the cognitive and attitudinal states of the characters represented within it. Moreover, in the case of pure instrumental music there is the possibility of ordering successive emotional appearances in ways suggestive of subtler or more complex states. Where deep sadness gives way gradually to joy and abandonment, it may be reasonable to regard the transition as consistent with acceptance and resolution. As well, it is important to recall the variety that can be imposed on the more general frame of the work's expressive profile via the performer's interpretation of the piece. Performers control many fine shades of phrasing, timing, dynamics, and articulation, and these features play a highly important expressive role within the performance. There is no inconsistency in maintaining both that the expressive scope of musical works is limited and that there is huge diversity and plasticity in the manner in which this expressive schema can be elaborated (or contradicted, or undermined) in the course of its realization in performance.

Other replies seek to bite the bullet by acknowledging music's limited expressive powers and by rejecting claims for its ineffable subtlety. As was observed at the outset, if expressiveness is to be predicable of the music, there must be a wide coincidence in judgments of expressiveness by suitably qualified listeners under appropriate conditions. It is only with respect to broad categories of emotion—happiness versus sadness, for instance—that this consensus is achieved. This is not to deny the importance and interest of the idiosyncratic responses of the individual (see Chapter 6), but it is to suggest that these are more revealing of the person who has them than of the music itself.

A further observation might help clarify what is at issue. Appearance emotionalists do not deny that there is an astonishing subtlety and multiplicity in the expressiveness of musical works. They claim, however, that this nuanced variety applies to the manner of musical expression, not to the identities of the emotions thereby presented (Davies 1999a). It is fallacious to reason from the fact that differing musical works are each expressive to the conclusion that each work therefore must express a different emotion; and it compounds the fallacy to infer that the differences between these emotions are ineffable simply because we cannot agree on the emotion terms that would capture their distinctness. Of course it is true that the expression of sadness in the funeral march in Beethoven's Third Symphony is not the same as that in the slow movement of Mahler's Fifth, but this is not because each expresses some emotion other than sadness in general. And if we find it hard to think of qualifying terms that capture how the two movements differ, this may be because it is the wrong type of description that is being sought. These works differ in the musical specifics by which each expresses the same general emotion. To capture the difference, it is not necessary to qualify *what* is expressed but, instead, to describe *how* the musical means for bringing about this result diverge in their detail. The difference, to put it bluntly, lies in the notes and how they work together, not in the identity of the emotion that gets presented.

The last of the objections I consider argues that appearance emotionalism cannot account adequately for the emotional responses music's expressiveness elicits from the listener. The objection can be presented as a dilemma: given the tenets of appearance emotionalism, either the listener has no basis for an emotional response to the music's expressiveness or the response is an inappropriate one. The first horn of the dilemma can be developed this way: while we have every reason to respond to others' emotions and feelings, mere appearances of emotion, recognized as such, give us no basis for an emotional response. We are not deeply moved by the sight of weeping willows, even if their bearing strikes us as sad looking, precisely because their appearance does not signal that any sentient being is suffering. And the second horn notes that, even if listeners do respond, for instance by mirroring what the music expresses, the music is not the object of their response, since they do not believe (or imagine) that it has the emotion-relevant qualities that are required. If sad music makes us feel sad, we are not sad *about* the music because we do not believe that it suffers or that its expressiveness is somehow unfortunate or regrettable. But in that case, our response is not of the standard, cognitively informed and directed kind, and it is thereby not a response about the music as such (Kivy 1999).

Kivy (1990) would take on the dilemma's first horn. He denies that sad music makes listeners feel sad, or that happy music can cheer them, unless they are pathological. When listeners report such things, their self-reports are mistaken. Kivy does not deny, however, that listeners can be intensely moved by music. They experience emotions for which the music is an appropriate object. They are moved to awe and delight by the music's beauty, to admiration by the composer's skill and ingenuity, to disappointment by the performer's ineptitude.

Kivy is correct, of course, in holding that music is a source of many responses for which it becomes a proper object by satisfying beliefs relevant to those responses. I am reluctant, however, to follow him in his assertion that listeners are never moved to respond to music's expressiveness with echoing emotions. It would be very surprising if their self-reports were systematically mistaken. As well as personal and anecdotal evidence for the kind of emotional osmosis the existence of which Kivy denies, there is experimental data in support of it, both as regards catching the mood of other people (Hatfield, Cacioppo, and Rapson 1994) and of music's producing mirroring reactions (Gabrielsson 2002). (See Chapter 4.) Some emotional responses can be generated through a kind of contagion, even in the absence of the cognitive and attitudinal elements that accompany them in the default or normal situation. I contend that music provides a case in point. It is far from inevitable that sad music calls forth a sad response, or happy music a happy one, but this happens frequently. It is not pathological for someone to choose a joyous musical work in the hope of sloughing off a depressed or sad mood.

This now leaves us facing the dilemma's second horn. Its first challenge, recall, is that the mirroring response to music's expressiveness is unacceptably aberrant. If the sadness we feel on hearing sad music is not about something we believe to be unfortunate and regrettable, it lacks the cognitive component essential to genuine sadness. A reply could suggest emotions lie on a continuum, rather than forming a unified, invariant class. At one end are emotions in which the cognitive elements are necessary, even dominant; examples would be envy and patriotism. Without the appropriate beliefs—for instance, that someone else has something I lack and desire, or that the action or quality I take to be admirable is attributable to my country—it cannot be envy or patriotism I feel. But at the other end are emotions in which the cognitive aspects are less important or sometimes are circumvented. They are likely to include emotions we share with non-human animals that lack our cognitive capacities. These emotions may be adaptively helpful precisely because of their 'fast and frugal' nature. Given the power of emotions as triggers for action, when it is best to shoot first and ask questions later there may be an advantage to emotions that do not require cognitive appraisal of the situation and of the options it presents as a prerequisite to their motivating a response. Sadness, happiness, fear, and anger seem to be regarded as falling into this category by psychologists (such as Ekman 1992) who write of emotions as 'affect programs' operating independently of cognition. But the claim need not be that sadness and happiness are always independent of the cognitive states of the person who experiences them, but merely that they may be so sometimes. In short: the mirroring response to music is aberrant only if one assumes inappropriately that cognition always plays a central or necessary role in emotional experience. Mirroring responses to music's expressiveness are clearly consistent with a broader view that rightly acknowledges the centrality of cognition for only some emotions or for only some contexts.

So far so good, but another problem seems to remain. If the sadness one feels on listening to sad music does not take the music or some other thing as its emotional object, then it is not about anything (Madell 2002). In that case, the response must be an objectless mood; it must be vague and undirected. As such, it might always be produced in some other way. It is only contingently related to the music and is bound to detract from concentration on it. The reply: it is true that the mirroring response does not take the music as its intentional or emotional object. The response is not *about* the music, and it does not involve believing (or make-believing) that there is something about the music's expressiveness that is unfortunate and regrettable. But this does not entail that the response is objectless, vague, and without any target. The music is the perceptual object and cause of the response. The response develops and unfolds as the music, which is its focus, does. What is important is not that the listener's response of sadness is *about* the music but that it is *to* the music and tracks the music's elaboration through time. A sad response that mirrors a sadness presented in the music's dynamic profile is locked on to the music in the way just described, even if that response is not also tied to the music via the usual kinds of sadness-relevant beliefs.

Hypothetical emotionalism

The alternative to appearance emotionalism on which I concentrate here, hypothetical emotionalism, holds that what makes it true that the music expresses an emotion, E, is that a qualified listener imagines of the music that it presents a narrative or drama about a persona who experiences E. We hear music as presenting the life or experiences of a persona who is subject to various emotional events or episodes; and the music expresses these emotions because it has the power to lead us to imagine such things.

As a theory of musical expressiveness, hypothetical emotionalism is offered not merely as a heuristic that will facilitate the listener's perception of the music's expressiveness. More is claimed than that listeners might better recognize and appreciate the expressiveness of the work if they think of it as strings controlling the inner life of some human puppet. The hypothetical emotionalist is committed to this stronger position: it is a necessary condition for hearing the music's expressiveness that listeners imaginatively project into it a persona whose situation or inner life it then portrays. Jerrold

Levinson's formulation (1996a: 107) of hypothetical emotionalism makes this strong commitment explicit: 'a passage of music P is expressive of an emotion or other psychic condition E *iff* [i.e., if and only if] P, in context, is readily and aptly heard by an appropriately backgrounded listener as the expression of E, in a sui generis, 'musical,' manner, by an indefinite agent, the music's persona.'

Hypothetical emotionalism differs from appearance emotionalism about the conditions under which claims about music's expressiveness are true. In particular, these rival accounts disagree about the kind and content of the response that is called forth from 'an appropriately backgrounded listener.' In the one view, the listener is said to imagine a persona undergoing appropriate emotional vicissitudes; in the other, the listener is said to experience a similarity between music's dynamic pattern and human experiences that are expressive without regard to felt-emotions. At a more general level, the two theories are alike in that both regard musical expressiveness as an objective, response-dependent property possessed literally by the music. In consequence, hypothetical emotionalism can also claim the advantages I listed earlier as accruing to appearance emotionalism; namely, it preserves a connection between musical expressiveness and (imagined) human feeling; it does not characterize expressiveness as irreducibly and mysteriously metaphorical; and it explains how expressiveness is immediately present in the music. But are there any further advantages it claims over appearance emotionalism? There are two.

Hypothetical emotionalism is better suited to admit to the sphere of musical expression the full range of human emotions and experiences, including ones that normally presuppose a complex cognitive aspect. This is because the persona that is to be imagined is a human being, who has desires, beliefs, attitudes, and the rest. It should not be surprising, then, that hypothetical emotionalists have been keen to argue that music is sometimes capable of expressing 'higher,' cognitively subtle and complex emotions, such as hope (Levinson 1990: ch. 14, Karl and Robinson 1995a) and cheerful confidence turning to despair (Robinson 1998).

Second, hypothetical emotionalism might seem better situated to explain why the listener is sometimes moved to an emotional response, since the listener is confronted not merely with appearances displaying the characteristics of emotions but with a person who undergoes psychological states and experiences expressed via the music. Admittedly, hypothetical emotionalism is not yet clear of the woods, because the person to whom the listener reacts is a figment of the listener's imagination, and there are many well-known problems in trying to account for our reacting emotionally to stories about people we know not to exist. Still, whatever difficulties remain, it might be thought that fictional people inhabiting worlds spun from the material of musical works are closer to the human realm of feeling than are appearances of emotion transposed to an inanimate universe of pure sound.

The proponent of appearance emotionalism could dispute these claims for the greater plausibility or desirability of hypothetical emotionalism. In its fully developed form, appearance emotionalism allows rich and subtle expressive powers to extended, complex musical pieces. And it is highly questionable that the cognitively complex setting required by the hypothetical emotionalist in accounting for the listener's reaction to music comes closer to the psychological reality of that familiar experience than does the theory of emotional contagion or osmosis put forward by the appearance emotionalist. But let us bypass these debates in order to focus on the important one, which concerns the overall plausibility of hypothetical emotionalism as an account of music's expressiveness. I argue that it fails in its most central assumptions. The most direct objection to hypothetical emotionalism asks how listeners know what to imagine when it comes to putting the persona they have envisaged through the relevant emotional hoops. If the music guides this process, then surely this means that the music is already successful in expressing the emotions that are to be grafted onto the persona's life. If I am to imagine that the persona is sad, won't this be only because I have already recognized expressions of sadness in the music? In that case, hypothetical emotionalism is both circular and redundant (Scruton 1997). Or on the other hand, if the music provides no guide to what is to be imagined, how can the content of that imagining be truly ascribed to the music as a property it possesses?

The hypothetical emotionalist can make this reply: the music does prompt and constrain what is to be imagined, but not by anticipating the expressive content that belongs to the music through the listener's imaginative engagement with it. Jenefer Robinson (1998) develops the response: the music's dynamic tension causes in the listener sensations or feelings of being pushed, prodded, pulled, dragged, and stirred. These primitive responses are largely non-cognitive. They fuel and direct the narrative that listeners construct about the experience of the persona they hypothesize as residing in the music. So it is true that listeners know what to imagine only on the basis of responses they have to the music, but it is not true that these responses are the emotions they go on to attribute to the imagined persona.

Though hypothetical emotionalism can dodge the charge of question-begging circularity, it faces two further major objections. The first simply doubts the empirical claim that all those who are qualified to predicate expressiveness to music do so on the basis of imagining a persona as subject to a narrative directed by the course of the music. The second denies that what is supplied by the music sufficiently controls what the listener may imagine, with the result that the process described by the theory should lead to an idiosyncratic medley of experiences, not to general agreement on the basis of which expressiveness could be attributed to the music. Of course, the hypothetical emotionalist is not committed to the implausible suggestion that everyone will independently imagine exactly the same when they give fictional life to a persona as they listen to the music. It is sufficient that listeners agree in their judgments about what the music expresses as a result of pursuing this imaginative process, even if each conjures up a distinctive scenario. Allowing this, the present criticism doubts that agreement in listeners' judgments about musical expressiveness could be explained by appeal to the control exercised by the music over what can be concluded on the basis of what is imagined.

The first objection is empirical. What goes on in people's heads as they listen attentively to music and correctly recognize its expressive character is very varied (DeNora 2000). Some may allow the music to direct their imaginings about the psychological experiences of a persona, but many who arrive at informed judgments about the music's expressiveness apparently do not imagine the things required by hypothetical emotionalism.

The second objection can be developed as follows: there is no constraint on the number of personas imagined as inhabiting a musical work. And there are innumerable coherent narratives about them that would coincide with and reflect the progress of the music. So long as these different narratives all license the same judgment about what the music expresses there need be no difficulty for hypothetical emotionalism, but there is no reason to suppose this will be the case. Where one persona bursts with joy, another might be imagined blowing his or her top; where one persona is pictured as growing increasingly despondent, a series of others might be envisioned as independently sad; where one persona overcomes fear to show courageous defiance, another moves from uncertainty to conviction, a third puts aside troubles and turns to something more positive, a fourth is gripped by a strange passion, a fifth first questions and then reaffirms his or her faith, a sixth reflects on the contrasting personalities of his children, and so on. These various stories do not fall under a single archetype and there is no basis for supposing that they will lead 'readily and aptly,' to use Levinson's words, to agreement concerning the music's expressive character. Music is too indefinite to dictate the content and form of such narratives so that they might issue in the sorts of intersubjectively congruent judgments that justify the view that music is objectively expressive of emotion (Davies 2003: ch. 10).

Conclusion

The assumption driving many theories of musical expressiveness is that there can be expressiveness only where there is an agent—the composer, the listener, or a persona imagined in the music—who feels emotion and displays this. I accept that composers sometimes express their emotions in the music they write, but they do so not by discharging their feelings through the act of composition but by appropriating and shaping an expressive potential already inherent in the musical materials on which they work. I allow also that listeners sometimes are moved to experience what they hear expressed in the music, but the music has its expressiveness independently of this reaction. As well, a listener might sometimes entertain the thought of a persona in the music, but I deny that the apprehension of musical expressiveness depends on such imaginings. For myself, the experience is one of hearing the music as possessing appearances of emotion, while regarding it as neither alive nor as haunted by a persona. The virtue of the account for which I have argued is that it makes sense of this experience, which I hope and believe is a common one. There is a familiar kind of expressiveness that pays no regard to experienced emotion, as when we find a face mask, or bodily bearing, or willow tree, or house front presenting an expressive appearance. Music is expressive in that way, and it is powerfully so because it is deliberately created to have the relevant properties.

What does this analysis contribute to our understanding of expressiveness in art more generally? First, it provides a basic model for understanding expressiveness in abstract genres of painting and image-making, sculpture, and dance. Also, it should draw attention to the fact that many works of art have an expressiveness of their own; they present an expressive point of view that cannot be predicated of the work's characters, narrator, creator, or performer. This is an easily overlooked but important fact about narrative and other representational artistic forms.

2
Music and Metaphor

A simple and intuitive argument suggests that attributions of expressiveness to purely instrumental music without associated titles, stories, or sung words are metaphoric.[1] It goes as follows: (1) Only sentient creatures can have and express emotions such as sadness; (2) music is non-sentient; (3) so music cannot have and express emotions such as sadness; (4) yet, despite realizing the truth of (1)–(3), we say such things as 'the music is sad' or 'the music expresses sadness,' referring to purely instrumental musical pieces; (5) so these attributions must be metaphoric rather than literal. Saam Trivedi (2003a: 259, see also 2008) puts the point bluntly: 'to say music literally is sad seems to imply that music literally or really has mental states such as sadness, which is just false.' Nick Zangwill (2007: 393) observes: 'it is still not the case that descriptions of music in emotion terms refer to real emotional mental states ... which the words taken in their literal sense would suggest.'

Probably Roger Scruton is the most dedicated 'metaphoricist,' though his reasons for holding the view go far beyond the simple argument offered above. For example, he writes (1983: 85): 'it seems to me that in our most basic apprehension of music there lies a complex system of metaphor, which is the true description of no material fact. And the metaphor cannot be eliminated from the description of music, because it is integral to the intentional object of musical experience. Take this metaphor away and you cease to describe the experience of the music.' But he also employs (1997: 154) a version of the simple argument: 'we face the question whether this [musical] sadness is the same property as that possessed by a sad person or another property. It surely cannot be the *same* property: the sadness of persons is a property that only conscious organisms can possess.'

In this chapter I review objections to the soundness of the argument with which we began. Those arguments tend to focus on the truth or otherwise of (1): only sentient creatures can have or experience emotions, such as sadness. Later, I review and reject two ways of challenging (1) before defending a third.

---

[1] Many of the arguments that follow could be applied to song, opera, film, or drama with musical accompaniment, program music, and so on, though sometimes the issue does not arise because the work contains characters who express or display their feelings partly through the music they are given. In any event, the issue is at its clearest when we focus on purely instrumental music.

Other issues

First, however, I mention in order to put aside a more radical view presented by Nelson Goodman (1968). In his account, an artwork is expressive if it metaphorically possesses a property and that metaphoric property is used to denote its literal equivalent. For instance, a musical work possesses or presents the metaphoric property of being sad and thereby it denotes or refers to literal sadness. In other words, his claim is not that *descriptions* of music as sad are metaphoric, but rather that it is the *music* that is metaphoric in the manner in which it exemplifies sadness.[2] I have criticized Goodman's theory elsewhere (Davies 1994a: 139–50). Here, my focus is on those who insist that it is descriptions using emotion words to characterize music that are metaphoric.

Also beyond my remit is a view presented recently by Christopher Peacocke (2009a, 2009b), according to which metaphor can enter non-linguistically into our perceptions. Before getting to the musical case, he illustrates the general thesis by reference to a painting of pots by Francisco de Zurbaran.[3] He says the depicted pots are often seen as a group of people and this involves seeing them metaphorically as a group of people, because isomorphisms between the domains allow the sub-personal transfer of properties from one domain to the other, which is a fundamental process on which metaphor relies. Though isomorphism underpins the perceptual experience in which the pots are seen metaphorically as people, it does not enter into that experience. Because the experience is perceptual, it is distinct from that in which someone sees the pots and imagines that they are people, Peacocke maintains. And he goes on to suggest that hearing expressiveness in music typically involves a similarly perceptual process.

I will not attempt to develop the objection, but the difficulty I have with this view is in understanding the central claim, which is that the concept of people enters into the *perceptual experience* of the pots. Peacocke denies that the painting is experienced as a depiction of people. (Rightly so, since no one would claim *that* as the content of their visual experience of the painting.) Presumably there must be, as it were, a people-slanted perception of the pots. But when I reflect on the phenomenology of my experience of viewing the painting, I cannot locate any such perceptual content. Rather, it seems to me that I do exactly what Peacocke denies, namely, I see the (depicted) pots and entertain the thought of that seeing that it is a seeing of (depicted) people. The content of the painting does not then look different to me, but I think differently about the way it looks.[4] The mechanism Peacocke proposes—cross-domain

---

[2] Others who write of music as a metaphor include Ferguson (1960) and Putman (1989).

[3] I focus on his non-musical example because, as will become apparent, I think music can literally possess its expressive character, so I do not think a special kind of perceptual or imaginative act is involved in recognizing that character. As a result, I would dispute the parallel Peacocke draws between this example and the musical case.

[4] I allow that what I imagine or believe can influence how I interpret what I see. If I imagine that Mona Lisa has just seen her secret lover enter the room, her smile will likely strike me as less enigmatic and more smirkish. But Peacocke holds that the change is in the content of perception, not in the interpretation of what is seen.

transfer and isomorphism—could underlie and make apt my imagining. If so, there is no need to invoke a special metaphoric mode of perceiving or, for that matter, a special metaphoric mode of imagining.[5]

Rejected approaches

One way of addressing the argument with which we began is by identifying some person who experiences an emotion that is given expression in the music. In other words, even if the music is non-sentient, it might stand to some sentient person's emotion as its expression. 'The music is sad' or 'the music expresses sadness' is to be parsed as saying 'the music expresses this person's sadness,' and that claim is both true and literal, not metaphoric.

An obvious candidate for the role of the sentient and emotional person is the composer, the idea being that she gives expression to her emotion and conveys it to the work via her creation of that piece.[6] Yet this view faces apparently devastating objections. It is not the case that all expressive music is composed by people undergoing the emotions heard in their music. Some composers were delighted to be commissioned to write the sad requiems they produced. Besides, even if it is true that the composer feels an emotion, successfully intends to convey this to the music, and thereby gives expression to her feeling, plainly this act of expression is of a complex and sophisticated variety. The music she writes does not stand to her sadness as do the tears to which she gives way. Her tears are primitive, direct, and thereby transparent, expressions or symptoms of her sadness. By contrast, she designs the music to have a character allowing it to express her emotion. But how is she able to succeed? On the most plausible account, she appropriates its inherent expressive potential and harnesses this to give a higher-order expression to her emotional state. And the crucial point here is that her successful use of this potential does not explain how music could have the potential she exploits.[7]

It is as if the composer expresses her sadness not by venting or showing it in the usual fashion but by picking up the mask of tragedy and holding it before her face. Such an act does indeed express her emotion, and does so in an elegant and sophisticated manner. But she succeeds only because the mask has an expressive character independent of her use of it, so we cannot explain how it has that character by reference to her act of expression. The problem with the mask of tragedy is no different from that of the

---

[5] For criticism of Peacocke's account of 'perceiving metaphorically-as,' see Budd (2009), Snowdon (2009).
[6] In some cases the performer might be a more apt candidate for the person who creates musical expressiveness in the process of giving expression to his emotions. I do not rehearse the case here because, when suitably translated into talk of performances rather than works, it faces the same kinds of difficulties as that involving the composer.
[7] For further discussion, see Davies (1994a: ch. 4, 2007: ch. 16).

musical case. We are forced to ask how lifeless wood can be sad or express sadness, just as we ask how sadness can be heard in sounding notes.

Another potential subject for the emotion heard expressed in the music is the listener. It might be suggested that she feels an emotion that she then projects onto the music. But this view is implausible in obvious ways. Listeners need not be moved in order to hear the music's expressiveness. And if they are moved, they distinguish their feelings from what the music expresses and regard their affect as a reaction to the music's expressive character, not vice versa.

Alternatively, the sentient subject of the emotion expressed in the music might be make-believed. There are two possibilities. The listener imagines of herself that the music is the expression of an emotion she feels, or the listener imagines of the music that it is inhabited by a persona whose feelings (actions, thoughts) are portrayed in the music.[8]

I suppose it is possible to imagine such things and doing so might be helpful in coming to hear what the music expresses. One might ask oneself, for example, 'If the music were to accompany a film about a person, what kind of person would he be and what would he feel?' But it is very unlikely that such imagining is inevitably and unavoidably implicated in hearing music's expressiveness. Moreover, there is the concern that purely instrumental music could not sufficiently control the content of what is imagined to explain the interpersonal agreement we find among listeners about what broad categories of emotion it expresses. Alternatively, if we agree in relevant ways about what kinds of things to imagine, there is the worry that this is because we identify the music's expressiveness and are guided by that, in which case the music is expressive independently of our imaginings. And finally, there is the problem that none of this explains what provoked the original argument to the effect that describing music as expressive is metaphoric. To say we imagine of the music that it is an expression of our own feelings or of those of a persona does not explain how musical sounds unconnected with primary, natural displays of affect could coherently sustain the appropriate state of make-believe.[9]

So far I have considered and rejected the challenge to (1) in our earlier argument that involves locating an agent who undergoes the emotion given expression by the music. A second strategy is to argue that musical emotions are sui generis. In particular, the view might be that the music's sadness just is its possessing a distinctively musical quality that is literally present and that is not connected to the world of human feeling and sentience. In other words, terms such as 'sad' have different, non-synonymous meanings and uses when applied respectively to music and to sentient creatures. The musical quality could have been labeled 'blerkness' instead.

The problem with this position is that we do intend and recognize a connection between the sadness of music and human sadness. Not only is the use of emotion terms

---

[8] A version of the first view is presented in Walton (1988). The most emphatic statement of the second position is found in Levinson (1996a: ch. 6, 2006); see also Ridley (1995a), Robinson (2005).

[9] For more detailed critical discussion of these views, especially the second one, see Chapter 1 and Davies (2003: ch. 10).

intended, it seems to be ineliminable in that no non-synonymous paraphrase is apt to capture the musical quality that is named. Moreover, without the connection with human feeling, it becomes mysterious why listeners find blerkness in music so emotionally moving and value it as they do.

Literal, not metaphorical, attributions

This takes us to the third way of disputing that music cannot express emotions because it is non-sentient: if the musical property is possessed literally rather than metaphorically, what we need is a literal use of emotion words that preserves a connection with their application to felt emotions but extends that use to characterize qualities of non-sentient subjects, plus the argument that it is this same use that applies to music.

I have suggested that these conditions can be met. Here is the view I defend: there is a familiar, literal use of words such as 'sad' in which they are not used to refer to a felt emotion. We might say that a person cuts a sad figure or that his face looks angry, say, without believing or assuming he feels as he looks. We are referring not to his feelings but to his comportment or physiognomy; in other words, to how he appears. And this use involves an extension of the primary one in which we use the same terms to refer to felt emotions. An angry-looking face is one that looks much as it would if its owner felt angry and showed this in his face; the person whose comportment is sad-looking moves much as he would if he felt sad and betrayed this in how he carried his body.

Clearly the words have a meaning in this extended use that is closely related to the ones they have in their primary one, though the reference is to appearances of faces, bodies, and the like, not to felt emotions. In other terms, the words have not acquired some quite different homonymous meaning, but instead have a new application.[10] This new use is secondary in at least two senses: we could not teach a child the secondary use before she had acquired the primary one and, had the outward show of felt human emotions taken a different form, we would not apply the secondary use to the kinds of characteristics or displays that we currently do.

It is because of the intimate relation between the secondary or extended use and the primary one that we cannot replace the emotion terms involved with non-synonymous paraphrases. And as a clear sign that the secondary use is literal, we regularly find it listed alongside the primary one in dictionaries.[11]

---

[10] Zangwill (2007) attributes to me the view that 'sad' is a dead metaphor when predicated of music and objects that the word retains its primary meaning in the musical case rather than acquiring a new one as would happen when the metaphor dies. But this misrepresents my position. I hold that there is an intimate connection between the word's meaning in both its primary and secondary uses. For a similar response to a similar argument by Scruton (1997: 153–4), see Budd (2008: 175).

[11] At one time I might have invoked Wittgenstein's discussion of secondary senses (1967 Part 2: §xi) in characterizing this extended use, but the interpretation of his comments and their application to aesthetics are not straightforward or uncontroversial. For discussion, see Budd (2008: 129–30, 148–9), Scruton (1974: 50–2), Sharpe (2000: 44–8), Tilghman (1984: ch. 7).

There is a technical term for the linguistic phenomenon in which a word has many closely related meanings: polysemy. For instance, we refer to a philosopher's opinion as a view, position, stance, or approach. And if we look up the word 'view' in the *Concise Oxford Dictionary*, we find the fifth meaning of the noun is 'an opinion,' which is linked to two further sub-meanings: 'a mental attitude' and 'a manner of considering a thing.' Now, according to linguists, polysemy, unlike homonymy, is preserved across languages, which clearly suggests that the network of a word's related meanings is conceptually deeply rooted.[12] Moreover, language is riddled with polysemy. Consider 'riddled' in the previous sentence and 'preserved,' 'clearly,' 'network,' 'deeply,' and 'rooted' in the one before that. My claim is that to call a bodily appearance sad, where this does not involve reference to felt emotion, is to adopt a literal use of a polysemous word.

We do not confine our ascriptions of what I call emotion-characteristics in appearances only to the human realm. Basset hounds are sad-looking dogs and dolphins have happy faces. Note that this is not relative to their native ways of showing emotions. Rather, it is because we experience their appearances as resembling the relevant human ones that we make the attribution. And we do not predicate emotion-characteristics only of appearances presented by animate subjects. To return to an earlier example, the mask of tragedy presents a sad face and willow trees can look bent down with pain and suffering.

My claim, then, is that it is this same literal use of emotion terms that applies to music. We experience music as presenting emotion characteristics in its aural appearance and attribute them accordingly. But on what basis do we do so? As is clear from earlier examples, we do so because we experience music as presenting an appearance that resembles characteristic human behavioral displays of affect.

A presently dominant theory within the psychology of music holds that we hear emotion in music because of experienced similarities between musical parameters—such as tempo, energy, attack, and contour—and prosodic features of expressive speech.[13] I am sure this view is established by the empirical data, but I am not sure it is the whole story or even the most important part. While it can account for local, short-term effects, I doubt that it explains sustained levels of expressiveness that depend on musical elements, such as larger-scale melodic and structural features.[14] The position I prefer identifies as the source of music's expressiveness resemblances experienced between the music's dynamic motion and human comportment, rather than between its tone and the sound of expressive speech.[15] Happy music generally progresses in a fashion that is sprightly and confident, open-textured, tonally unambiguous, and with

---

[12] Bach writes (2001: 39): 'considering that the adjectives in [a list of different examples one of which is 'sad person, sad face, sad day, sad music'] have counterparts in other languages with a similar range of uses, it is not because of ambiguity (linguistic coincidence) that these adjectives have their different uses.'

[13] See Juslin and Laukka (2003), Juslin and Västfjäll (2008a). For a review and discussion, see the symposium in *Behavioural and Brain Sciences*, 31 (2008).

[14] The experimental design adopted by Juslin and his colleagues neutralizes or eliminates such effects by focusing on versions of a single, short piece, 'When the Saints Come Marching In.' For comment, see Chapters 3 and 5.

[15] For perceptive criticisms of my position, see Stecker (1999) and for a response, Davies (1999a).

balanced phrasing and emphatic cadences. Sad music typically drags itself along, is dense in texture and downcast, and is often clouded with tension, discord, and delayed or interrupted resolutions.

Metaphor all the way down?

At this point the proponent of the view that it is metaphoric to describe music as sad is likely to protest. The description of music as involving motion, and all the particular terms by which this is indicated—as when we say music is jagged, tense, smooth, hesitant, energetic, and so on—involve the use of metaphor. If our thinking of music as expressive depends on our entertaining this web of metaphoric descriptions, it must be that the attribution to music of emotional expressiveness is also metaphoric. After all, if some combination of metaphoric descriptions can be taken as premises entailing a conclusion, that conclusion had better be read metaphorically as well.

Here are some illustrative examples: 'tones, unlike sounds, seem to contain movement. This movement is exemplified in melodies, and can be traced through a "musical space", which we describe in terms of "high" and "low." It seems fairly clear that this description is metaphorical.... We must recognize that the idea of musical space, and of movement within that space, is a metaphor' (Scruton 1983: 80–1). 'We call music sad, [it is suggested], because it moves slowly, stumbles, droops, and so on—just as sad people do. But these are not real analogies, since music does not *literally* droop or stumble, any more than it is *literally* sad' (Scruton 1997: 153). 'Since "delicate," "balanced," "high," and "moving from note to note" are clearly metaphorical descriptions of music, we should treat "angry" similarly' (Zangwill 2007: 392).

One long-standing critic of such views is Malcolm Budd, who takes Scruton as his prime target. Scruton argues that metaphors of expressiveness and motion are ineliminable from descriptions of music. Budd counters that live metaphors are always eliminable;[16] they can be replaced by newly invented literal technical terms or by non-synonymous (possibly metaphoric) paraphrases. If Budd is correct about the replaceability of live metaphors, his argument could run in either direction: he could agree that the description is ineliminable and conclude that the terms are not used metaphorically, or he could agree that they are replaceable and argue that they are used metaphorically. In fact, he goes both ways. He accepts that the use of emotion terms cannot be eliminated without loss of sense from accounts of music's *expressiveness* and disagrees with Scruton's view that such terms are used figuratively, and he appears also to accept that descriptions of musical *movement* as spatial are metaphoric but then argues against Scruton that they are eliminable (Budd 2008: chs 6, 8, 9).[17] To be more precise,

---

[16] See Grant (2010) for arguments against the thesis that some ideas or thoughts make an indispensable use of metaphor.

[17] Budd first published these views in the 1980s, but I refer to their later incarnations because Budd further developed his position there.

his view in this second case is that the use of spatial terms in characterizing pitch, say, were once metaphoric but with the death of the metaphor, the relevant terms took on a literal meaning that is distinct from and therefore homonymous with their spatially related meanings. 'For pitch as such, it seems clear that the terms "'high" and "low," "higher" and "lower," do not import an essential reference to relative spatial height. Even when these terms first came to be used (as metaphors) to characterize the pitch of sounds they were doing duty for predicates—predicates we lacked—standing for a specifically audible characteristic of sounds; and now, when these terms are used to characterize the pitch of sounds, we no longer lack the predicates, for "high" and "low," in this use, have become them' (2008: 161). Similarly he writes (2008: 166): 'the fact is that "movement" is not restricted to mean change in spatial location, but can be used to mean change along a non-spatial continuum or with respect to some discrete variable, no reference to spatial movement being intended or implicated.' While I agree with Budd about expressiveness, I do not share his rejection of music's spatial character, though I think musical space is more like mathematical topographic space than geographic space.

Budd's argument for the eliminability of reference to spatial movement in music is as follows: the identity of a tone is tied to its pitch, so it cannot be that we hear tones moving toward or away from each other on the pitch continuum. As they hear the progression of a melody, listeners do not imagine the tones are going from place to place. 'In listening to a melody we do not hear tones as moving along some (indeterminate) spatial dimension, nor do we hear something other than the tones moving in this manner' (2008: 163).[18] Budd proposes a more plausible model: a melody is a temporal gestalt with a beginning and end. Its movement is temporal, not spatial. I agree that musical progress is that of a temporally unfolding dynamic process rather than that of a re-identifiable individual that changes its spatial location, and have argued that the former model of motion both is no less common in general use than the latter and is the one that applies to music (Davies 1994a: 229–37).[19] We talk of the economy running down or speeding up, of inflation as stagnant, and the like.

The crunch case, as Budd realizes, is not that of melodic motion but rather that of harmonic depth, where temporal progression is not at issue. Scruton argues (1997: 32) that chords are heard as made up of notes occupying different points in acoustic space. True to his earlier theme, Budd rejects (2008: 167) the suggestion that the description must be spatial. We can think of chords as spread along a non-spatial pitch continuum.

On this matter I am more sympathetic to Scruton than to Budd. We hear notes at the interval of an octave as the same but at different pitch locations—this is sometimes

---

[18] According to Scruton (2004), it is not the tones that move but the melody that moves through them, but I take it that Budd intends to reject this option in his closing phrase.

[19] Scruton refuses to acknowledge any model of movement other than one involving spatial displacement. 'What exactly is meant by "merely temporal" movement? What is supposed to move, from where to where? If this is not metaphor, I do not know what is' (2004: 187).

put as saying they share the same pitch class or chroma (Patel 2008a: 13)—and most cultures describe the separation using spatial terms (Davies 1994a: 232), such as 'high,' 'low,' 'big,' 'little,' 'thin,' 'fat.'[20] Within this musical space, different notes can be more or less stable (within a tonal or modal system, for instance), and the dynamic temporal unfolding of music is generated as patterns of fluctuating tension through the interaction between tones.

Budd and I agree that the use of terms like 'high' and 'low' in referring to pitch do not have the same application as when they are used to refer to physical (geographic) locations or relations, and we agree that the terms are literal in their application to music. The difference is that Budd thinks their musical application is homonymous whereas I think it is polysemous. For Budd, they refer to a distinctively musical characteristic of sounds and that characteristic can be recognized for what it is without being experienced as spatial. Hearing music as spatial is not integral or necessary to hearing music as music. By contrast, I claim that in the musical case these terms have meanings closely related to those they have in referring to physical locations or relations and I say this is so because we experience pitch as bearing that similarity. It is significant, I believe, that the same spatial terms are used cross-culturally to indicate this dimension of pitch, because this is what separates polysemy from homonymy and is what shows that the usage, rather than being parochial and contingent, gestures toward an aspect of how music is bound to strike us as human listeners. For this reason, I do not think terms other than these spatial ones could have seemed natural to those trying to characterize their experience of the music.[21] This is not to say that musical space is like or coextensive with physical space, but that does not entail that there cannot be an intimate relation between the meanings of the terms in their respective domains of application. So, when Budd insists that it is not essential to experiencing the relevant musical qualities that one hears the music as spatial, I agree and I disagree. I agree that this is not an experience of physical (geographic) space, but I disagree that it is not an experience of space and movement within that space. It is an experience of a musical space that can be thought of as analogous to mathematical topologic space.[22]

---

[20] The recognition of octave equivalence appears to be universal among humans (Higgins 2006), but we share the capacity with other animals and birds, so it is almost certainly one that is useful for ordinary sound processing rather than one that is targeted directly at music.

[21] In the political case, which position was first labeled 'left' would have been contingent, but this seems not to be the case in labeling the pitch continuum in terms of height. In other words, the pitch continuum comes to us as directionally ordered, rather than being structured solely in terms of non-directional contrasts. Perhaps that is because the vocal production of high notes requires more muscular tension than the production of low notes. Here it might also be relevant to invoke Johnson and Lakoff (2003)—see also Franklin and Tversky (1990)—on the way in which experiences of bodily vertical and lateral orientation structure our perception and description of other phenomena, though I would resist their account of such descriptions as metaphoric.

[22] I am not sure that I want to get into the argument about whether this experience is necessary or unavoidable. These strike me as not the right criteria. It would be sufficient for my view if such experiences seem natural, are common, and can be conveyed to others without requiring elaborate explanation or justification.

If Scruton is correct to maintain that it is hard to know how one would describe certain features of music except through the use of spatial terms that preserve a close connection with the meaning they have when used by navigators and geographers, it does not follow that he is also correct in holding that this usage is metaphoric or that it justifies the mysterious kind of intentionality he attributes to the experience. Indeed, there is every reason to think the terms are literal and that their polysemous use across a wide spread of domains is commonplace. Relations within many hierarchies, processes, or continua are described in spatial terms. In mathematics, we say that some numbers are higher or bigger than others; in politics, we hold that some views are to the right or left of others; and so on. When we do this, we are mapping relations between elements in a spatial domain, not tracking the displacement of an individual in geographic space. And these various uses are part of the public, shared language, not idiosyncratic or vivaciously figurative. In other words, they are recognized not as live metaphors but as sharing closely related literal meanings. It is no more metaphoric to describe a note's pitch as high than to call the temperature high, a salary high, or someone's social status high.

So, in my view there is musical space and progress within it revealed by the music's temporal unfolding, but, or so I claim, appropriate descriptions of music along these lines are literal, not metaphoric. Moreover, these literal meanings retain close connections with the meanings of the same terms as they are applied to physical space and other domains of space. They are not technical terms within folk musicology that have quite different, homonymous meanings from those they have in the other contexts I mentioned.

Action and purpose in music

At this point the metaphoricist might again object. To hear the music in terms of resemblances that would justify our finding it expressive, we must animate it. We must hear something like human action rather than inorganic process. But this business of animating inanimate sounds must be metaphoric at heart. Scruton writes (1983: 100): 'understanding music involves the active creation of an intentional world, in which inert sounds are transfigured into movements, harmonies, rhythms—metaphorical gestures in a metaphorical space. And into these metaphorical gestures a metaphorical soul is breathed by the sympathetic listener.' Zangwill observes (2007: 393): 'I do not recall having heard the following descriptions of music, but I can think of music I would want to call "perturbed," "remorseless," "hesitant," "nervous," "insistent," "vibrating," and so on. These are clearly metaphors.' He claims that these are live metaphors because newly minted by him, and that it is ad hoc to say different things about live and allegedly dead metaphors, such as that the music is sad.[23]

---

[23] Zangwill also claims (2007: 392) that 'delicate,' 'balanced,' 'high,' and 'moving from note to note,' are 'clearly metaphorical descriptions of music.' For reasons previously outlined, I see no reason to think these usages are not straightforwardly literal.

Now, Zangwill's descriptions strike me as hackneyed rather than novel. Music is described in such terms all the time. It is of course true that we can create live metaphors in describing music—the soloist is an eagle soaring above the orchestral valley—but that says nothing about how we should regard Zangwill's more mundane examples. I also think that it is crucial, not at all ad hoc, to distinguish live from dead metaphors, precisely because what is merely intimated by the former becomes literal in the latter (Davies 2007: ch. 15).

I agree that we describe music in terms more suited to purposive action than random motion and that recognizing the aptness of such descriptions may be essential to experiencing music as expressive. If that is what animating the music amounts to, then we animate the music in hearing it as expressive. But what lies behind this? Scruton and Zangwill seem to think a kind of metaphoric projection is involved. I return to their views below.

Vivifying the music

Many authors testify to our apparently unavoidable inclination to animate music. In a view that recalls Daniel Dennett's 'intentional stance' (1987), Peter Kivy (1989: 172–5) speculates that we are hard-wired to animate the world and that is why we hear expressiveness in music. Charles Nussbaum (2007: 47) argues that, partly due to the physiology of hearing, the internal representations employed in recovering the musical structure from the musical surface specify motor hierarchies and action plans, which, in turn, put the listener's body into off-line motor states that specify virtual movements through a virtual terrain or a scenario possessing certain features. The psychologist Patrik Juslin and his colleagues (Juslin and Laukka 2003, Juslin and Västfjäll 2008a) speculate that many musical instruments are processed as super-expressive voices by brain modules. In a recent experiment by Nikolaus Steinbeis and Stefan Koelsch (2009) that is interpreted as showing that we are especially primed to find expressiveness in humanly produced artifacts, areas of the brain dedicated to mental state attribution were stimulated when participants listened to what they (rightly) believed to be humanly composed music and were not similarly stimulated when they listened to what they (mistakenly) believed to be computer-generated music. (For a non-musical analogue, see Reeves and Nass 1996.)

Of course, the response to such positions is a simple one. These accounts all attempt to identify the causal mechanisms underlying our tendency to hear resemblances between action, purpose, and human life in music, but do nothing to show that our characterization of music in such terms could be literal. Trivedi puts the point this way (2003b: 110): 'while resemblance gives us the causal story behind expressiveness, telling us that resemblance is what causes or allows music to be heard as sad, it does not tell us how something *inanimate* or insentient such as music can be sad or happy (or otherwise expressive of emotions), which is the basic problem of expressiveness.'

A crucial consideration, however, is that these causal processes are not personal and idiosyncratic but rather aspects of our shared human nature. They underpin our shared way of experiencing what we hear and how the world comes to us in perception, and this implies the literalness of our descriptions of music's expressiveness.

We hear purpose and action in music because we approach it as humanly created and designed. The emotion terms and action words that we find apt for describing some of these experiences of music are also part of our common language; they are used interpersonally and recorded in dictionaries. Even if we would not teach the ordinary meanings of these terms starting from the musical case, once children master that ordinary use they are easily able to learn to extend this ordinary meaning to subtler, richer contexts, including the musical one. These are the hallmarks of the polysemous use of literal language. We can assume that this process of extending ordinary uses of terms denoting mental states and actions goes back to those who first became sophisticated language users, or in other words, to the dawn of humanity.

By contrast, live metaphors are singular, creative uses of language without an interpersonal basis or fixed meaning. They challenge others to search for their significance and it is not obvious that there are determinate limits to what that significance might be, nor is it likely that they prompt the same or similar paraphrases from everyone. When I coin a novel metaphor, I creatively project something I imagine onto the world and invite others to do the same in working out what I mean. But a person's description of music as sad does not involve a novel, creative use of language that provokes others to try to puzzle out what she could be driving at, given how incongruous her choice of words appears to be. When something is simply our shared way of experiencing music and sound, rather than talking of imagination and projection, it is more to the point to consider how what we all perceive is structured and filtered by our evolved perceptual, cognitive, behavioral, and affective systems.

Response-dependence and anti-realism

Of course, musical qualities are of the kind called response-dependent. That is to say, they are adequately represented only by concepts whose conditions of application essentially involve conditions of human response. The concept of musical sadness, for instance, is the concept of the music's disposition to produce the listener's recognition of sadness under appropriate conditions of listening. If sentient creatures with perceptual, cognitive, and affective systems like ours had never existed, music (or music-like sounds) would not have been experienced as sad, grass would not have been experienced as green, and rainbows would not have been experienced as beautiful, though music-like sounds, grass, and rainbows possess the relevant dispositional qualities even where the conditions actually obtaining do not allow the realization of those dispositions.

It is widely accepted, however, that response-dependence does not undermine objectivity. Nor does it entail the version of anti-realism according to which judgments about the relevant qualities necessarily involve a feeling, emotion, or attitude on the part of the judger and, to that extent, are always projected. This anti-realist view (wrongly) equates literal possession of a quality with the mind-independence of that property and then denies the mind-independence of the relevant aesthetic properties. But, as I indicated, there is every reason to resist this equation and the anti-realism that goes with it. All the parameters of sound, pitch, and volume for instance, are response-dependent, but it would be revisionary to be anti-realists about these, and there is no evidence that Scruton or Zangwill denies the reality of these first-order acoustic properties.

They both think that some further kind of mind-dependence is involved when we hear music. For Scruton, it is an unasserted thought in terms of which we hear note sequences as, say, melodies, and for Zangwill, it appears to be some kind of valuation inherent to the experience.[24] I am not convinced by their arguments and do not share their anti-realism about higher-order aesthetic properties. It is not necessary to settle that debate, however, in order to reject the claim that descriptions of music's expressiveness are live metaphors, because anti-realism concerning higher-order aesthetic properties in no way requires that descriptions of such properties must be metaphoric.

In brief

I have outlined my reasons for believing that talk of both musical motion and musical expressiveness is closely connected with usages of the relevant terms established in non-musical contexts. These non-musical usages refer both to temporal process in terms of motion and space, but not to the spatial displacement of particulars, and also to the ascription of emotion-characteristics to appearances without the attribution of felt emotions to the bearers of those appearances. The musical case involves an extension of the ordinary meanings of the terms, but this polysemous expansion is one that our natural history prepared us for in our ancestral past. The relevant uses are recorded in dictionaries and have the robust interpersonality, familiarity, and teachability of meaning that characterize literal, not live metaphoric, discourse.

---

[24] Zangwill writes (2007: 396): 'theories other than the aesthetic metaphor thesis have a problem with explaining the *direct* way that emotion descriptions typically function as reasons for evaluations. The evaluative reason-giving aspect is *intrinsic* to the emotion description because *what* is described is an *evaluatively* charged feature. But any literalist or emotion theory must deny this.' I have to confess I find this quite baffling. I do not see how the relation between expression and evaluation is such that only metaphoricism can account for it, but perhaps that is because I have no idea what is meant by the insistence that the relation is direct.

3

Cross-cultural Musical Expressiveness: Theory and the Empirical Program

In the initial sections of this chapter I outline the theoretical background for a research program considering whether the expressiveness of a culture's music can be recognized by people from different musical cultures, that is, by people whose music is syntactically and structurally distinct from that of the target culture. I then examine and assess the cross-cultural studies that have been undertaken by psychologists. Most of these studies are compromised by methodological inadequacies.

Affect programs

Psychologists have described a set of six basic affect programs: those for fear, anger, happiness, sadness, surprise, and disgust (Ekman 1992). Affect programs are characterized as involving appraisals, affective states, and distinctive behavioral displays of these. They are programmatic in being automatically triggered and universal.

We should be careful not to equate affect programs with full-blooded emotions. Affect programs are common, perhaps even necessary, elements in emotional episodes of happiness, disgust, and the like, but there can be more to these emotions, especially cognitively, than is covered by the affect program. Moreover, emotional episodes are themselves often only parts within a complex and temporally extended state that is the emotion proper. Nevertheless, in what follows I begin with affect programs.

Because of their distinctive behavioral displays, we can predict that we should be able to detect the basic affective states of members of other cultures so long as the automatic displays of their states are unimpeded, and empirical evidence bears this out.

Though the display is automatically triggered, it might be suppressed or 'restructured'. If this occurs quickly, it is unlikely that cultural outsiders will be able naturally to read the affective significance of whatever behavior takes place. The suppression or restructuring of standard behavioral displays of affect can be fast when it is no less

---

First published in Elisabeth Schellekens and Peter Goldie (eds), *The Aesthetic Mind*, Oxford: Oxford University Press, 2011, 376–88.

automatic than the behavior it supplants. And it can become automatic as a result of implicit or explicit socio-cultural training or conditioning. Nevertheless, because of the value of being able to communicate and recognize these fundamental affective states, we might anticipate that their distinctive displays are not all or always immediately cloaked by culturally shaped substitutes. The anticipated upshot is this: for the most part, we should be able to recognize the basic affective states of individuals from other cultures by the universal behavioral displays that characterize them, but we should not presume that this cross-cultural recognition will always be possible.[1]

Music and the affect programs

I now turn to the case of music and focus on 'pure' or 'absolute' music, which is to say instrumental music without literary titles, sung words, or accompanying pictorial depictions or verbal descriptions. Such music is widely recognized as being emotionally expressive, by which I mean that it seems to embody a certain emotional tone, appearance, or character in the way it sounds, independently both of how it arouses the listener (if it does) and of associations, whether shared with others or idiosyncratic, that it has for the listener. The range of emotions such music expresses is limited: happiness, sadness, anger, and their cognates are common; pomposity or sassy sexuality might also be possible.[2] Notice that happiness, sadness, and anger belong to the set of basic affect programs. And for that matter, behavioral patterns of sassy sexuality and pomposity may also be cross-culturally recognizable, because they deal in aspects of sexuality and status that have long had significance in the evolution of our species.

An aside: some philosophers suggest that the attribution of sadness and other emotions to music must be metaphoric, because plainly it is not literally true that music is sentient.[3] By contrast, I regard this usage as literal. This literal use is not homonymous; it is not as if 'sad' has become a technical term in folk musicology that retains no connection from the realm of human feeling. Rather, it is polysemous; the word 'sad' has many closely related meanings. Having acquired the primary use, in which 'sad' refers to a felt emotion, the meaning is extended to cover behaviors, appearances, occasions, and states of affairs. It is no less literally true that the music is sad than that the mask of tragedy and the face of the basset hound present sad appearances, that bottles have mouths, and that the exchange rate moves up and down. Most dictionaries record the secondary use of emotion-terms in relation to the character and mood of artworks, which is a good sign that the relevant attributions are not live metaphors. Note also that words that are polysemous in one language tend to be likewise in another, whereas homonymy does not hold constant from language to

---

[1] This prediction is borne out by the empirical data summarized in Elfenbein and Ambady (2002) and, for vocal displays of emotion, in Juslin and Laukka (2003).
[2] Empirical studies confirming these observations are too numerous to cite. The following are representative: Krumhansl (1997), Gabrielsson (2002, 2003), Juslin and Sloboda (2010).
[3] See Scruton (1983, 1997), Trivedi (2003a), Zangwill (2007). For criticisms other than the ones given here, see Chapter 2 and Budd (2008).

language and the live metaphors used in one language can be absent from another. So it is significant that most cultures attribute emotional or expressive character to their music. This suggests that the usage, rather than being parochial and contingent, indicates how music is bound to strike us as human listeners. Terms other than emotion-words would not have seemed natural to those trying to characterize their experience of the music.

We might now speculate as follows: the widely made claim that music is a universal language often includes the idea that perception of the expressive character of music is unaffected by both the listener's and the music's cultural origins. In other words, we can be expected to recognize the affective character of the music of other cultures fairly often. (Given that we do not understand anything of their language, we might now be listening to songs and the like, not solely to instrumental works.) And experience also suggests that some kinds of music in other cultures can be expressively opaque to the outsider. So, in both these respects, the cross-cultural recognition of the expressive quality of music parallels the cross-cultural recognition of basic affective states. Moreover, certain universal principles of structure, organization, continuation, and closure are universal to all musics (see Higgins 2006, Thompson and Balkwill 2010).[4] So, if these play a role equivalent to that of the characteristic behaviors that universally betray basic affective states, and if these musical universals can also be subject to cultural suppression or restructuring, so that sometimes their fundamental expressive import becomes disguised, we might try to develop the analogy yet further.

We arrive at this conjecture: some (systematic) applications of universal musical principles somehow play the role of invoking, representing, or referring to the primitive behaviors that universally display basic affective states, and this is one, fundamental route by which music gets to have an expressive character. The universal significance of these musical applications usually facilitates the recognition of musical expressiveness across cultural boundaries and musical genres, styles, and kinds, though these applications can be subject to local inflections that make the expressiveness of the music then produced unfathomable to all but those steeped in the particular musical tradition and culture in which the music is made.

Reservations and qualifications

There are two reasons for being wary of the fantasy that was just sketched. Here is the first: it is widely held that languages are structured according to deep, universal principles and, of course, languages are universal among humans, but it does not follow that we can understand each other's languages. Even if music is universal in its occurrence and is governed also by universal structural-cum-perceptual principles, it

---

[4] Of course, opposed to this line of thinking there is a long tradition of skepticism regarding musical universals, based on an anthropological perspective that sees all biological grounding overruled and superseded by contingent cultural considerations. For an example, see Walker (1996).

cannot be assumed that the expressive character of foreign music will be any more accessible to us than is the import of utterances made in the foreigner's native language.

Some of the differences between music and language mitigate this first concern, however. The structural universals displayed by languages do not require semantic transparency between languages. This is not an issue with 'pure' music, however, because it has no semantic content; its 'meaning' depends purely on its syntactic, tonal, and timbral properties. Besides, the structural universals characterized for language by Noam Chomsky are deep indeed, not part of the phenomenology of following linguistic utterance, whereas what is universal to different musics and how they are experienced is accessible and much nearer the surface.

The second reason for doubting that music's expressiveness might be modeled in terms of the basic affect programs is that it expresses only some of them. Music can be sad, happy, or angry. Despite its non-sentience, we say the music is sad, or that it expresses sadness, or that its expressive mood is one of sadness, and we do not mean by this merely that it is saddening, though it may be that too. But the other basic affect programs do not seem to be susceptible of expression in pure music. Music can be surprising, disgusting, or even frightening—that is, it can elicit (and even be the object of) surprise, disgust, or fear—but we would not say of it that it is surprised, disgusted, or frightened.[5] Haydn's Surprise Symphony is designed to startle the audience, but the symphony is surprised by nothing. And if someone expressed the view that a musical piece was disgusted, we would be hard pressed to guess what he might be trying to say.

This runs against the view implied earlier. If music expresses, say, sadness through exemplifying acoustic structural or perceptual principles that operate to display sadness by invoking, representing, or referring to the primitive behaviors that universally display the basic affective state of sadness, then, one might think, it should be able to do the same for each of the other basic affective states.

Consideration of the musical means by which musical expressiveness is achieved, and comparison then with basic affect-program expressions, allows us to address this concern and to refine our proposal. The primitively expressive behaviors highlighted by psychologists in discussing the operation of affect programs concern expressions of the face, but the expressiveness of music does not seem to be physiognomic in its genesis. For instance, if a certain kind of smile, as opposed say to a grimace, is characteristic of the unreflective display of happiness, it is not as if music is happy by imitating or depicting such a smile, and this might allow us to explain why it expresses only some affect-program emotions. In music, expressiveness seems to be rooted in dynamic patterns or processes of tension and movement, rather than in the relative disposition of elements like those found in a facial array or expression. So, by way of filling out the account proposed earlier, it is plausible to suggest that the universally expressive behavioral displays that music is experienced as resembling (and thereby, the

---

[5] Music often plays a vital role in horror movies, but it does so typically by building tension and suspense or by being brutal, not by expressing fright as such.

emotions it is experienced as presenting) have a temporally extended, processional, dynamic character, rather than a static physiognomy. Now, if besides their distinctive facial expression, some but not all the various basic affects have other expressive displays more akin to the musical kind, this would explain why only some of the basic affects are amenable to expression in music.

Surprise is typically short-lived. And while disgust and fear might persist, they do not possess distinctive patterns of behavioral expression over the longer term. Fear behaviors, where the fear's object is not immediately present, indicate a general nervousness or anticipatory tension. These are states that music can express—for instance, with disjointed, darting phrases, or with throbbing discords that call for future resolution—but these states are too general to count distinctively as of fear or disgust. And while aversive behaviors are also typical of fear and disgust, whether movement amounts to fleeing from or drawing toward depends on the location of its target or object, and nothing sufficiently specific counts as the object of musical expression. By contrast, happiness and sadness do have characteristic demeanors, carriages, gaits, ways of moving. Happiness tends to be fast rather than slow, tension-free, light rather than heavy, whereas sadness is the reverse, dragging, clouded, heavy with unresolved tension. What is more, the expressive significance of these ways of moving is apparent even to the observer who sees another's expressive movement yet does not know the object to which this is a reaction. Anger is similar, though usually more short-lived.

In light of this, it seems plausible to suggest that music presents the appearances of sadness and happiness because it is experienced as progressing in ways that are typical of the non-physiognomic expression of such states in a person's carriage.[6] And we can now also explain why it does not express disgust or fear. These do not have distinctive gaits or carriages, or do not have them at least unless the third-party observer is aware also of the emotion's object and its location. And to return to the previous argument, if the gaits of sadness and happiness are universally distinctive, we should be able to recognize these emotions in the progress of foreign kinds of music, unless the music in question alters or subverts the universal musical principles that most naturally shape its dynamic character.

How music is expressive

Notice that, while many of the earlier claims about music's expressiveness were agnostic about how it is expressive, replying to the worry that music expresses only some of the affect-program emotions forces engagement with that issue. So it is important to acknowledge that experimental work by psychologists sometimes assumes other models for musical expressiveness.

One alternative locates the musical features that are the source of music's expressiveness not in the way music is experienced as moving but in the way it is experienced

---

[6] I have defended such a view in Chapter 1 and Davies (1994a, 2003: Part 3).

as resembling prosodic features of expressive speech.[7] If the expressiveness of spoken utterances depends not only on their semantic content but also on prosodic features of pattern, duration, accent, volume, tempo, pitch variation, and contour, and if different basic affective states are matched by distinctive groupings of prosodic features, perhaps music is expressive by being experienced as presenting the relevant prosodic cues. And again, if the affective import of these prosodic cues is universal, we should be able sometimes to recognize the relevant affects in the progress of foreign kinds of music, unless the music in question alters or subverts the universal musical principles that most naturally shape its dynamic character.

In favor of this view, there is strong evidence that verbal and vocal displays communicate their expressive tones (especially where these are the affect-program emotions) to people of other cultures who have no semantic clues about what is being uttered. Though these data are suggestive for what we might expect in the musical case, there are insufficient data regarding that case to test whether cross-cultural communication of musical expressiveness depends on music's imitating expressive prosodic features (Juslin and Laukka 2003: 280).

This theory is clearly plausible, but how does it tackle the worry that only some affect-program emotions are expressed in music? Earlier, I suggested that this could be explained by the facts that music is expressive via its pattern of movement and that only some affect programs typically have temporally extended expressive displays. Is a similar argument available to support the prosodic account of music's expressiveness? Are the temporal and dynamic structures of the characteristic vocalizations of only some affect-program emotions sufficiently extended to permit the expression of only some affect-program emotions by musical means? I doubt this. Prosodic features can be extended through repetition and the like, but expressive prosodic features tend not to be temporally extended. Overall, it is less clear on this account of music's expressiveness than on the one presented earlier why music is limited in the range of affect-program emotions it expresses.

Most tests of the prosodic theory adopt a method that filters the expressive effects of structural features, such as the pattern of melodic and harmonic succession, which are responsible for the temporal play of tension and resolution. They do this by holding those factors constant; they use as examples different performances of a single, short piece, with the musician instructed to play it sadly, angrily, happily, and so on. In consequence, proponents of the theory give pre-eminence to prosodic over structural features in contributing to music's expressiveness and they attribute the expressiveness

---

[7] See Juslin and Laukka (2003). They hold that vocal expression is an evolved mechanism based on innate and universal affect programs that develop early and are fine-tuned by prenatal experiences. They predict: (a) communication of emotions is cross-culturally accurate in vocal expression and music performance, (b) the ability to decode basic emotions develops early in ontogeny, and (c) similar patterns of emotion-specific acoustic cues are used to communicate emotions in both vocal and musical communication channels. To test these claims they reviewed 104 studies about the vocal communication of emotion and 41 about the communication of emotion in music.

to *performance* properties rather than to *work* features. There is no reason why the two theories are not complementary, however, and many of the prosodic features identified as expressive could belong to the piece rather than to its individual interpretation if they are called for by the piece's composer.[8]

Neonates and music

I now briefly consider a further approach to the study of what if anything is universal in musical expressiveness. Instead of comparing adult listeners raised in different cultures, one might study neonates. If they are innocent listeners, and if they detect the expressive character of the music they first hear, whatever their culture, it looks as if music has a pre-cultural expressive dimension.

Though I am not aware of specific studies of neonates' reactions to 'foreign' music, there is work on their responses to 'good' and 'bad' melodies and to 'concords' and 'discords,' and their reactions are sometimes characterized as having (or detecting) an emotional character, for instance because of the frontal hemisphere in which they are processed, the one being associated with negative evaluations or experiences and the other with positive ones.[9]

Nevertheless, I think there are significant problems with the interpretation of the results of such experiments. To begin, it is not clear that neonates are musical innocents. They receive a fair amount of exposure to their culture's music while in the womb. And it is not obvious that their reactions are to music as such, as opposed to revealing biases related to speech processing or to auditory processing more generally. In addition, the interpretation of the behaviors or brain scans observed is surely controversial.[10]

Similar issues arise with studies of individuals whose musicality is affected by specific neural deficits (whether accidental or congenital). It is not accepted that such studies point to what in undamaged participants would be universal and innate capacities that are specifically musical (Justus and Hutsler 2005, McDermott and Hauser 2005, Patel 2008a). In any case, few of these studies deal with music's expressiveness and none is cross-cultural or based mainly on people in non-Western musical cultures.

A theoretical program for empirical research

We are not out of the woods yet, but we are some way toward establishing a theoretical underpinning for an experimental program. And it is noteworthy,

---

[8] For other criticism of the prosodic theory, see Patel (2008a: 345–8), who also notes the lack of neuro-imaging data in favor of the theory.

[9] For instance, see Trehub et al. (1990); Trainor and Trehub (1994); Zentner and Kagan (1996); Trehub (2000, 2003); Justus and Hutsler (2005); Thompson and Balkwill (2010).

[10] For elaboration of some of the reservations expressed here, see McDermott and Hauser (2005), Patel (2008a: 377–86).

I think, that psychologists have pursued the analysis of music's expressiveness along the lines I have indicated, by considering if music has a prosodic character and by considering the affective relevance of what I have called its carriage or gait.

The program I have envisaged relies on two empirical claims: that we can often correctly identify the expressive character of foreign music and that sometimes we cannot do so because of ways in which the normal modes of musical expression are tweaked within the local musical tradition. Psychologists have ignored the second, taking no interest in the ways musical cultures set out to disguise or mask their music's expressiveness to outsiders. But they have attempted to study the first claim, that is, to look for cross-cultural correlations in judgments and reactions to music's expressiveness. As I shall show later, the results of this research program have so far been limited, inconclusive, and inadequate. Before I get to that, though, I indicate some lines of research that I think should be put to one side.

Motherese

There is cross-cultural recognition of lullabies, as distinct from other kinds of song, and it has been suggested that expressive communication is part of what makes lullabies distinctive (Unyk et al. 1992, Trehub et al. 1993a). The experimenters found that prosodic features in the style of presentation (Trehub et al. 1993b) rather than dynamic pattern and structure appeared to be responsible for the recognition and the expression. I doubt, however, that this supports the prosodic theory of musical expression. Whereas that theory holds that music is expressive by imitating prosodic features of natural vocal expressions of basic emotions (by adults, under the force of those emotions), the prosodic features that account for this lullaby effect more likely derive from the inflections of Motherese or Infant-Directed Speech, a sing-song, exaggerated vocal style adopted by mothers (and fathers) of neonates in all cultures. Anne Fernald (1992) observed that descending pitch contours, which are characteristic of lullabies, dominate in speech used to soothe infants. As a result, the expressive effect of lullabies is more likely a result of their elaboration of Motherese than of their specifically musical character. So, these studies should not be offered in support of the hypothesis that *musical* expressiveness is cross-culturally recognizable.

Similar doubts are likely to arise with respect to cross-cultural recognition of the grief expressed in musicalized renditions of wailing and keening. Unless the musical intrusion is highly stylized, it is possible that the expressiveness lies more in the universal manner of vocalizing grief than in anything the music contributes to this.

The point I have been making is this: even where there is cross-cultural recognition of expression and that expression involves music or has a musical character, before one can credit the music with even partial responsibility for the transmission of affect it is necessary to control for other modes of universally recognizable auditory expression that could mediate the communication of affect. This was one reason for focusing on instrumental as against vocal music. I suggest that a similar consideration should lead us to discount results based on lullabies and laments.

Actual cross-cultural studies

I now turn to empirical studies that offer the hope of confirming the cross-cultural transmission of musical affect. (For an excellent overview, see Thompson and Balkwill 2010.) Some of these do seem to bear out the phenomenon. Laura-Lee Balkwill and William Thompson (1999) had thirty Western participants listen to twelve Hindustani raga excerpts that were agreed by Hindustani experts to express joy, sadness, anger, and peacefulness. These listeners were sensitive to the expression of joy and sadness, somewhat less so for anger, and least for peacefulness. Their judgments of the emotions expressed related significantly to judgments of psychophysical dimensions (tempo, rhythmic complexity, melodic complexity, and pitch range). A similar result was found with Japanese listeners to Japanese, Western, and Hindustani music (Balkwill et al. 2004). Meanwhile, Carol Krumhansl (2002)[11] compared British folk, Chinese folk, and atonal songs, and compared Western musicians with Finns with respect to Finnish spiritual folk hymns and vocal Saami music. The results she lists come close to what I have suggested. She concludes (2002: 49): 'in sum, these results support the idea that music draws on common psychological principles of expectation, but that musical cultures shape these in unique ways.' Thomas Fritz et al. (2009) found that Mafa (Africans from a remote area of Cameroon) without prior exposure to Western music could distinguish between happy, sad, and fearful Western music at better than chance, with happy music recognized more consistently than sad or fearful music.

If these studies are suspect, they are so in the ways that most psychologists' studies are. They rely on a limited set of musical examples. The examples are brief and are stripped of their musical context. As well, they are often presented under laboratory conditions that are not normal for (or conducive to?) the appreciative enjoyment of music. And they typically require choices between descriptors provided by the experimenter.

It should be noted that the brevity and absence of a temporally extended musical context for the excerpts is likely to be especially unfortunate in the study of cross-cultural responses. Whereas a listener can easily pick up and make sense of a musical excerpt when the style and kind of music is already native to her, access to the organizational principles and expressive character of unfamiliar styles of music can be expected to require a much longer exposure. In addition, the use of forced choice alternatives may be problematic in assuming that all cultures apply the same affective categories to music (Benamou 2003). And it is not sufficient to point to the 'successful' cross-cultural identification of music's expressive character, supposing this occurs, as

---

[11] Reporting on Krumhansl (1995), Krumhansl et al. (1999), Krumhansl et al. (2000).

the sign that these worries are misplaced. The thesis that expression may rely on universal musical elements is supported only if the participants have an appropriate experience of the music, and not if entirely inappropriate modes of listening or categorizations of musical affect fortuitously elicit the 'correct' identifications.

A further consideration is the degree of similarity between the music of the cultures being compared. For instance, if the topic cultures share very close tonal/modal systems, and if expressiveness can be affected by the music's mode as is often assumed, successful cross-cultural recognition of expressiveness might not be generalizable to musically more distant cultures.[12]

Problems and complications

In other published studies, methodological flaws cast doubt on the credibility of the results claimed. Sometimes these flaws are widely found and are not specific to cross-cultural studies. For instance, while the goal of Andrew Gregory and Nicholas Varney (1996) was to compare what Western and Indian listeners identified as the music's mood and character, instead of asking about that, they asked about what the listener felt on hearing the music. It was plain throughout that they took these two very different questions to mean exactly the same. A similar confusion is present in the design of the trials conducted by Alice-Ann Darrow et al. (1987), in which participants matched descriptors to the music. Some of the descriptors (mournful, dignified) had implications for the music's expressive character. Others (exciting, soothing) concerned the evocation of response as against expressive character. And yet others (fanciful, dramatic) fell in different categories. And Fritz et al. (2009) seem to slide from musical expressive qualities (happiness and sadness) to the listener's response when they consider fearfulness, which must be the music's power to cause fear or to be apt, say, for a horror movie, and not the property of its being frightened.

Unlike some philosophers, I do think that music can elicit an emotional response that echoes its own expressive character and that this process parallels other cases of emotional contagion as described by psychologists (see Chapter 4). But I doubt that a thirty-second excerpt is likely to elicit this response usually, and in any case, it is surely obvious that the listener's response need not correspond to the music's expressive character. What does (thirty seconds of) Vivaldi's 'Spring' express? A certain *joie de vivre*. What does the Spring excerpt make you feel? Perhaps frustration because the movement is cut short, or disappointment at the musicians' poor interpretation, or boredom because you have already heard the piece a dozen times this week, or

---

[12] This may be an issue with Fritz et al. (2009), given that many African musics south of Sahara employ modes not unlike the Western major and minor. The authors of the study provide no information about the musical system of the Mafa. And in any case, the conclusion they draw on the basis of data from one African group—that the emotional expressions conveyed by the Western musical excerpts can be universally recognized, similar to the largely universal recognition of human emotional facial expression and emotional prosody—is overly strong.

irritation because that excerpt, like Barber's Adagio, is used so often by experimental psychologists, or sadness because this was the music playing when your child died.

A second fault is that of assuming music's expressiveness is always and solely a matter of contingent association. A particularly striking example of this occurs in an experiment done by Gregory and Varney (1996), who believe that expressiveness is based on learned association. So, in asking their participants what season is depicted by Vivaldi's 'Spring' and the monsoon raga 'Rag Kirvani,' they equated (1996: 47) spring with the monsoon season because there is 'the same association with renewal and joyfulness.' But if the expressiveness of music depends on its dynamic character, as I have already suggested, and if spring in Italy and the monsoon in India manifest dynamically distinct patterns of weather, as seems likely, that both are associated with renewal might be irrelevant to their expressive characters. So, the lack of a significant correlation, which was the outcome of this part of the experiment, should not be interpreted as proving a failure of cross-cultural agreement about the music's expressive character, though this is how the experimenters read it.

Other methodological problems are specific to cross-cultural studies. One is the limited number of musical cultures that have been compared and the tendency to concentrate on 'high,' literate musical cultures, such as those of the West, India, China, and Japan, as against small-scale, oral, tribal traditions. Balkwill and Thompson (1999) and Gregory and Varney (1996) compare Western and Indian musics. Balkwill (2006), Balkwill et al. (2004), Darrow et al. (1987), and Etsuko Hoshino (1996) compare Western and Japanese subjects. E. Glenn Schellenberg (1996) and Krumhansl (2002) compare Western and Chinese subjects.

A further methodological risk is that of confusing political with musico-cultural boundaries. Contrasting French with German listeners does not produce a musically significant cross-cultural comparison, for example, because the national styles present in their musics differ more as dialects than as languages. The relevant comparisons must be across musical divides. This may be an issue with the studies by Krumhansl and others (1995, Krumhansl et al. 1999, 2000) comparing British folk and Finnish spiritual folk hymns with Saami yoiks.

Another difficulty results from the globalization of (popular and film) Western music: non-Western participants are already musically bicultural (McDermott and Hauser 2005), whereas Western participants tend to be musically monocultural and thereby are ignorant of the non-Western music the experiment exposes them to. In consequence, most studies are not fully cross-cultural and they lack the symmetry and two-directionality that would be required for the most satisfactory tests. (Fritz et al. (2009), who explicitly acknowledge the issue, are a notable exception, though the part of their study concerning expressiveness was one- rather than two-directional.) Of course, the problem might be avoided if the comparison were between, say, the musics of Inuit and of tribal Australian aboriginals, but all studies so far involve Western music.

Here are some examples: Darrow et al. (1987) compare non-music majors in both the U.S. and Japan with respect to excerpts of various styles of Western and Japanese music. As they allow, while the U.S. listeners were unfamiliar with Japanese music, the Japanese listeners had considerable experience of Western music. They suggest this familiarity might explain the higher agreement in descriptors chosen for the Western examples, but in that case the comparison is not genuinely cross-cultural. The same problem arises also in a study by Hoshino (1996) involving female Japanese, who associated emotional characters with Western major and minor modes and various Japanese modes. (For another example, see Balkwill et al. 2004.)

A more glaring instance is by Gregory and Varney (1996), who were supposedly comparing subjects from European and Asian cultural backgrounds. Whereas the Europeans were students of the University of Manchester, the Asians were of Indian descent but bred and raised in Bradford, England. They were enrolled at a college of Further Education. In addition to the issue of the lack of genuine biculturality raised above, this selection of participants introduces predictable differences in the socio-economic status of the two groups (ethnic majority at university versus ethnic minority at a college) that may be relevant to how subjects respond to music (or to psychologists).[13]

Gregory and Varney's conclusion was that there is a significant correlation between Western and Indian listeners for Western classical music and New Age music and also between male and female listeners, but that there is a lack of agreement over the season for which music is appropriate. For the reasons given, however, it is hard to accord this conclusion much credibility.

Where to from here?

Cross-cultural studies of listeners' reactions to 'foreign' music are in their infancy. When one discounts methodologically questionable experiments, few remain. These do appear to support the hypothesis argued here, that cross-cultural recognition of musical expressions of basic affect-program emotions is sometimes possible, but that conclusion is far from established.

Thompson and Balkwill (2010: 782–3) outline the direction for future empirical tests of the extent to which musical expressiveness is cross-culturally recognizable. They acknowledge the need to investigate if universal cues of musical expressiveness can be culturally overridden, which I identified earlier as a question that so far has been ignored. They invite models and theories concerning the mechanisms or structures responsible for the existence of culture-transcendent connections between psycho-physical cues and emotions. And they anticipate further comparison between affect in prosodic speech and in music.

Of course the relevant facts will be settled by empirical studies rather than by philosophical speculation, but the credibility of those studies will depend on how they address many of the issues I have highlighted here. For instance, it is crucial to

---

[13] McKay (2002) faults Gregory and Varney (1996), and also the study by Hoshino (1996), on this score.

separate questions about the music's expressive character from ones about the listener's response, to work with musics that involve quite different modal systems and sonic ideals, and to test listeners who are unfamiliar with the other culture's music under conditions that provide them with the opportunity to bootstrap their way to an appreciative grasp of how the music they are hearing is organized.

In addition, some of the considerations I have raised point to the need for new lines of research. For instance, psychologists might test why music expresses only some basic affects, given that the ones it does not express also have distinctive prosodic as well as physiognomic expressions. And rather than focusing exclusively on parallels between expressive music and prosodic speech, which tend to be local and short-term, they might pay more attention to large-scale expressiveness and its possible connections with musical structure and movement.

4

Emotional Contagion from Music to Listener

I have long been interested in the expression of emotion in music and in the response this calls forth from the listener. I do not subscribe to the so-called arousal theory, according to which 'the music is sad' is true if and only if the music disposes a suitably qualified and interested listener to feel sad. I regard music's expressive properties as possessed independently of their effects (see Chapter 1 and Davies 1994a: 184–99). Nevertheless, as I argued in the early 1980s, I do think that music's expressiveness can induce an emotional reaction and that, in the interesting case, the listener is moved to feel the emotion that the music expresses; sad music tends to make (some) listeners feel sad and happy music to make them happy. I call this a 'mirroring' response and describe the communication of emotion from music to listener as emotional 'contagion' or 'infection.' In other words, we tend to resonate with the emotional tenor of the music, much as we catch the emotional ambience emanating from other people. I am not wedded to the medical metaphor, however; I also describe the connection as involving transmission, communication, or osmosis.

Reflecting on the musical case not only enhances understanding of the listener's response, it provides a novel objection to the cognitive theory of the emotions favored by many philosophers and invites critical consideration of the models for human-to-human emotional contagion proposed by psychologists. As I try to show, the most common accounts of emotional contagion should be developed and refined in light of analysis of emotional contagion in the musical case, which recommends, for example, that we distinguish attention from non-attentional modes of emotional transmission and, in general, we should avoid defining the phenomenon reductively in terms of the routes and mechanisms of communication.

The nature of emotional contagion

What characterizes emotional contagion? Intuitively, the hallmarks are these: one emotional state, appearance, or condition is transmitted to a person (or creature)

The material amalgamated in this chapter was first published as 'Infectious Music: Music–Listener Emotional Contagion,' in P. Goldie and A. Coplan (eds), *Empathy: Philosophical and Psychological Perspectives*, Oxford: Oxford University Press, 2011, 134–47 and 'Music-to-listener Emotional Contagion,' in T. Cochrane, B. Fantini, and K. Scherer (eds), *The Emotional Power of Music*, Oxford: Oxford University Press (forthcoming).

who comes to feel the same way; the display of the first emotional state plays a causal role in the process of transmission and the first emotional state must be perceived, either attentionally or non-attentionally, by the emotion's recipient; however, the responder does not hold about the first emotional state beliefs that make it an appropriate intentional object for the response in question.

Emotional contagion should be distinguished from some conditions that are outwardly similar in that *A* and *B* experience the same emotion. The following do not fit the characterization of emotional contagion that was just offered: we both feel the same emotion because our emotions have a common intentional object about which we both hold the same emotion-relevant beliefs. (We both react with fear to the nearby charging lion or we both laugh at the same joke.) I react to your emotion by feeling the same because I believe the basis of your reaction will also provide me with a reason to react similarly. (Seeing you flee in terror, I do the same without waiting to discover what you are terrified of, or I begin to share your humor at a joke you are about to tell.) Your emotion is the emotional object of my response and our emotions are the same. (You are angry that we are delayed and I am angry that you are angry because you promised you would not lose your temper.) I try to work out what you are feeling by imaginatively simulating your situation or I use knowledge of your character and circumstances and thereby empathically share your state. And finally, emotional contagion is distinct from the case in which our recognizing that we share some reaction modifies that reaction, for instance, by augmenting it—people laugh thirty times more often when they are with strangers who also display their amusement than when they are alone (Provine 1996)—or by coloring it—as when we feel a sense of community, or, alternatively, become self-conscious and embarrassed to react as the other does.

Emotional contagion does not always occur when two people share the same emotion, or even when this sharing is caused by one person's emotional state impinging on the other. What is crucial, as I have noted, is that the mirroring response does not take the initial emotional state, appearance, or condition as its emotional object and does not involve the kinds of beliefs about that state, appearance, or condition that are distinctive to emotions of the kind elicited. Even if it arises via contagion, however, that other people are similarly affected may trigger the effects of sharing, such as an amplification of the response.

To consider such responses in more detail, it is relevant to situate them against the background of the dominant philosophical account of the emotions.

The cognitive theory of the emotions

In the 1960s and 1970s, philosophers (Kenny 1963, Solomon 1976, Lyons 1980) developed what became known as the cognitive account of the emotions. Emotions are object-directed states characterized in terms of the beliefs under which their intentional objects are subsumed. For example, if I am afraid for myself I am afraid *of* or *about* something—a rise in the mortgage rate, say—and I *believe* that a rise in the mortgage rate will injure me or otherwise affect me adversely. A rise in the interest rate is the *intentional object* (or *emotional object*) of my fear, and the belief that the intentional object of my response will injure me or otherwise affect me adversely, a description sometimes known as the *formal object* of fear, is what characterizes the response as fearful. Similarly, for my emotion to be one of envy I must believe that another possesses something that I desire and do not have, and so on.

Though proponents of the theory occasionally suggest that the nature of the belief is sufficient to determine what emotion is involved, the more circumspect view is that the relevant belief is necessary and that no other condition is also sufficient. In other words, other conditions might be necessary for an emotion's being one of fear—for instance, a disposition to fight, freeze, or flee—but among the conditions that are jointly sufficient for an emotion's being fear is the condition that the relevant beliefs, ones about dangers posed by the emotion's object, are present. It is the centrality that this theory accords to the role of belief that led to its being called a cognitive account of the emotions. The cognitive theory stresses the cognitive dimension of emotions, their intentionality or object-directedness, and the public aspect of the expressive behaviors that are in part constitutive of them, and contrasts with a purely physiological, often pneumatic, view that sees emotions as inner stirrings that precede cognition and are distinguished one from the other by their distinctive phenomenological profiles.[1]

A number of fairly obvious putative counterexamples can be ranged against the cognitive theory of the emotions. Phobias either involve beliefs not appropriate to the emotion's object or are impervious to beliefs that should block the response. Reflexive affective responses of the kind sometimes called by psychologists quick and dirty or fast and frugal also seem to operate independently of, and be unaffected by, the responder's belief systems. As Darwin (1889 [1998: 43–4]) famously observed, he flinched in fear of a striking snake even as he knew it was separated from him by an unbreakable glass barrier. Meanwhile, emotional reactions to fictions recognized as such, as when I feel sad at Mimi's death in *La Bohème*, or to counterfactually entertained scenarios, as when I feel sad as a result of imagining a world without birds, also do not involve beliefs that should be crucial: that Mimi exists or existed and therefore suffered the fate depicted or that the earth will be bereft of birds. As well as these cases, all of which question the claimed tie between the emotion's kind and the content of the beliefs of the person who experiences it, there are others denying that emotions necessarily take emotional objects. Apparently there are objectless moods and feelings, as when one is gloomy but

---

[1] For a subtle account of the issues written with the advantage of hindsight, see Solomon (2003). And note that there is a much weaker form of cognitivism to which many psychologists subscribe according to which emotions involve appraisals of one's self or situation, where these appraisals may be very fast, automatic, and not present to consciousness. In other words, there is cognitive (or at least bodily) processing but there need not be the adoption of propositional attitudes such as belief.

not about anything in particular or where one experiences an undirected sense of dread or foreboding.

There are a number of replies the cognitivist can offer. Emotional reactions that are based on irrational or otherwise mistaken beliefs are inappropriate to the way the real world is but are not otherwise unintelligible. And reactions that do not engage the responder's beliefs perhaps should not be put together with full-blooded emotions. In this view, reflexive reactions either are not emotions at all or they form a minor, peripheral class within the wider group in which cognitively founded, object-directed emotions are central and paradigmatic.[2] As for moods and anxieties that appear to be objectless, it could be argued that they take relatively general objects rather than specific ones (Goldie 2000: 143)—one is depressed about the condition of the world at large, though not at a particular part of it (Solomon 1976: 172–3)—or that their objects are unconscious (Lyons 1980; for discussion, see Lamb 1987). Or again, perhaps the claims of objectless moods and dreads to unequivocal standing as emotions should be doubted.

Meanwhile, our responsiveness to what we know to be fictional characters and situations has attracted a spread of theories. There is the option of denial. Kendall Walton (1990, 1997) stands by cognitivism. He holds that *fictional emotions*—by which he means not that the states are merely imagined but that they occur in the context of games of make-believe prescribed for the consumption and appreciation of fictional works—are not kosher, despite their emotion-like phenomenological and physiological profile. An implausible alternative is Samuel Taylor Coleridge's suggestion that one suspends—or in contemporary jargon, puts off-line—one's awareness of the fictionality of the events shown or described. There is the proposal that the response is non-rational, either because beliefs in the existence of their objects are absent or, for other reasons, because one does not believe one's responses can affect or engage with the object of the response. Colin Radford (1975), who endorses this proposal, apparently thinks irrational reactions can be tolerated by the cognitivist as exceptions that prove the rule. Alternatively, Alex Neill (1993) argues that cognitivism does not require the belief that the fictional target of one's emotional response exists in the actual world. According to Neill, one can pity a fictional character provided one believes that the character exists in a pitiable situation in the world of the fiction. Another attractive suggestion (offered in Lamarque 1981, 1996, Carroll 1990, 1997, Feagin 1996) recommends modifying the cognitive theory to allow that the relevant cognitive role can be played sometimes by make-believe, not only by belief. The emotional

---

[2] If emotions serve adaptive functions, as is widely claimed (Plutchik 1980, Lazarus 1991, Le Doux 1996), and if we share many emotions with less cognitively sophisticated species, as seems hard to deny, the cognitive theory does look to be parochial and narrow. On the other hand, Griffiths' (1997) conclusion, that 'conceptual analysis' provides no coherent account of cognitively sophisticated emotions and that the notion of them is incoherent because psychologists' methodologies cannot deal with them, seems equally biased.

evocativeness of fictions entertained as such then no longer calls the cognitive theory into doubt.

Music-to-listener emotional contagion as a counterexample to the cognitive theory

There are many mechanisms by which an emotional response to music might be induced. Patrik Juslin and Daniel Västfjäll (2008a) identify six, of which emotional contagion is only one, the others being brain stem reflexes, evaluative conditioning, visual imagery, episodic memory, and musical expectancy. Some of these—for example, increased tension when a prediction about the course of the music is defeated or the reflex induction of a startled response by an unexpectedly loud chord—perhaps should not count as emotions. And others—for example, happiness when music triggers memories of a happy occasion—reveal more about the experiences of the listener than the nature of the music. Anyway, it is the example of emotional contagion on which I will focus. It is important because it is a fully fledged emotion that is directly connected to and is revealing of the music's expressive character. More important for the philosopher, perhaps, is that the mirroring response is intriguingly problematic in two respects: such responses are counterexamples to the cognitive theory of the emotion because they lack emotional objects and because they cannot be justified in the usual way and to that extent appear to be non-rational.[3]

It is widely accepted that even purely instrumental music can express or present the appearance of emotions such as happiness and sadness. It is also generally acknowledged that happy music sometimes makes people feel happy and sad music sometimes makes them feel sad, or in other words, that there is sometimes music-to-listener emotional contagion. Music can give rise to an affective reaction that mirrors or echoes its own expressive character. But, and here is the point, those who are saddened by sad music are not sad *about* or *for* the music. The music is the perceptual object and cause of the sad reaction. Indeed, the music is the attentional focus of the response, which tracks the expressiveness as it unfolds in the music's progress.[4] However, the music is not the emotional object of the listener's response—the response is *to* the music without being *about* it—because moved listeners do not believe of the music that it satisfies the formal object of sadness.[5] In other words, they do not believe it suffers or is otherwise unfortunate or regrettable. They might regard the slow movement of Mahler's Fifth Symphony, say, as expressing a profound sadness, and on that account, as a magnificent human achievement that should be celebrated, not mourned, yet hearing it inclines them to share in its sadness.

---

[3] See Davies (1994a, 2003: chs 8, 9, 11).
[4] The disposition to echo the music's expressiveness might be overridden, though, in light of a broader view of its expressive character. I might not be cheered by the occasional happy moments because I recognize them as the work's overall pattern contradicted by the predominant sadness of unalloyed joy.
[5] Philosophers interested in analyzing the emotions sometimes discuss the musical case without noticing how peculiar it is in this respect; see Wilson (1972: 82–5) for an example.

Some psychologists, including Juslin and Västfjäll (2008a), identify emotions as involving appraisals and objects that are appraised, even where contagion is involved.[6] Let me make clearer what I mean by saying that music is not the *emotional object* of the listener's mirroring response. Though it is true that background music of which the hearer is not consciously aware might affect her feelings by way of contagion, this is not the relevant case. And though the intentional object of one's response can drift apart from its perceptual object under conditions of error, as when one fears the presence of a lion when one mistakes the shadow of a mop for the shadow of a lion, that again is not the relevant case. Rather, the important point is that even where the mirroring response of sadness targets and tracks the music, one is not sad *for* or *about* the music. The *emotional object* of the emotion is the object that is perceived with belief as falling under the emotion-relevant description; for instance, where the emotion is one of fear for oneself of another, its emotional object is what one believes to be dangerous to one's wellbeing. While the listener's contagious response of sadness is reflected back to the sad music and in that sense takes the music as its object, and while this response clearly involves appraisals of the music's expressive character, the music is not the *emotional object* of the response because the listener does not believe of the music what would make it the intentional object of a sad response, namely, that the music is unfortunate, suffering, or regrettable. The music is not brought under the characterization that picks out the *emotional object* of sadness. And provided that nothing else is brought under that characterization, the response lacks an emotional object though the music remains its perceptual object.

The lack of an emotional object also seems to bear on the rationality of the response. Typically, we justify our emotions by showing that their emotional objects have the emotion-relevant qualities that we believe them to have. I justify my fear for myself by pointing to the dangerous qualities of the apparently hungry lion that shares the room with me, for instance. But in the case of the mirroring response, the listener does not hold beliefs about the music appropriate for her response to its expressiveness. She cannot justify her response of sadness in the usual way, by indicating what is unfortunate and regrettable about the music or its expressiveness.[7]

The apparent non-rationality of the contagious response seems to fit the case in which the listener is unconsciously affected by background music she is not aware of hearing. It is less appropriate, though, to the example in which the listener focuses on the music and its expressiveness and comes to feel the same way as a result, because we often would acknowledge such a response as evidence that the listener follows the music with understanding. Before exploring this issue, we should consider further the differences between attentional and non-attentional emotional contagion from music to listener.

---

[6] By the way, I agree with Robinson (2008) that Juslin and Västfjäll frequently depart in their (2008a) paper from the definition of emotional contagion they give there.

[7] There is a third issue, specifically about the sad (rather than the happy) mirroring response, that I will not consider here, namely, why we enjoy and return to music that makes us feel sad. For discussion, see Davies (1994a: 307–20).

Attentional versus non-attentional music-to-listener emotional contagion

It may be useful to distinguish two types of emotional contagion in which music could take part. Music is played as background sound in stores and elevators where it serves to calm those who encounter it. To produce its effect it must be heard. Typically, though, it is not listened to. It is the perceptual object of the response, but the person calmed by it may be oblivious of this fact and may remain unaware throughout of the musical wallpaper. The sense of wellbeing experienced as a result of this barely aware or subconscious perception is not appreciated as a response to its cause and is not directed to the background music. In other words, the music generates an objectless mood that reflects its own, calm expressive character.

The second kind of music-based emotional contagion is the one I described earlier. The music is the object of attention and is inevitably recognized as the source (or one of the sources) of the response it calls forth. The listener responds *to* the music, though the response is not *about* the music. The response is experienced as occasioned by and linked to the music, not as some undirected mood.[8]

To say the response is attentional is, of course, not to maintain that the person subject to emotional contagion attends to or is even aware of the causal mechanisms responsible for the transmission of affect. Typically she is not. She attends to the source of contagion, the music's expressive character, without following the process by which this affect becomes one she shares. In many cases, however, the attention she pays to expressions of the source emotion plays a crucial role in opening her up to the relevant triggers of emotional communication.

Film music may turn out sometimes to involve attentional contagion and at others non-attentional contagion, or to involve the first more often with one group of viewers than with the rest. Many moviegoers are not aware of the film's accompanying music as they hear it, while others are aware of but not focused on the music, yet both kinds of viewer are liable to be emotionally primed by the music they hear. At other times, the music draws attention to itself and clearly establishes an emotional tone for (or tension against) the movie action that is to follow. If there is emotional contagion in either case, it is non-attentional in the first and attentional in the second. As well, some members of the audience may be inclined to listen more often and more carefully to the movie's music, in which case if they are infected by the music they are likely to be conscious more often of its working on their emotions.

---

[8] Madell (2002) objects to accounts of music's expressiveness like mine and Kivy's (1989) that they leave the listener's response only loosely tied to the music. He cites Radford (1991), and the objection does seem relevant to Radford's view, in which music is a cause of objectless moods that are about 'everything and nothing.' The objection does not have much force against the position I defend, however, which stresses the attentional dependence of the response on the music's expressive development.

Challenges to the view that the listener's attentive response sometimes involves emotional contagion

Not all philosophers of music agree that the mirroring response to music's expressiveness involves contagion. Kivy, who is a dedicated cognitivist, at first (1987, 1989) denied that anyone (apart from the pathological) is ever saddened by sad music.[9] This view dismisses the testimony of many music lovers as well as the experimental results of psychologists' studies.[10] Later (1993, 1994), Kivy ameliorated his position, accepting that music weakly tends to move some listeners. Radford (1989, 1991) allowed that music can produce a generalized, objectless reaction but seems to take as his model the case of non-attentional emotional infection, and thereby mischaracterizes the important musical case. Jerrold Levinson (1996a: ch. 6, 2006; see also Robinson 2005) argued that music is expressive because we experience it imaginatively as a narrative about an indefinite persona we hear as inhabiting it. He suggests that sometimes our responses are to the fate of this persona. Or finally, instead of proposing a rival account, one can file it in the 'too hard' basket: 'and only music, with its capacity not only to go beyond words but to exist only beyond words, can provide an explanation of why we respond the way we do to it. We are confusing the issue further by attempting to package this emotive understanding in terms of language, or in terms of objects and beliefs. Perhaps this is where both music as well as emotion should, as Wittgenstein suggests, be passed over in silence' (Worth 2000: 106).

I find all these alternatives unconvincing and have argued against most of them elsewhere.[11] I will not recapitulate those discussions, except to make this observation: I suggested earlier that it is plausible to maintain that our responses to fictional novels, dramas, paintings, and movies involve making believe that one is seeing (or hearing about) actual events, and that this grounds the response. Moreover, we then can justify the rationality of the response by reference to what is true in the fiction, that is, to the truths that the audience make-believedly entertains under the artist's direction. If the response to music's expressiveness can be assimilated to the response to fictions, we thereby have a method for addressing the former's problematic aspects. In effect, this is the strategy adopted by those who argue that we make-believe of the music that it

---

[9] Kivy conflates the arousal account of music's expressiveness—music expresses an emotion E if and only if it arouses (or tends to arouse) E in a suitably qualified listener—with the claim that music sometimes arouses echoing responses in the listener. He writes as if he can demonstrate that music never arouses a mirroring response if he can show that the arousal theory is false. These views should be kept apart, however. There is no inconsistency in maintaining (as I do) both that music's expressiveness does not depend on its arousing any emotion (and hence that the arousal theory is false) and also that music regularly does arouse the emotion it expresses.

[10] Krumhansl (1997) sets out specifically to test Kivy's position and concludes he is wrong to claim that listeners do not experience the emotions they recognize in music. For empirical evidence of contagion from music to listener, see Evans and Schubert (2008), and for a review of the psychological literature see Gabrielsson (2002). See Kivy (2006) for his critique of Krumhansl's experiment.

[11] See Chapter 1 and Davies (1994a, 1994b, 2003: chs 8–11).

contains an emoting persona to whom we then respond; they make the response to the music of a kind with the imaginative response to fictions.

In my view, this strategy is mistaken. One may treat work of pure music as the occasion for an imaginative reverie, but I do not think that the appreciative listener always does so. Her response is directed not to a make-believed fiction that the music conjures up but to the music's expressive character, simply perceived as such. And she identifies that response as mirroring the music's expressive character though she does not regard the music as satisfying the description that normally would justify her reaction.

So what are we to say about the peculiarities of such a response?

The objectless non-rationality of the contagious response?

The contagious response provides a counterexample to the cognitive theory of the emotions but that fact counts against the theory, not against the emotional legitimacy of the contagious reaction.

As I noted, the cognitive theory is faced with a number of troublesome cases, such as moods and phobias. At least some of these seem to qualify as emotions, and that suggests that the cognitive theory is not all-encompassing, even if it does apply to many paradigm cases. Musical-to-listener emotional contagion is a new kind of counterexample that was not widely recognized as such. This does not mean that the musical case is one peculiar to the aesthetic context, however, which is a good thing because the application of emotion terms under circumstances that bear no resemblance to the wider circumstances of their use, as in talk of sui generis artistic emotions or responses, is rightly regarded with suspicion by contemporary philosophers of art. It is a commonplace of folk psychology that emotional contagion is familiar as a response to our fellow humans. We often catch or are affected by the mood of others. Moreover, the outcome is not necessarily diminished when we move to modes of expression that do not involve sentience. It is widely acknowledged that the weather and colors can affect our emotions and that we predicate expressive properties to both the weather and to colors.

As for the second issue—that the listener does not have the beliefs that could justify her response—I admit that it has some force. It is not obvious that we should criticize someone who is not moved to sadness by sad music, because it is not as if he thereby betrays callousness or lack of sympathy. But we can also argue that, if the mirroring response does occur, it can be justified, not by reference to emotion-relevant beliefs but rather in the sense that no other non-cognitively directed response is equally apt. By comparison with the person who is typically cheered by sad music and depressed by happy music, but without believing or make-believing about either anything that makes it a fit object for happiness or depression, the person who is cheered by happy music or saddened by gloomy music seems normal and has the appropriate response.

Or to make the point differently, there seems to be a place prepared in our natural history for the mirroring response in a way that is not true for alternatives that are similar in also not being cognitively directed. It is for this reason that the listener's response can be taken as indexing her sensitive comprehension of the music's character.

We might draw a parallel here with emotional responses to what are known to be fictions. As noted earlier, some philosophers regard these as paradoxical and irrational. After all, why should I fear the movie monster that I know not to exist and, hence, to be unable to harm me? Whatever one says in answer to this paradox, it seems reasonable to suggest that it is more rational to fear the monster than the cowering, little old lady that it is threatening in the film.[12] In the same way, it is more rational to be saddened by sad music and gladdened by happy music, even if I think the music expresses no one's feelings in either case and even if I hold no other emotion-relevant beliefs about the music, than it is to feel the reverse.

Robinson's criticisms of my account of emotional contagion

Jenefer Robinson shares my view that music can be a source of emotional communication of the contagious kind, but she disagrees with my account of this. In this section I outline her objections and respond to them.

Robinson writes (2005: 385): 'Davies's account cannot be quite right for two reasons. For one thing, emotional contagion normally occurs automatically without our being aware of what's happening: the expression is acquired automatically by some form of motor mimicry. *Recognition* of the expression is not necessary as Davies stipulates, and may even prevent or moderate the effect of contagion.'

This first objection insists that emotional contagion normally does not depend on one's recognizing the expressive character of that to which one responds. By this, I take it that Robinson holds that emotional contagion is commonly non-attentional, so the attentional response I characterize cannot be 'quite right.' But this has to be wrong. Robinson cites with approval the work of psychologists Elaine Hatfield, John T. Cacioppo, and Richard L. Rapson and indicates them as her primary source on emotional contagion. Apparently, Robinson overlooks this: 'people should be more likely to catch others' emotions if their attention is riveted on the others than if they are oblivious to others' emotions' (Hatfield et al. 1994: 148). These psychologists go on (1994: 148–52) to provide compelling evidence for the truth of this hypothesis. And common sense and experience suggest that one is more likely to catch another's mood by recognizing his emotions and signals of affect than by being unaware of them. Filmmakers know this and

---

[12] For discussion of the alleged paradox of responding emotionally to what are recognized to be fictional characters and situations and of the rationality of such responses, see Davies (2009).

focus spectators' attention on characters' expressive facial features in order to elicit emotional contagion or empathy (Plantinga 1999, Coplan 2006).

In fact, Robinson regularly cites psychologists' experiments in which the subjects were asked to listen to—that is, attend to and recognize—the music's expressive character. The experimenters measured the subjects' physiological or behavioral responses or obtained self-reports afterwards. One of Robinson's favorite cases is an experiment by Carol Krumhansl (1997) of exactly this kind: the physiology of half the subjects was monitored as they attended closely to the music, while the other half recorded their emotional responses as they listened. Robinson (2005: 395) also mentions Dale Bartlett's review (1996) of 130 studies showing how listening to music produces physiological effects in listeners. The vast majority of the studies listed by Bartlett are recognitional. In only a tiny minority is the music played as background while the subject focuses on something else, such as a puzzle task, for instance. Robinson offers these recognitional experiments as evidence of a kind of emotional contagion she labels the 'jazzercise effect.' So, she cannot consistently maintain against my view that emotional contagion in the musical case is normally non-attentional.

It is true, as I noted earlier, that the listener subject to emotional contagion is usually oblivious to the way the affect is transmitted. Nevertheless, her recognition of and attention to the music's expressiveness primes her to catch the music's mood. Her focus on the music's expressive character encourages and invigorates the transmission of affect, as is indicated by experimental evidence both for emotional transfer from person to person and from music to person. So, there is nothing amiss in my suggestion that music is involved in attentional emotional contagion. Indeed, one would expect this to be usually more powerful and reliable than non-attentional contagion from musical sources.

Robinson's second objection is as follows (2005: 388): 'on Davies's account music is *like* an expression of emotion—just as is the configuration of the basset hound's face—but it isn't one really. We are programmed to respond with sadness to an expression of sadness in another human being. The fact that we are probably programmed to respond to other human faces (on the grounds that sad *human* expressions usually indicate sad humans) probably has no implications for our responses to doggy faces. (After all, if living with a basset hound were like living with a depressed person, would normal folk choose a basset hound as their life's companion?) And by parity of reasoning we are probably not programmed to respond to musical sounds by virtue of the fact that they are *like* expressions of emotion in some way.'[13]

It seems to me that these are empirical claims and that the evidence favors my view rather than counting against it. To take a non-musical case, I surmise that when we are cheered by a warm and jolly décor, this is most easily explained as involving contagion. Presumably the

---

[13] Robinson is correct that I regard music as expressive by virtue of its presenting appearances of emotion. I do allow that the real emotions of the composer can be expressed in his or her work, but I also hold this to be a sophisticated act of expression achieved via the composer's appropriation of the expressive character of the music he or she writes (see Davies 1994a, 2007: ch. 16).

original source of the cheerfulness of yellow and the gloominess of grey is the weather, and it is not difficult to understand why we might be programmed to react positively to sunny weather and to be depressed by rain and fog. Though the interior décor of a house is never likely to be mistaken for the local weather, nevertheless, it inherits the positive and negative values of the weather and we respond via contagion to this.

As this case testifies, our valuations and responses to our natural environments, as well as to our human cohorts, can become generalized and applied over a range of contexts. Synesthetic generalizations are common in the musical case, in particular. We conceive of music in terms of human, spatial, and other categories. Timbres are warm, metallic, dark, and brittle; rhythms are jagged or square; notes are high or low. Melody and music in general contains movement, conflict, statements, questions, dialogue, wit, and humor. The progress of music makes sense much as human behavior does: we do not regard it as mechanically determined, yet we expect to be able to understand each event in terms of what went before. We anticipate that the music will present a coherent pattern much as we anticipate that a person will act in character, though both can also be bafflingly unpredictable on occasion. Above all, we hear in music humanly created emotional expression. The *image* of human expressiveness is often as evocative as the real thing. There are good biological reasons for this fact. Our first reaction as social creatures that rely on our mind-reading abilities is to respond to the outward show as a window on the human soul. That is how (and why) we react to expressiveness in music: it is no less a human form of expression, though it is a far more sophisticated one, than weeping is.

Few deny that music often powerfully calls from them an emotional echo of its own expressiveness. I think we respond directly to that expressiveness—and not that we respond to a persona we imagine to inhabit the music, for example—so I do not find it at all implausible to regard that response as suggesting we find music evocative of contagious responses.

Of course, we can become inured to the effects of contagion through overexposure. No doubt that is why basset hounds do not drive their owners to suicide via contagion. Peter Kivy, in a commentary on a draft of this chapter, described this concession as 'utterly devastating' for my view, because we have resided with sad music our entire lives and therefore should never respond to it via contagion. I do not agree. We react to the expressive detail of particular works (Davies 1999a). Our emotions may be gripped when we return after a suitable period to a given work, despite having been exposed to other, similarly expressive pieces in the meantime.

Criticism of Robinson's 'jazzercise' model of musical contagion

As we have seen, Robinson's second objection to my account of music's contagious powers fares no better than the misconceived first. How well does her own theory of musical expressive transmission by infection stand up? I find it confusing. What she offers as the primary example of musical contagion either looks like something else or supports a view like mine, as I now demonstrate.

Robinson's jazzercise effect, which illustrates her model of emotional contagion, works like this: music arouses physiological changes; the subject aware of these changes looks for and latches on to cues in the environment and responds emotionally to them. Robinson's model here is a notorious experiment performed by Stanley Schachter and Jerome Singer (1962).[14] The experimenters used a drug to induce arousal in their subjects. These subjects, who were unaware of how or why their bodies were stimulated, matched their emotions to a stooge who behaved angrily with his situation in some cases and who cheerfully horsed around in others. Robinson writes (2005: 401): 'my proposal is that at least sometimes music plays a role similar to that which the epinephrine played in Schachter's famous experiment. It *arouses* listeners and puts them in a bodily mood or state. But, as in the experiment, listeners have no good explanation for their state of arousal. Why, after all, should music make me feel anxious or fearful? ... So what they do is what the subjects in the Schachter experiment did: they look around for an appropriate label for their vaguely felt affective state, and they *label* their state of arousal depending on the context they bring to the experience.'

Here is the process Robinson describes: the music causes me to feel tense, say. Perhaps matters end there; I feel an objectless irritability. Alternatively, I find myself thinking of tomorrow's dental appointment and thereby come to identify my reaction as one of apprehension. Or again, perhaps I pick up on the affective tone of those around me, so that I come to share their all-too-apparent irritation.

Now, the first two cases—unfocused irritability and apprehension at tomorrow's dental appointment—are not ones of emotional contagion. I experience an objectless mood in the first and an object-directed response of the ordinary, cognitively founded kind in the second. And if the third example—I pick up on the irritation of others—is one of contagion, the communication of affect is not to me from the music, but to me from people in my environment. In all these cases, the music is relevant because it heightens my physiological condition and in that way disposes me more than might otherwise be the case to adopt an affective stance, so that I come to experience a mood or to resonate emotionally with some aspect of my environment. But the music is always remote from the response. It plays a role in making me receptive to emotional experience, but this role might have been played instead by three cups of espresso or a shot of adrenaline. Certainly, the response is not made *to* the music.

I do not deny that people sometimes react affectively in the way just described or that music sometimes initiates the process by which this occurs. I agree, that is, that

---

[14] I call the experiment notorious because the methodology is suspect, the results have proved difficult or impossible to replicate, and the interpretation of the outcome is contested. For a review of psychologists' criticisms, see Carlson and Hatfield (1992). Philosophers have often discussed the experiment; for recent critical comments, see Griffiths (1997), Prinz (2004).

music can affect the listener's physiological state in ways of which she is not directly aware and that this can lead her to interrogate her wider environment for cues as to the character of her affective state. For the examples previously described, however, I deny that the response involves catching the music's expressive character. If contagion occurs, it does not directly involve the music. So, when developed this way, Robinson's would not be an account of *musical* contagion.

How could the music play a more prominent role? Schachter's experiment has been taken as an instance of emotional contagion (as in Hatfield et al. 1994: 111–13) because the subjects tended to catch the confederate's emotion. If the music not only initiated the change in the listener but also participated in her reaction, much as the confederate did in the experiment, the result would involve contagion, the transmission of affect from the music to the listener. Moreover, the suggestion is plausible. It would not be surprising if the listener latched on to the music to which she is attending already, and in particular, to the emotional character she recognizes in the sounds it presents. Her attention to the music then closes a causal circle: the music affects her physiology, which makes her attend more closely to what it expresses and disposes her to account for her own reaction in similar terms. This description is consistent with a very familiar case—we are physiologically affected by events in our neighborhood, which makes them perceptually and cognitively salient, which leads to our taking them as the intentional objects of our emotion—except that, for music, where we are aware that its sadness, say, is not an appropriate object for our sympathy, it is the echoing response, not sympathy, that is elicited.

Is this how Robinson's account should be understood? As I say, this story is one of emotional contagion via music and is plausible.[15] Nevertheless, it cannot be the interpretation Robinson wants for her view, because it describes the emotional contagion produced by music as normally of the attentional kind. Moreover, this story matches my own theory of the echoing response, which Robinson would rather reject.

Despite Robinson's doubts, I remain convinced that the idea of attentional emotional contagion provides the most convincing characterization of the emotional reaction of the listener who attends closely to an instrumental work and, as a result, finds herself inclined to be moved to mirror the music's overall expressive character.

Psychologists on emotional contagion

I now turn from philosophers to psychologists. Many psychologists are not interested in the intentionality and cognitive subtlety of emotions. They prefer to focus on physiological changes (e.g., in the autonomic nervous system, body chemistry, neurological activity, or sub-muscular movements) or on behavioral displays (e.g., facial expressions) that can be accurately measured without relying on self-reports. Much work has been done to show that there are basic affects—fear, anger, happiness, sadness, surprise, and

---

[15] I am not convinced, however, that physiological change *always* precedes perceptual inspection and cognitive evaluation, as this account implies.

disgust—that have universally recognizable facial displays and that are modular in the sense that they are triggered and operate independently of conscious reflection (Ekman 1972, 1980, 1992).[16] These are called 'affect programs,' though it is not uncommon for psychologists to proceed as if this technical term designates all that is covered by the word 'emotion' in its ordinary, day-to-day use.

As well, psychologists and others have long been interested in empathy, sympathy, mob psychology, social conformity, and emotional communication, but emotional contagion was not usually distinguished from other versions of these modes of emotional engagement.[17] It was not until the 1990s that emotional contagion was isolated as a specific focus of study.

The previously cited *Emotional Contagion* by Hatfield, Cacioppo, and Rapson came in 1994.[18] Of course, they studied the human-to-human transmission of affect, not the response to music. And their primary interest, unlike mine, was in the mechanism causally responsible for inducing in one person what is felt by the other. Their definition of primitive emotional contagion occurs in this passage (1994: 5): 'the focus in this text is on rudimentary or *primitive* emotional contagion—that which is relatively automatic, unintentional, uncontrollable, and largely inaccessible to conversant awareness. This is defined as the tendency to automatically mimic and synchronize facial expressions, vocalizations, postures, and movements with those of another person and, consequently, to converge emotionally.' They emphasize mimicry and feedback in explaining emotional contagion.

'Proposition 1. In conversation, people tend automatically and continuously to mimic and synchronize their movement with the facial expressions, voices, postures, movements, and instrumental behaviors of others.

Proposition 2. Subjective emotional experiences are affected, moment to moment, by the activation and/or feedback from such mimicry.

Proposition 3. Given Propositions 1 and 2, people tend to 'catch' others' emotions, moment to moment' (1994: 10–11).

---

[16] Note that non-cognitive reactions of these kinds were discussed above as possible counterexamples to the cognitive theory of the emotions.

[17] Wheeler (1966) was among the first psychologists to attempt to distinguish contagion from other types of social and emotional influence. An appropriate subtlety is apparent in some recent empirical studies of empathy, for instance, which portray empathy as more sophisticated than, and as involving a different degree of self- and other-awareness from, emotional contagion. See Decety and Jackson (2004), Decety and Hodges (2006). For a philosophical account of some of the relevant distinctions, see Goldie (2000: ch. 7), and for discussion of the difference when the response is occasioned by films, see Coplan (2004).

[18] The cover of their book shows a wonderful picture from the 1937 All-Ireland Road Bowls Championship. The bowler and scores of onlookers are shown attempting to use body English to control the course of the (out of shot) bowl's movement. The authors identify this as 'an example of postural mimicry' when clearly it is no such thing. Everyone's eyes are fixed on the bowl, not the bowler, and each, independently of the rest, is attempting to guide its course. There is behavioral coincidence with, not mimicry of, the bowler.

The idea, then, is that, when dealing face to face with another, I tend to mimic his behavior and facial expressions without being aware of doing so; I 'read' my feelings off from my facial expressions and behaviors; so, I come to feel the way my interlocutor does.

Hatfield, Cacioppo, and Rapson defend the premises of their argument. Some psychologists regard facial feedback as singularly important in this process, while others see other factors sometimes as equally relevant. When they review the psychological literature, Hatfield, Cacioppo, and Rapson (1994: 53–63) find strong experimental evidence in favor of the facial feedback hypothesis. Evidence for vocal and postural feedback is positive, but the tie is not so close as that with facial expression (1994: 63–76).[19] They conclude (1994: 52–3): 'subjective emotional experience is affected by feedback from facial, vocal, and postural muscular movements, as well as by feedback from instrumental emotional activity. We also expect subjective emotional experience to be influenced by feedback from the facial, vocal, and postural movements that are *mimicked*.'

In a different work, Teresa Brennan proposed a quite different mechanism of transmission as crucial (2004: 68–9): 'if contagion exists (and the study of crowds says it does), how is it effected? Images and mimesis explain some of it...but olfactory and auditory entrainment offer more comprehensive explanations.... Research on chemical communication and entrainment suggests answers centered on the analysis of pheromones, substances that are not released into the blood but are emitted externally.' Pheromones play a role not only in sexual behavior but also in communication, she argues.[20]

Now, if there is emotional contagion between music and humans or between house décors and humans, it cannot be facial mimicry that underpins it because music and house décors do not present a human physiognomy, and it cannot be the detection of pheromones that cause it because music and house décors do not emit pheromones. Rather than abandoning talk of emotional contagion for such cases, where it seems fitting, we need to focus on what is distinctive to the musical case.[21]

When psychologists searched for an analogous role for music in the induction of emotion, it was in the context of testing how background music affects the mood and

---

[19] Later in the book, however, they allow (1994: 159): 'people vary greatly in the extent to which they rely on facial, vocal, and postural feedback in determining what they feel.' For a review of work on facial feedback in mood contagion, see Adelmann and Zajonc (1989).

[20] The experiments cited by Brennan concern the regulation of human female ovulation and show how exposure both to men's and women's perspiration affect the cycle. As well, there is interesting work she does not cite indicating that females detect male MHC (major histocompatibility complex) alleles (and vice versa). A male with MHC alleles differing from a given female's alleles thereby signals his capacity to father children with stronger immune systems. Women prefer such men at the peak of monthly fertility, but otherwise take as partners men with MHC alleles nearer their own. For discussion, see Milinski (2003), Thornhill and Gangestad (2003).

[21] Note that Hatfield et al. (1994) take care to identify their topic as *primitive* emotional contagion and they allow that cognitively more complex forms of contagion are possible. Nothing in their account commits them to analyze non-primitive emotional transmission in terms of the causal mechanisms they highlight for primitive emotional contagion.

behavior of diners and shoppers and in the use of music as therapy.[22] Neither kind of study specifically targets music-to-listener emotional contagion, as opposed to more general interactive effects between music and mood, and in many cases the concern is with effects that do not involve the hearer's attention to the music as such. As a result, these studies do not provide useful paradigms for the study of emotional contagion where this results from the listener's close attention to the music's expressive character in a context of trying to follow the music with understanding.

Psychologists concerned with music-to-listener emotional contagion of the attentional variety tend to return to the human-to-human model. According to Juslin and Västfjäll (2008a: 565): emotional contagion 'refers to a process whereby an emotion is induced by a piece of music because the listener perceives the emotional expression of the music, and then 'mimics' this expression internally, which by means of either peripheral feedback from muscles, or a more direct activation of the relevant emotional representations in the brain, leads to an induction of the same emotion.... Recent research has suggested that the process of emotional contagion may occur through the mediation of so-called mirror neurons discovered in studies of the monkey premotor cortex in the 1990s.'

The problem with this is that it appears to turn what is supposed to be literal for human-to-human contagion into something metaphorical. It is not as if the music has muscles the movements of which can be mimicked, or a premotor cortex with neuronal activity that can be mirrored in the brains of listeners. Because of their apparently metaphorical character, the explanatory power of such characterizations of the relevant mechanisms is questionable.

Yet, as I noted earlier, talk of emotional contagion seems perfectly apt in such cases. In part this is because talk of musical movement, pattern, tension, and expressive appearances is literal, or so I would maintain (see Chapter 2). Such attributions are secondary, in that the meanings of the relevant terms are not first taught by reference to such examples, but once the secondary extensions of these meanings are acquired, the terms have the kind of shared interpersonal use that live metaphors lack. For instance, dictionary definitions of words like 'sad' frequently mention the case of music or art, whereas live metaphors do not appear in such reference works. Moreover, while metaphors can easily be replaced with non-synonymous terms, talk of spatial movement and the use of emotion-terms in describing the music's character seem to be ineliminable. If this is so, talk of listeners mimicking the music is not merely poetic; even if there are no musical muscles or neuronal patterns to be imitated or mirrored, there can be musical movement and process, patterns of tension and release, and the like.

---

[22] For discussion of the use of music in marketing, see Milliman (1982, 1986), Bruner (1990), North and Hargreaves (1997). Shatin (1970) discusses the use of music to control and change the listener's mood; see also Bunt and Pavlicevic (2001) and the practical guide to music selections associated with desired emotional responses edited by Capurso et al. (1952).

How then does emotional contagion operate in the musical case? That is for scientists to discover, but it is possible to offer some speculative suggestions. I favor the view that music is expressive because we experience it as presenting the kind of carriage, gait, or demeanor that can be symptomatic of states such as happiness, sadness, anger, sexuality, and so on.[23] If contagion operates through mimicry, we might expect the listener to adopt bodily postures and attitudes (or posturally relevant muscular proprioceptions) like those apparent in the music's progress.[24] Vocal mimicry, in the form of subtle tensing or flexing of vocal muscles, would also be a predictable response to vocal music or to acts of sub-vocal singing along with instrumental music.[25] And where the flux of music is felt as an articulated pattern of tensing and relaxing, this is likely to be imaged and mimed within the body, perhaps in ways that are neither sub-postural nor sub-vocal. Finally, there is the possibility that music works on the brain, not only by eliciting physical-cum-physiological changes that nudge the subject as she becomes aware of them toward affective appraisals and responses, but also more immediately, by directly stimulating cortical regions linked with emotional recognitions and responses.[26] Many and diverse routes of emotional transmission might be involved, perhaps simultaneously.

In brief

That music sometimes leads the attentive listener to share the emotions she hears it as expressing calls into question the cognitive theory of the emotions, because the listener does not believe of the music's expressiveness what would make it an apt emotional object of the response and she does not pick up on some other aspect of the environment as the response's emotional object. This phenomenon is best understood as involving emotional infection or osmosis. Emotional infection requires perception of the music's character but may be non-attentional or attentional. The mirroring response of the music-focused listener is of this second variety. She is very likely to identify the music's expressiveness as the cause of her response because her reaction tracks her following of the music and recognition of its expressive character, but she is

---

[23] For details see Chapter 1 and Davies (1994a: 221–58, 2003: ch. 9). For empirical work on the human capacity to identify a person's emotion by observing only the abstract form of human motion (that is, motion as displayed only as light points on an otherwise invisible body), see Grammer et al. (2003).

[24] For relevant empirical data, see Janata and Grafton (2003).

[25] For relevant empirical data, see Koelsch et al. (2006). Juslin and Laukka (2003) and Juslin and Västfjäll (2008a), who postulate that the response to music can be explained as involving emotional contagion, make the comparison not with facial mimicry but with the communication of affect through vocal cues. See also Neumann and Strack (2000). And see Patel (2008b) on how this hypothesis might be tested via brain imaging. Simpson, Oliver, and Fragaszy (2008) suggest their brain-imaging results—that instrumental music is not processed by parts of the brain concerned with the voice—show that contagion is not a mechanism for the arousal of emotion by music. Their conclusion is unwarranted because they do not consider alternatives to the suggestion made by Juslin and his fellow researchers that music is experienced as a super-expressive voice. (Juslin and Västfjäll [2008b] reject their criticism for other reasons.)

[26] For further discussion of related possibilities, see Cochrane (2010).

unlikely to be aware of details of the causal mechanisms that forge the connection. The evocative power of purely instrumental music to call forth such a reaction does not depend on the listener's taking the music as expressing someone's felt emotion. As social beings, we are primed to detect and react to mere appearances or presentations of emotions (provided we judge that cheating is not an issue).

It is a mistake to identify emotional contagion with the causal mechanisms that activate it, as psychologists are prone to do. There is a lesson philosophers have learned from functionalist theories of the mind: a given state or process might be realized in different ways by different systems. That process or state should be identified in terms of its functional role in the system's operation or ecology rather than in terms of factors that are contingently dependent on the form in which the system exists or on the materials of which it is built. This lesson is appropriate to the case in hand. Emotional contagion should be characterized in terms of what is distinctive to the affective relation, not solely in terms of its underlying etiology (or etiologies). Here is the relevant account: *emotional contagion involves the arousal in B by A of an affect that corresponds either to an affect felt and displayed by A or, where A is non-sentient, as for the case of music and house décors, to the expressive character experienced by B as displayed in A's appearance, and while B's arousal must derive from A's displaying the relevant affect, so that A's affect is the perceptual object of B's reaction, A's affect is not the emotional object of B's response, because B does not believe (or imagine) of A's affect what is required to make it an appropriate emotional object of the response B experiences.* We can be agnostic about the mechanism of transmission. Between humans, there are many possibilities, from subtle facial mimicry to the detection of emitted pheromones. Between music and humans, or home décors and humans, different causal routes might produce the relevant outcome.

5

Once Again, This Time with Feeling

The arbitrariness of so many virtuosos is partly responsible for the excess of expression marks to be found in the works of composers who thus hoped to forestall distortion and misinterpretation. Yet, complete control over the performer is not only impossible but also undesirable. The only remedy is to improve the education of performers in matters of musical style and taste. The most common fault is the application of a Romantic, that is, a highly expressive treatment of non-Romantic music, such as the works of Bach, Mozart, Beethoven. The deplorable result is an overdoing of all nuances: the use of *prestissimo* instead of *allegro*, of *larghissimo* instead of *adagio*, of *fff* and *ppp* instead of *f* and *p*, of frequent *crescendi* and *decrescendi* instead of an even level of sonority, of numerous *rubatos, ritardandos,* and *accelerandos* instead of strictly kept tempo, etc. In view of all these tendencies nothing seems to be more important for the student than to learn to play without expression. Only the pianist who has learned to play Bach's *Chromatic Fantasia* or Beethoven's *Apassionata* in the most rigid way will be able to add that amount of nuances and shades which these works properly require. (Apel 1966: 252)

Prelude

How does the performer communicate the emotional expressiveness imparted by the composer to his music? The response to this question will depend on one's view of performance. For Western works specified notationally (to which I will restrict the following discussion), a plausible position regards musical performance as analogous to quotation. The performer's task and intention is, by following the composer's score, to repeat or re-create an 'utterance' made originally by the composer and, thereby, to convey what he meant by it. The response will depend also on one's theory regarding the manner in which music is expressive of emotion.

Expressive performance as feeling or simulation

One such account, known as the *expression theory*, has it that music is expressive of an emotion just in case the composer experienced that emotion and gave vent to it

First published in *Journal of Aesthetic Education*, 38 (2) (2004): 1–6.

through the act of composition. The work, his 'utterance,' betrays what he felt. In that case, the performer's task is to quote the composer's utterance in a manner that betrays the same emotion. Rather than merely mouthing what he says, she will invest it with the passion that would be typical of someone's giving direct expression to her experience of the relevant emotion. She might adopt either of two approaches to this end. Like the 'method' actor, she might induce an equivalent emotion in herself and affirm what she quotes as an expression of her own feeling, this being one she shares with the composer. Or she might simulate the expression of the appropriate emotion. She articulates the composer's utterance as if she felt what he did.

According to the *arousal theory*, music is expressive of a given emotion just in case the audience is aroused to an experience of that emotion as a consequence of listening to and following the music. In that case, the performer's goal is to move the auditor to an appropriate emotional response by 'quoting' the composer. One of the most compelling ways of doing so would be by eliciting an empathetic reaction. Provided the performer demonstrates the appropriate feeling with sufficient ardor, she can rely on the natural human sympathy of the audience to kindle in them a reaction echoing her own emotion. Accordingly, she should proceed as already described, either by inciting herself to the appropriate emotion and showing it in her manner of playing or, at least, by acting as if she is in the grip of that emotion, even if she is not.

There are grounds for rejecting both the emotivist and arousal theories of musical expressiveness (see Chapter 1 and Davies 1994a: ch. 4), but independent of those reasons, it should be apparent that what these accounts imply about the manner of performing music expressively is unconvincing. Musical performance, if it is to be successful and compelling, very often demands of the player such a high degree of concentration and clarity of mind that she has neither the time nor the inclination to indulge in emotional extremes or sophisticated simulations of them. If she were gripped by powerful emotions, these may get in the way of her performing; at best, they would be ancillary, not integral, to her main goal, which is to play through the work correctly, from beginning to end. The same goes for the suggestion that the performer engages in an elaborate game of emotional pretense. Performance calls for concentration on the business of sounding the work. The player needs to focus, not to emote and not to simulate experiences she does not have. In other words, the story told above is psychologically implausible, given what we know already about the physical demands on and state of mind of performers in general.

And it fails in another way. Notice how inconspicuous it makes the music. The emphasis falls on the state of mind of the composer, of the listeners, and of the performer, as if the actual notes and their sequence are of small concern. To return to the analogy introduced earlier, it implies that musical expressiveness resides entirely in or results exclusively from the manner of utterance or quotation, not at all in or from the *content* of what is uttered or quoted. The leading alternative theories of musical expressiveness avoid this last complaint because they connect music's expressiveness to concrete details of its structure and content, thereby implying that the performer communicates the music's expressiveness by delivering an accurate performance, not by betraying emotions she feels or pretends to feel.

Expressive performance as playing the notes

The theory I favor (Chapter 1 and Davies 1994a: ch. 5) holds that emotions are literally presented by music. The emotions expressed by music are not psychologically experienced states; instead, they are expressive appearances. Just as basset hounds are sad-looking, so music is sad-sounding. Music is sad-sounding not because it mimics sounds like those that might be wrung from someone who feels sad (though it may do so sometimes); rather, this is so because it presents a sad demeanor via the manner of its progress. Sad music is slow, dragging, dark, downcast. (If these once were metaphors, they have long since died and become literal, I maintain; see Chapter 2.) As I put it, music is expressive by presenting emotion-characteristics in its aural appearance.

Other theories tie music's expressiveness to properties literally possessed by the music, even if they are less inclined than the last to locate music's expressiveness squarely within it. Again, the key properties are dynamic ones. Through a process of imaginative engagement with these, the listener hears expressiveness in the music. Just what is to be make-believed varies from theory to theory. According to one view, the listener is to make-believe of what she hears that it is an awareness of an emotion she feels (Walton 1988). Another version maintains that the auditor is to entertain the existence of an imagined persona and to hear the music as an expression, in a fashion that is distinctively musical, of that persona's emotions and psychological states (Levinson 1996a: ch. 6, 2006).

Fortunately, we need not adjudicate between these competing theories because their entailments in regard to the performer's role in communicating music's expressiveness are similar. To the extent that the music's expressiveness either is an objective property of the music, or supervenes on (other) objective musical properties, the performance will be appropriately expressive so long as it realizes the relevant properties. To do so, the performer must follow the score accurately. What, if anything, she feels, or seems to feel, is beside the point. For the audience, what then is needed is perception, not arousal. This perception must be cognitively informed. As with other complex cultural artifacts, music will be fully grasped and understood only by the listener who is able to locate the work against the background of its socio-musical context, and who is thereby aware of the traditions, conventions, practices, canons, paradigms, and the rest of what it presupposes (see Chapter 7).

If their emotions are irrelevant, why is it so commonly said that a musician will not be able to play a piece well until she can *feel* it, and why do we assume that the true music lover will be deeply moved by what she hears? Regarding the performer, I think the 'feeling' referred to is not emotion but, rather, the kind of practical knowledge that makes sensitive playing possible. This knowledge is not of propositions, but is of applied skills. The musician does not need to *know that* one or the other thing is true of the music; instead, she needs to *know how* to sound the notes so that they form a compelling, unified whole, and so on. We talk of *feeling* here not because emotion is involved but rather because the knowledge required is frequently non-propositional and thereby inarticulable (see Chapter 7). As for the music lover, nothing I have said so far denies the propriety of her emotional reactions. Indeed, she has much to respond to: the music's beauty, majesty, and the rest, along with the power and interest of the performer's interpretation. As well, she is liable to find the music's expressive mood contagious (see Chapter 4). What I have denied is only that her ability to perceive what the music expresses depends on her being aroused to feel the same.

The performer's contribution to the performance's expressiveness

The present analysis is not yet satisfactory, however. It undervalues the performer's contribution to the performance's expressiveness by implying that she need only copy or re-create was has been achieved already by the composer. Yet we know that many performances of a piece might all be faithful to the composer's work while differing in important, though often subtle, ways in their expressiveness. These variations, which sometimes are all that distinguish great from mediocre performances, are attributable to the performer's interpretation, not solely to the work. (It begins to look as if a better analogy is with translation than with quotation; see Chapter 12.) So far, the creative contribution of the performer, qua interpreter of the work, has not been acknowledged.

Composers of Western classical works write scores. These should be understood not just as descriptions of the work's contents but also as prescriptions. In effect, the composer says: make this so! Unless it is deficient in being incomplete, ambiguous, or indefinite in crucial respects, a score fully specifies the scope of the work it is of. Nevertheless, it underdetermines many of the concrete details of a performance. For example, convention may dictate that a melody should be decorated in a stylistically appropriate manner, but no directions in the notation show what is to be done. In that case, the work contains decorations, but no particular set. A faithful performance will decorate the melody but, subject to the appropriate stylistic limitations, it is for the performer to choose what she will play. Many of the fine details of performances are left to the performer's discretion, and the ways she handles them comprise her interpretation of the piece (see Davies 2001a).

The general point just made applies also to the specific case of musical expressiveness. Work-determinative features specified in the score usually settle the broad emotional tone of the work (because they also settle the dynamic shape and progression of the work). But this is susceptible to many shades of articulation that depend on interpretative decisions taken by the performer. These can arise at all levels—at the microcosmic, regarding nuances of attack, phrasing, and volume for motives, figures, and melodies—and at the macrocosmic, regarding balance, emphasis, and patterning for chunks, sections, and movements. The performer might work to highlight and make more precise a given expressive tone; equally though, she might exploit possibilities for ambiguity and equivocity for their interpretative effect. In any case, she provides a creative input by adding a dimension of fine-grainedness in expressive detail that goes beyond the work's expressive character. The expressive disposition of her accurate performance interpretation will transmit the work's expressiveness, but, inevitably, will also comment and elaborate on that expressiveness in doing so.

Can the performer give the performance an expressive character that is entirely absent from the work itself? I doubt that she can usually do so, assuming that the performance is faithful, integrated, and plausible as a rendition of the work. But there are these possibilities: a powerfully expressive work might receive a performance that is so quiet and detached that it distances itself from the essence of the work, with the result that it parodies or ironizes what is expressive in the work. And a work that is playfully witty or deliberately coarse for the sake of humor could be played in a deliberately dull, straight fashion that makes the piece seem clumsy and inept in its expressiveness and character. Such performances, even if they are faithful at the most basic level, traduce the works they are of, however.

A Pedagogical moral

There is a pedagogical moral to be drawn from the above. As I have observed, performers are often urged by their teachers (or conductors) to play 'once more, this time with feeling.' It would be easy to be misled by such a phrase. It should not be understood as exhorting the performer to emote about the music. Performers who do emote about the music are liable to lose control of their performance, while performers who look as if they are in the grip of intense emotions are likely to distract the listener's attention from the music. Rather, when she is instructed to play with feeling, the musician is being called upon to use sensitivity in her interpretative judgments. And that is, indeed, something she will need if she is to play very well. It is the practical skill underpinning this sensitivity that the teacher should cultivate in the pupil. The education of musicians should focus more on technique, nuances of interpretation, and 'authentic' modes of playing than on self-expression or on sharing the music's expressive moods.

6

Musical Meaning in a Broader Perspective

Musical meaning has been an ongoing concern of philosophers, musicologists, and semiologists. Expressiveness and representation have been much discussed during the past two decades. Despite this, the debate concerning musical meaning has been limited to considering what music conveys, how it does so, and what it means for it to do so. These questions ask what music refers to (or denotes, signifies, stands for), or what it represents (or depicts, describes), or what is expressed through it. Without playing down their differences, one can see that these notions all imply a conception of meaning according to which a meaning-bearer communicates a content that exists independently of itself. In principle, the same content could be communicated just as well by numerous other meaning-bearers. The meaning-bearer is merely a vehicle for the meaning it communicates.

This picture of meaning has only limited application to music. Music does not always convey 'extra-musical' contents. Many compositions do not refer beyond themselves. Music's capacities for representation are limited. Though music's expressive power is considerable, expressiveness is absent from many musical works of great value.

One might conclude that, at root, music has no meaning. Kivy argues this way (1990: 8–9): because music has no semantic content—despite its quasi-syntactic structures—musical meaning does not exist 'as a reality of listening.' His conclusion is inescapable only if one restricts the notion of meaning to the linguistic model. Ordinary language allows for a more generous use of 'meaning,' however. Most people agree that (good) music makes sense and can be said to have meaning.

In this chapter, we explore several notions of musical meaning that do not accord with linguistic or semiological frameworks. We begin with formal meaning. Accounts trying to reduce this to linguistic or semiological meaning are flawed, we argue. Instead, progress and structure within musical works can be explained in terms of reasons like those that justify human actions. Next, we describe an even more fundamental, non-discursive kind of meaning in music, *experiential formal meaning*.

Co-authored with Constantijn Koopman and first published in *Journal of Aesthetics and Art Criticism*, 59 (2001): 261–73.

Later, we turn to the subjective significance music has in human life. With *meaning-for-the-subject*, we concentrate on the idiosyncrasies of musical experience. The meaning music has more widely for all human beings, rather than solely for individuals, then is discussed as *meaning-for-us*.

Formal musical meaning

A number of theorists hold that musical meaning comes from the specific properties of musical form. They use expressions like *formal meaning* (Alperson 1987: 16). Malcolm Budd, whose term is *intramusical meaning*, writes (1995: 127): 'the core of musical understanding—of hearing music with understanding—is the experience of what I shall call the intramusical meaning of a musical work, that is, the work's audible musical structure, the musically significant relations (melodic, harmonic, rhythmic, and so on) that obtain amongst the sounds and silences that compose the work.' In a similar vein, one of us refers (Davies 1994a: 48) to the *formal significance* of musical ideas. This type of meaning consists in the coherence of the structure of the work; to understand the musical work is to understand how it is put together. Neither Budd nor Davies has elaborated this notion of formal or intramusical meaning.

Other authors distinguish formal (or intramusical) from extramusical meaning. Leonard B. Meyer has coined the terms *designative* and *embodied* meaning. He observes (1956: 35): 'a stimulus may indicate events or consequences which are different from itself in kind, as when a word designates or points to an object or action which is not itself a word. Or a stimulus may indicate or imply events or consequences which are of the same kind as the stimulus itself, as when a dim light on the eastern horizon heralds the coming of day.... The former type of meaning may be called designative, the latter embodied.' According to Meyer, debates on musical meaning have centered around designative meaning, that is, music's pointing to extramusical objects and concepts. Though more important than designative musical meaning, critics have ignored embodied musical meaning, which occurs when parts of a musical work 'indicate' or 'point to' other parts (1956: 32–5). After Meyer, various theorists have proposed similar distinctions: Wilson Coker (1972: 61; *congeneric* versus *extrageneric meaning*), Jean-Jacques Nattiez (1990: 102ff; *intrinsic* versus *extrinsic referring*), Roman Jakobson (1971: 704–5; *introversive* versus *extroversive semiosis*), Lucy Green (1988: chs 2, 3; *inherent* versus *delineated meaning*), and Winfried Nöth (1990: 431–2; *endosemantics* versus *exosemantics*).

Though we approve of the distinction, we object to the way in which intramusical meaning, no less than extramusical meaning, is characterized in a quasi-linguistic or semiological manner. For instance, Meyer holds (1956: 34) that formal meaning results from referential relations within the musical work: 'anything acquires meaning if it is connected with, or indicates, or refers to, something beyond itself, so that its full nature points to and is revealed in that connection.' While Coker draws on the semiological theory of C. S. Peirce in employing the term 'icon' to analyze *congeneric* musical meaning (1972: 61) as 'those resultants of a dominantly iconic sign situation in which someone interprets one part of a musical work as a sign of another part of that same work or a diverse musical work.'

Despite the widespread view that formal meaning can be assimilated to linguistic or semiological frameworks, we do not believe that attempts to do so are convincing. The relationships between parts of a musical work are relationships of implication that should not be conflated with the linguistic or semiological notions of reference, denotation, or signification.

In observing that musical relationships have the character of implications, we agree with one of Meyer's central ideas (1956, 1967: ch. 1). Music features stylistic conventions. These determine that some progressions are likely, others less so, and still others impossible. In tonal music from the classical period, a chord on the fifth scale degree is more likely to lead to one on the first than the sixth degree, while a progression to the fourth is excluded. To be sure, stylistic conventions may be broken. The impossible may become possible and the improbable more likely. In fact, as several authors have noted, the attractiveness of a musical composition significantly depends on its breaking conventions, thus bringing about the unexpected. Nevertheless, the set of stylistic orthodoxies is resistant to change. A composer can disobey only a limited number of rules if her music is to remain understandable, or even recognizable, as music. Though not unassailable, conventions regulate musical practices by defining the musical game that can be played.

In music, structural patterns are subtle, multi-dimensional, and multi-hierarchical. They involve development as well as iteration. As these patterns unfold, they create implications at all levels of the composition. For example, in tonal music within the classical tradition, a large melodic leap usually is followed by a continuation in smaller steps in the opposite direction. A thematic phrase of four measures ending on a dominant chord is likely to be followed by four more measures concluding on the tonic. An exposition of two themes, the first in the tonic and the other in the dominant, leads us to expect a development section after which both themes are recapitulated in the tonic. And at the highest level, a fast opening movement of a symphony, a sonata, or a string quartet is likely to be followed by a slow piece of at least half its length. We hear earlier events as having consequences for the proper order and treatment of later ones, though it usually is the case that, at any given moment, more than one continuation is apt.

However, relationships of implication should not be conflated with referential relationships, as Meyer does (1956: 34, 1967: 5–14). An analogy from the visual domain might help to make this clear. Consider patterns comprised of dots or geometric figures. Because principles of gestalt perception (like those of good continuation and completion) apply to such designs, we consider the placement of particular dots to have implications for the proper location of other dots; several dots may be grouped into higher order gestalts that are themselves patterned. As with musical notes taken in relation to larger wholes in which they are elements, the observer might identify some dots as misplaced, or might judge some continuations as wrong, with others as more or less appropriate. We do not usually take one part of the wallpaper to *refer* to another, however, despite the implied iteration of the gestalt. Similarly, we should not assimilate relations between a work's musical elements to linguistic reference. Such connections are on the psychological level of perception rather than the linguistic level of signification or denotation.

This can also be seen from other differences between musical relations and linguistic reference. In a linguistic context, reference involves non-reflexive relationships between the meaning-bearer and what it stands for; by contrast, the relationship between musical entities (themes, rhythms, chord progressions, etc.) is reflexive. Within a work, musical events implicate their successors and vice versa. Second, musical entities are not vehicles for referring beyond themselves, but are parts of the very thing communicated. We treat words and signs as transparent to their meaning, ignoring their intrinsic features, but we attend to the formal properties of musical events for their own sake. Third, whereas meaning-bearer and meaning are related in language through an act of abstract conjunction by which the former comes to stand for the latter, relationships between parts of a musical work are established simply by their being concretely perceived as belonging together within the same perceptual field.

In short, the differences between intramusical relationships and referential ones are so fundamental that it is misleading to 'explain' formal musical meaning in terms of linguistic or semiological notions. When used of music, 'reference' and related terms have been stripped of the content they have in their original, linguistic setting and have been invested with a psychological rather than a semiological significance. Also, there is no reason to adopt the terminology of *icons*, as Coker does. We should not be more tempted to think of new occurrences of the theme as icons of its earlier statements than to think some windows of a palazzo are icons of its other windows.

Although relations of implication cannot be equated with referential relationships of language, they do provide us with the key to an alternative account of formal musical meaning. In terms of the relations between its parts, we can provide reasons why a work develops this rather than that way. Moreover, these reasons have a distinctive character: they are like those with which we explain human actions.

We account for most phenomena in terms of involuntary causal mechanisms. We explain rain by a story about water evaporating, accumulating into clouds, condensing again under the influence of falling temperature, and precipitating in the form of drops. With humanly made objects like machines, besides pointing to causal mechanisms we also refer to the intentions of the creator. In the case of musical works, however, we do not restrict ourselves to these two kinds of explanations. More typically, we explain musical works as displaying a kind of internal rationality (Davies 2003: ch. 9). Musical works cohere in specific ways that can be explained because, like human action, their progressions are ruled by implications. Events happening later in the piece can be understood by relating them to what has come earlier; in view of its antecedents, an event is the right (which is not the same as the most probable or the only possible) progression of the piece. And events in the beginning of the piece can be explained as connecting to later parts and to the work as a whole. Explanation here is in terms of coherence. The coherence of the parts of the piece at all levels enables us to explain the function of the various parts in the whole. (See Chapter 7.)

Because we can explain what happens at a given point in the music by reference to what occurs on either side of it, it is not inappropriate to talk of 'the meaning' of the music and of its temporal progress. In the context of formal meaning, the question: 'what is the meaning of event x in piece y?' should not be taken as a request to specify some referent z which could be identified as the meaning of x. Typically, it is a request to elucidate the way event x coheres with the rest of piece y.

Experiential formal meaning

The fact that we can explain music in terms of reasons provides a sufficient justification for speaking of musical meaning. However, there is a more fundamental sense in which music can be said to have meaning. To understand music as meaningful, it is not necessary that we can explain the progression of the music. Meaning can be understood immediately in the musical encounter, without reasoning at all. Music appears to have an experiential rather than a discursive logic. We do not merely perceive a succession of patterns in music. Instead, we experience the musical parts as connected into a dynamic whole. There is sense to the way music progresses. Music presents itself as a continuous process in which, at every moment, what we hear follows in a compelling way from what came before; that is, music proceeds not as the temporal succession of otherwise unconnected elements but as the unfolding of an integrated whole. One understands a piece's formal musical meaning when one appreciates the internal connectedness of its parts. Roger Scruton notes (1987: 171, 174) that music is primarily understood in response and that musical meaning is what we grasp when we listen to music with understanding. If we add to these observations that listening to music with understanding involves tracking the dynamics of musical forms per se, we can conclude that there is formal meaning in response, or *experiential formal meaning*, as we shall call it.

We take 'experiential formal meaning' to refer to the experiential potential the listener is able to realize when he responds to the music with understanding. It is the coherent dynamic content he discovers by focusing on the music's formal progress. In characterizing experiential formal meaning in terms of experiential or dynamic content, we acknowledge a limited, though significant, connection between this type of meaning and the linguistic model. In both, there is a fundamental distinction between, as Carl Dahlhaus puts it (1973: 39–40), what is present and what represented (see also Scruton 1997: 19). There is a difference between what a musical structure acoustically presents and what we can hear in it. Take, for example, the standard cadence in classical tonal music in which a chord on the fifth degree is followed by a chord on the first. We can make a distinction between the acoustic sounds and the tonal functions the experienced listener can hear in them. Someone with no background in the culture will hear successive clusters of sounds, not the dynamic connection between a dominant and a tonic chord.

In other respects, however, experiential formal meaning differs fundamentally from the linguistic and semiological models. Experiential formal meaning does not depend on musical form's communicating something that has no intrinsic connection with it; that is, musical form is to be grasped as such if this meaning is to be accessed. The experiential content is uniquely related to the musical form by which it is communicated. No other musical piece has the same experiential content as, for example, Mozart's Sonata Facile.

As we suggested, experiential formal meaning is connected to the dynamics of the musical encounter. As it unfolds, music features a complex of events that change and evolve, while interacting to form a complex whole. Theorists have tried to capture the dynamic character of musical progressions, often describing them as patterns of tension and release (see Meyer 1956, for example). Ernst Kurth (1991) and his followers use the terminology of 'musical energetics.' Building up and releasing energies in specific sequences, every work possesses a distinctive musical energetics. Other authors—Coker (1972: ch. 3), Scruton (1997: 352–64), Christopher Small (1998)—have used the metaphor of gesture to describe music's dynamic nature. Often these quasi-gestures are related to extramusical meaning, but there is no reason to do so; they are features of musical dynamics and can be appreciated as such, rather than being interpreted as conveying extramusical content.

Note that, while patterns of tension and release or energetic sequences and gestures are often attributed to the work, they are realized only through the imaginative response of the listener (see Scruton 1997: 16–96). These dynamic features are present in the work neither at the level of the acoustic signal nor in the notation that specifies the work. It is only in our experience that they are manifested. Even the phenomena of tone and movement, which are the very basis of musical understanding, feature only at the level of musical response. Nevertheless, these dynamic features are contained in the work and are part of its experiential formal meaning.

If experiential musical meaning is revealed only in the experience of the listener and depends on that response, in what sense is it an objective property of the music? Why do we attribute the meaning to the music rather than to the listener's experience? Here we might draw a parallel with what philosophers have called 'secondary properties,' which include colors, flavors, and similar qualities.[1] Only creatures with the appropriate sensory apparatus, and perhaps also with needs that depend on color discrimination, perceive green. Yet we predicate the color to the grass, not to the experience to which it gives rise in appropriate observers. This is because there is considerable interpersonal agreement in the color judgments made by observers, with the result that such judgments are more informative of what is viewed than of what may be idiosyncratic to the spectator or to the conditions under which the perception occurs. One way of construing the color property is as a causal power, that is, as the capacity to produce experiences eliciting the appropriate judgments from suitably equipped or qualified observers. Music's meaning can be construed as analogous. Although it is

---

[1] Scruton (1997: 160) takes musical qualities to be a specific class of tertiary qualities, which are different from secondary qualities in that their perception also involves intellect and imagination.

response-dependent, it is an objective property of the music because there is agreement in the relevant judgments of suitably qualified listeners under appropriate conditions.

As the use of 'understanding' suggests, it takes more to be a comprehending listener than to be a perceiver of colors, though. Whereas our capacity to perceive colors is innate, our ability to grasp a musical work's experiential meaning results from a (largely unconscious) learning process in which we become acquainted with the conventions of the musical tradition to which it belongs. Only those who have internalized the conventions of the work's style, genre, and tradition are able to respond with understanding to it (Levinson 1996a: ch. 3).

The experience of the comprehending listener is governed by the form of the musical work. The character of the melodic and rhythmic motifs, the layout of the themes, the further development of the melodic and rhythmic substance, the harmonic progression, the successive arrangement of the various timbres, variations in loudness: all these features in their specific combinations guide the listener's experience. As the form unfolds and builds up a unified structure, so the responses of the listener develop into a unified experience. The consistent progression of musical substance intimates to him a coherent experiential structure.

This is not to say that a musical work completely determines the experience of the listener, however. Even if listeners all have a similar musical background and attend to the musical progression with full concentration, clearly their experiences differ widely. Musical experience may be thoroughly personal, as we will elaborate later. Nevertheless, this should not prevent us from seeing that music possesses a specific experiential potential. A work embodies a certain blueprint for coherent experience. As the listener follows the work, his responses take specific directions that are controlled by the properties of the musical sequence, so that the dynamics of musical form are matched by corresponding dynamics in the response.

Although we tend to speak separately of the dynamic features of musical form and of the dynamic musical experience, the two coincide in the musical encounter; dynamic form and dynamic response are realized in one and the same act. Dynamic musical form does not precede the dynamic response, because it is only through the imaginative response that the dynamic characteristics of musical form—like tension and release, and quasi-gestures—come into being. In musical experience, the constitution of dynamic musical form and musical response are two sides of the same coin.

The special way musical ideas are presented, repeated, alternated, contrasted, and transformed in each musical work results in every work's presenting a complex whole of dynamic qualities, which is experienced by the listener as a unique gestalt. This experience is ineffable; that is, it is finer-grained, subtler, and more complex than are linguistic concepts and propositional structures. That is no fault in language, though, which can perform the function of mediating and categorizing the world only because it is not isometric with direct perception of the world. Moreover, the ineffability of the experience of music's formal meaning does not have the corollaries sometimes claimed: that the contents of direct experience of music and of linguistic assertions about music constitute mutually exclusive domains and that direct experience of music communicates linguistically inexpressible yet deeply important truths about the emotions.

Our conception of experiential musical meaning bears a close affinity to Jerrold Levinson's views of musical understanding. He argues (1997) that understanding music is a matter of being able to follow the musical connectedness from point to point. To have a basic understanding of the music, a listener need not have a reflective awareness of large-scale structures. It is sufficient for him to experience the cogency of the music's progress from moment to moment. Knowledge of large-scale form can add a further dimension to his appreciation, but the pleasure he takes from this is relatively weak in comparison with, and also is parasitic on, that afforded by apprehending music in the moment.

Levinson devotes a small passage to the concept of musical meaning, suggesting (1997: 33–4) that musical meaning 'concerns the purely internal connectedness of music, its kinetic and dynamic content.' Our elucidation of the concept of experiential formal meaning is similar. We take the experience of coherent musical structure as the basis for ascribing meaning to music and we take music to have an experiential content that can be characterized as dynamic and kinetic. However, our conception of experiential meaning does not endorse Levinson's radical conclusion that the apprehension of large-scale formal structure is largely irrelevant to musical appreciation. In our opinion, one's awareness of large-scale structure, both on a reflective and an unreflective level, can be crucial to musical experience (see Chapter 7 and Davies 1999b). Nevertheless, Levinson correctly places the cogency of sequence, the connectedness of music as it develops from point to point, at the center of musical experience.

Finally, we admit that our account does not apply directly to certain varieties of contemporary music; for instance, 'non-teleological' aleatoric or minimalist pieces. Such music does not comply with the ideals of dynamic progression, evolution, and directionality. Nonetheless, our account of musical meaning is not completely irrelevant to understanding these works, because part of their significance derives from their willfully neglecting these ideals, which characterize not only Western classical music but virtually all musical traditions. Furthermore, the concept of experiential formal meaning can explain why music that lacks goal-directedness strikes many listeners as meaningless. These listeners are used to music that invites and guides their dynamic response. They are disoriented by non-teleological music that is experienced as not 'working' the way it should.

Understanding in response versus understanding through analysis

The distinctive character of experiential formal meaning can best be brought out by opposing it to the understanding of musical form we gain through analyzing a musical score.

In formal analysis, the work's elements are identified and separated, producing a picture of self-contained, static components timelessly linked by similarity, opposition, and the like. Formal analysis treats music as architecture, as if the piece's parts coexist in a timeless reality. By contrast, experiential formal meaning relates to dynamic experience as it unfolds in real time. When listening, we experience an ongoing musical process, not a sequence of isolated events. Caesuras in the music do not undermine this effect. Music presents a continuous flux of events to which we react with a corresponding flux of responses. Second, whereas analysis depends on conscious reflection on the work's make-up, experiential formal meaning is non-reflective and non-propositional. It resides in the response, not in an internal commentary. This leads to a third point. Whereas formal analysis is purely cognitive, feeling (not to be identified with emotion) plays a crucial role alongside cognition in realizing the experiential content of music. To grasp the musical work one has to feel the progression of the music. If one does not experience its sequences of tension and release, one does not have an adequate understanding of what is going on in the music. Comprehending experiential formal meaning calls for a response that engages both our cognitive and our affective powers. Fourth, whereas formal analysis adopts a distanced standpoint, experiential formal meaning requires total involvement in the music. One must be able to give oneself to the music and be prepared to be carried away by it if one is to apprehend fully its experiential meaning. Of course, this does not mean that peak experiences always occur. Sometimes the music is too weak to seize us or it may be simply without much pretension. But even then, our willingness to join in is presupposed. In other cases, we find the music not so much unappealing as repulsive, precisely because we feel that it abuses the empathetic stance it presumes from the listener.

Also, with analysis we approach music from the outside, that is, as an artifact put together in an ordered way. With experiential meaning we understand a work from the inside. We treat it in a significant sense more like a person than like an inanimate object. Stanley Cavell writes (1977: 197–8): 'but objects of art not merely interest and absorb, they move us; we are not merely involved with them, but concerned with them, and care about them; we treat them in special ways, invest them with a value which normal people otherwise reserve only for other people.... They *mean* something to us, not just the way statements do, but the way people do.'

There are several respects in which our experience of music is like that of a person. For instance, sometimes we hear the expression of emotion in music. At a more fundamental level, we find in music the kind of coherence and non-arbitrary progress that marks human action; it displays integrity and cogency in the manner of its unfolding. Moreover, we also respond to musical movement with empathy. It is only through *Einfühlung* that we can apprehend the experiential formal meaning of music.

Scruton observes (1997: 352): 'the human psyche is transformed by art, but only because art provides us with the expressive gestures towards which our emotions lean in their search for sympathy—gestures which we seize, when we encounter them, with a sense of being carried at last to a destination that we could not reach alone.' He uses both 'sympathy' and 'empathy' to characterize musical experience, without distinguishing the two. We prefer to describe experiential formal meaning in terms of empathy, defined by the *Concise Oxford Dictionary* as 'the power of identifying oneself mentally with (and so fully comprehending) a person or object of contemplation.'[2] Empathy is a broader notion than sympathy and does not presuppose the presence of a person to whom one responds.

Music affects us powerfully because we identify with it; it is in virtue of the empathetic responses they elicit that great works have such profound effects on us. Just as we extend our being by identifying with heroes, so we enrich our existence by engaging with music, but whereas an idol merely presents us with an image of a desirable life, music directly intimates an extended way of being alive. Our identification with the work can be so complete that the boundary between ourselves and it seems to disappear. The music's movement can seem to become our own. In our awareness there is no longer a form out there to be contemplated; the dynamics of the music overcome us, imposing their patterns on our experience.

The phenomenology of musical experience might lead one to hear in the work something of the composer's character and personality. That would not always be a mistaken way of hearing the music but, in general, one is no more justified in extrapolating from the music to the composer than one is in reading novels as autobiographical. Also, the phenomenology of the musical experience might lead one to hear in the work a narrative concerning the emotional life and actions of a persona. Again, that is one way of engaging with music that may assist in the listener's following its progress with understanding. In our view, it is a mistake to analyze musical expressiveness as requiring such imaginings, however.[3] Such approaches are natural to the extent that, where we find action and emotion, we also expect a human agent to whom these can be attributed. A persona is not in any way required, however.

The following should also be clear: the similarity between our experiences of music and of human behavior does not mean that music can be understood only in terms of expressiveness. It also resembles human action with respect to the coherence it exhibits and the empathetic response it elicits, and experiencing neither of these requires that one hear it as expressive of emotion. What music presents us with in the first place is not the expression of human life but an extension of it. Thanks to music, we are acquainted with modes of experience we would never dream of. We concur with Alan H. Goldman, who argues (1992: 42) that 'the peculiar value of music lies in its presenting us with an alternative world in which we can be fully engaged.' Our concept of experiential formal meaning explains how our response to the dynamics of musical form can be, and often is, fully empathetic without being a reaction to music's expressiveness.

A last difference between experiential formal meaning and analysis is that only with the former do we comprehend the music as compelling, as a process in which every event grows organically from the preceding ones (Levinson 1997). Through analysis

---

[2] Our use of 'empathy' should not be associated with Ridley's idiosyncratic distinction (1995a) between a sympathetic and an empathetic response, the former being associated with a mirroring response to the expressiveness of music, the second with one's hearing the music as a manifestation of a persona.

[3] One who does so is Levinson (1996a: ch. 6). For criticism of the idea that appreciation of music's expressiveness necessarily involves the invocation of a persona, see Chapter 1 and Davies (2003: ch. 10).

we can trace the connections between musical parts—the oppositions, the elaborations, the reductions, and so on—but such insights by themselves cannot establish that the music is convincing. A work may exhibit a bewildering range of ingenious relationships and lack any sense of cogency. Similarly, through analysis we can establish that the piece is coherent in the sense of its consistently following the conventions of a certain style, but such coherence should not be confused with cogency. Whether a work is compelling is revealed only in the experience it affords the qualified listener.

Do analyses not contain references to musical cogency and to other dynamic qualities of the work? They do, but such judgments are based on the analyst's actual or imagined experience of the music. On the basis of her musical experience, she is aware of the formal dispositions that underlie the listener's experience of musical cogency. Formal relations extracted from the score are not in themselves sufficient to account for the cogency or otherwise of the work at hand. In consequence, musical analyses, though they may enhance the listener's grasp of the work, cannot guarantee a basic understanding of it. To achieve such an understanding, one needs a sense of the experiential meaning of the work, of the organic connectedness of its parts. If this experience eludes us, a formal analysis probably will not help.

It is now time to tone down the opposition between understanding music through analysis and understanding music in response. Analysis often is informed by insights gained through experiencing the music and sets out to relate form in the score to experiential categories. These analyses aim to elucidate the structures that underlie our experience of coherence, balance, elegance, and so on. Also, musical analyses often refer to phenomenologically experienced features of the music, for instance, to tension and release, growth and decline, expansion and contraction, thickness and airiness. Again, such ascriptions depend ultimately on the analyst's musical experience and not solely on what is recorded in the score.

Conversely, understanding music in response features aspects associated with analysis. An awareness of large-scale form can be a part of the listener's response. In other words, musical experience does involve the static, timeless dimensions of musical form. Also, as we listen sometimes we reflect consciously on the work's structural relations. We agree with Levinson (1997), however: self-conscious reflection on the musical experience as it proceeds is less prominent for the average listener than some theorists would want us to believe. At base, experiential musical meaning is apprehended by moving along with the music from moment to moment rather than by cognizing a picture of the musical form as a whole.

Meaning for the subject

So far we have discussed musical meaning from the perspective of our experience of music's formal qualities. Now we turn to a more personal kind of musical meaning. *Meaning-for-the-subject*, as we call it, has to do with the place something takes in the individual's life or consciousness, with the specific way he experiences it, and with how this relates to his perceptions, feelings, thoughts, and desires. The meaning a thing has for a subject does not lie in its instrumentality—for example, as a vehicle for communication—but rather is existential. Like experiential musical meaning, meaning-for-the-subject owes nothing to linguistic and semiological models that explain meaning as a function of a sign's use in communication.

In considering meaning-for-the-subject, the comparison with the meaning other people have for us is again pertinent. Our relation to music parallels our relationship to human beings: as well as regarding music as subject to explanations like those we give for human actions and as inviting an empathetic response, we relate to it as a determining factor of our lives. Musical works are objects of concern, of special care. We treat them with intense affection, with reverence sometimes. We can be hurt by someone's expressing himself unfavorably on musical works we hold in high esteem. Our engagement with music is so fecund, versatile, and intense that it can be compared to the way we relate to our fellow human beings.

Meaning-for-the-subject is largely subjective. Music has an experiential formal meaning and, sometimes, also expressive or representational properties. Even if we restrict ourselves to these objective contents, there is ample room for personal interpretation and response. Moreover, there are numerous other dimensions—historical, psychological, social, political, ideological, etc.—that allow for readings of a more personal kind. For example, someone may think Boccherini's famous minuet is the ideal evocation of the wigtail period. Or he may consider the mathematical Prelude in A minor from the second book of Bach's *Well-tempered Clavier* as an exemplification of the composer's character, which he believes to be rigid. Or he may find the music of Richard Strauss, Reger, and the early Schoenberg to be overly decadent. Such examples can be multiplied endlessly.

The best example of a dimension of musical meaning that is idiosyncratic concerns the association of music with particular events in a person's life. A work may be particularly dear to him because it first awakened him to classical music. Or it may be that he used to play it with an absent friend. Alternatively, a person may hate a work or style because it recalls a disastrous episode in his life. The rejection of Wagner's music by survivors of the holocaust presents a marked example.

Though some musical pieces take a more salient position than others in our lives, all the works we know have a particular meaning for us. How a given work fits into one's life is a personal matter. For Ben, a classical work is interesting as an accompaniment for a film; for Liz, it is the catchy tune she knows from a commercial; for Nathalie, it is one of the many classical compositions that provide a pleasurable background for her work; for Arthur, it is an object of reverence that is to be addressed only when he can give his full attention to it.

Finally, the role played by music as a whole in one's life is highly individual. The extremes range from music's being the most cherished occupation in life to complete indifference to music of any kind. This last attitude, though, is very rare. Most people do appreciate engaging in musical activities of some sort and consider their doing so to contribute significantly to their lives.

So far, we have focused on the purely individual aspect of meaning-for-the-subject. Specific ways of musical behavior are often shared by groups of people, however, for example, when music contributes to the identity of a group. Teenagers are an exemplary case. They categorize their peers in ways that identify and value a specific way of life in which music is crucial. Members of the group love and hate the same types of music, go to the same concerts, buy the same CDs, talk in the same way about music, wear T-shirts of the same bands, and so on. As this case shows, the meaning music has for the subject is constituted both by meanings that are private and by ones that are shared with others. Instead of being objective properties of the music, both kinds of meaning are to be attributed to the subject.

Meaning-for-the-subject has attracted little attention in the philosophical literature. 'Why should philosophy concern itself exclusively with what is objective in the sense of being shared or common?' asks Kathleen M. Higgins (1997). She traces and criticizes the tendency to objectify music and its attendant corollary: the assumption that there is an aperspectival way of hearing music, free from the 'distortions' that result from taking a particular perspective. If aesthetics is concerned with when and why music has significance and with how music can have its fullest impact, it cannot afford to ignore the idiosyncratic nature of the musical response, she argues.

Higgins discusses several personal aspects of musical experience, for example, the perspective on a piece taken by a particular musician. She quotes an oboist saying that, for him, there are at least two ways of listening to a particular symphony: that of the first oboe and that of the second oboe. Also, a pianist complains that she cannot listen to piano music without focusing on technique. Then Higgins notes that our familiarity with a work influences our response upon hearing it. Prior knowledge of the original may lead a listener to concentrate more rigorously on a performance of a piano transcription of a Brahms sextet. A third example acknowledges the specific history of one's engagement with a work. For example, on a particular occasion one might have a quite new experience of the piece being played, so that one suddenly discovers more of its richness and complexity.

Higgins makes a number of interesting observations about these cases. Professional musicians sometimes have the most idiosyncratic perspectives. Also, though the reactions are idiosyncratic, they are motivated and conditioned by objective features of the music. Lastly, what is salient to listeners varies with their backgrounds. Whereas some people extol the private experience of music, others, including performers, see music as a social enterprise.

Meaning-for-us

In characterizing the meaning music has for a person, we have stressed its significance for the individual. Now we should ask if musical meaning has a wider scope. As well as meaning-for-the-subject, is there *meaning-for-us*? There is reason to think so. No human society is without music and there is hardly an individual who would not claim that music plays an important role in his life. The description of someone as without a shred of interest in music conveys an odor of criticism. Musical meaning-for-the-person is too haphazard and private to account adequately for the ubiquity of music, for its vital importance to the life of societies and to so many individuals. Indeed, the power and tenacity of musical meaning-for-the-individual probably depends on the deeper importance that music has in the lives of people. It is not an accident, after all, that music happens to be playing during rites of passage, courtship, war, and the rest. So, it should be possible to explain how and why music has meaning for humankind in general.

Apparently music answers to a deep human need. We might expect, then, that it serves a fundamental evolutionary function. But what could this be? The emotional heightening of human speech? This suggestion, and all the others that come to mind, strike us as unconvincing. Music making and listening do not contribute to the fitness of our species in a direct and obvious fashion.

Perhaps music is important to us not because it serves a single purpose but because it addresses a very broad spread of our interests and concerns. Perhaps it is significant because it is so versatile, contributing in small and different ways to a large variety of tasks and activities. Undoubtedly it does this, yet this fact does not explain the unity of music's appeal. Even if we do not all like the same kinds of music, we are agreed that it is music that is important for us and that its import is as music. Moreover, many people would claim that their enjoyment of music is an end in itself. This suggests that the approaches taken so far are mistaken in seeking a purely functional account of music's importance.

Here is a different kind of story. We are a social species. Our relationships with people are of deep evolutionary importance to us. We must be able to understand others so that we can live cooperatively with them, which we must do if we are to flourish and reproduce. In attempting to understand our fellows, we look for a coherent, unified pattern in their actions. We expect their response to their situation to be shaped by their reasons and character. To understand them, we must treat them as agents; what they do cannot be understood merely in terms of crudely mechanical causal processes. Our goal in understanding others, of course, is to be able to predict their future behavior. Often this is not easy to do. The problem is not just that a person can act irrationally or out of character, but that it is not simple always to predict, for the range of conduct that is in character, which will result. Though we strive with success to be mind readers, our talents are limited, so that sometimes it is only in retrospect that we see how a person's action is consistent with his character and circumstances.

Because of the abiding importance of sociality in our lives, we are inescapably motivated to seek coherence and pattern in human behavior, and we account for it in terms of the agent's reasons and character, not mechanically deterministic processes. So strong is it, that drive can overspill itself. It does so when non-human systems or processes attract our interest and reward our attention through their apparent simulation of human behavior, or because their nature seems to invite the sort of explanation that is apt for human action. Music is of this latter kind. Our fascination with music comes from an evolutionary function with which it is connected only indirectly.

A complementary account starts from the realization that, besides our ability to detect coherence, a capacity for empathy is a second crucial endowment of human beings. Empathy plays a pivotal role in reconciling two fundamental data of human life: our existence as self-contained units in a world of innumerably many similar self-contained units and the social nature of our relationships to others. Only by associating with others can the individual realize herself. Thus, one of the most important things a human being has to learn is how to develop solid relationships with others. For this, empathy is indispensable.

Strong relationships exist only on the basis of empathy. To develop the deeply rooted relationships a person needs in order to live a bearable life, she must be able to identify with the other. And while less intimate public relations sometimes can be approached in a more impersonal fashion, still there are many situations in which others' actions are comprehensible only from an empathetic stance. If people get emotional, for example if they are easily irritated or unexpectedly burst out in laughter, often we can understand them only by trying to put ourselves in their position.

Being able to deal with other individuals, and in particular being able to respond to the other with empathy, goes beyond survival or self-maintenance. Empathy allows the individual to flourish in ways unthinkable for the self-contained person. In terms of their depth and richness, empathy provides the basis for the most valued relationships in life: those of love and friendship. In terms of broadness, empathy allows us to expand our life by experiencing what it is like to live in circumstances that we do not know at first-hand. Artforms, like the novel and film, exploit this fact of human life. These media are attractive because, through our empathetic engagement with the characters they present, they allow us to share experiences we will never encounter in our normal lives.

As the case of music shows, empathy does not stop short with real-life persons or fictional characters, however. Our experience of musical form is empathetic; we identify ourselves with the movement of music. Like our motivation to look for coherence and pattern, our tendency to respond with empathy to music's form may be the happy outcome of an overflow of our social drives. By harnessing our indispensable capacities to perceive coherence in and to respond with empathy to human action, music presents us with a fascinating extension of experience, thereby adding significantly to the worthwhileness of our lives.[4]

To suggest that music is an inessential spin-off from evolution is not to deny its deeper meaning-for-us. In virtue of its tremendous appeal to our empathetic capacities, music can resolve the isolation we find ourselves in as individuals. The desire to

---

[4] I (Stephen Davies) am no longer comfortable with this view. Even if music originated this way, it could take on adaptive significance later. For my current thinking on this topic, see Davies (2010).

transcend the boundaries of the self is one of the Ur-themes of human life, as its prominence in myth and religion testifies. Many religions take the merging of the individual with a higher reality to be the ultimate purpose of human existence. Whatever one may think of them, such visions attest to an enduring tendency in human beings. The triumph of individualism during the last centuries has not been so complete as to obliterate the human desire to escape the confines of the ego.

When putting ourselves affectively in the position of another, ordinarily we remain aware of the boundary between ourselves and that person. With music, however, we can be carried away; we can approach the psychological state of self-forgetfulness. Music has this power, apparently, in virtue of, not in spite of, its abstractness; music provides us with an opportunity for unlimited empathy but at the same time it does not confront us with life-like situations featuring definite personas. The combination of deep affective and cognitive immersion with a situation in which concrete practical needs and interests are absent appears to produce the best condition for transcendent experiences.

The line of thought developed here can also account for a more down-to-earth dimension of musical meaning-for-us: music's tendency to promote coherence within social groups. In responding to music empathetically, we collectively give ourselves to something supra-personal, rather than identifying ourselves with some individual. Consequently, collective musical engagement provides an ideal picture of social coherence: there is both the coordination of individual actions and the intense devotion to something surpassing the realm of the individual. When successfully engaging in music as a group, we do not merely share a great experience, we also promote our sense of belonging together, our belief in our capacity for effective collective action, and our joint commitment to ideals that go beyond our private wellbeing.

Conclusion

We began with the experience of music's formal meaning and ended with what appeared to be a distinct, though equally non-linguistic, model of musical significance, one in which music has meaning for an individual through the way it contributes to the fabric of her life. This led to considerations in more general terms of how and why music has meaning for us. It does so because our experience of music is in important respects analogous to the way we experience human beings. First, music is more like a person in her actions than like a machine in its movements. Being programmed by evolution to be especially interested in understanding actions as forming coherent patterns, we respond to the dynamics of music in a way that parallels our reaction to human behaviors. Second, our response to the quasi-gestures of music is one of empathy. We identify ourselves with these gestures, appropriating them rather than relating them to some persona in the music. There are two more specific ways empathetic responses relate to the meaning music has for us: by providing a sense of liberation from the boundaries of the self and by promoting social coherence.

These admittedly speculative views provide a route for connecting the notions of formal meaning and meaning-for-us. Earlier we characterized the experience of following musical form with understanding and empathy. What was missing from that account was an explanation of why we would value the experience achieved by this mode of listening. And that was a significant lack if one wants to privilege the kind of listening that takes the detailed unfolding of the music as its prime focus and motivation.

As is now clear, the experience of formal musical meaning not only conforms to a model that subsumes our experience of the integrity and rationality of human action but also builds on the empathetic nature of human interaction. In light of these connections, it is easier to appreciate why an interest in following dynamic musical form could be a source of deep and lasting pleasure in its own right.

7
Musical Understandings

In this chapter, I investigate the various understandings expected of and evinced by an accomplished listener, the performer, the music analyst, and the composer. I confine the discussion to Western, purely instrumental music, mainly with the classical tradition in mind.[1] And I refer primarily to the Anglophone literature of 'analytic' philosophy of music. As will become apparent, my concern is with an analysis that maps what are meant to be familiar aspects of musical experience.

The listener's understanding

What is involved in listening to music with understanding and what is understood?

In the first place, the comprehending listener must be able to distinguish music from the non-musical noise and sound that envelopes it, both diachronically and synchronically. That is, she must know when the music starts and stops and, while it sounds, she must be able to separate it from background sound that coincides with the playing without being part of the music played. Plainly, the basis for these discriminations is not purely phenomenological, because many non-musical sounds are music-like, such as birdsong, while many musical sounds are noises, bangs, and squeaks that are not music-like. Musical works can contain parts for typewriters, anvils, cowbells, and cannons. Also, some musical instruments—castanets, cymbals, and Theremins, as well as ordinary melodic instruments used in unusual ways or at the limits of their ranges, as when a pizzicato is so violent as to slap the string against the instrument's fingerboard—produce grunts, clicks, crashes, shrieks, bangs, and whines. As well,

---

The material amalgamated in this chapter was first published as 'The Know-how of Musical Performance,' *Philosophy of Music Education Review*, 12 (2) (2004): 56–61, 'Performance Interpretations of Musical Works,' *Nordisk Estetisk Tidskrift*, 33/34 (2006): 8–22, and 'Musikalisches Verstehen,' in A. Becker and M. Vogel (eds), *Musikalischer Sinn: Beiträger zu einer Philosophie der Musik*, Matthias Vogel (trans.), Frankfurt: Suhrkamp Verlag (2007): 25–79.

[1] I do so for convenience and simplicity. Western classical music is the kind with which my reader is likely to be most familiar, and the idea that purely instrumental music—music without sung words, literary titles, or associated programmatic stories—presents a content that can be grasped with understanding is more stark and provocative than the alternatives. I believe, however, that a fuller account must consider non-Western music and the many popular Western varieties (and I have attempted this in Davies 1994a, 1999c, 2001a). I also accept that there is justice to the charge that philosophers may go wrong in ignoring the primacy of vocal music with texts (Ridley 2004).

musical performances contain silences and gaps between movements that may be indistinguishable from silences arising outside of musical contexts.[2]

Not all the sounds that are ambient to a performance or sounding of music are incidental to the music's production.[3] The use of musical instruments sometimes generates sounds that are not of the work that is sounded. Obviously this is the case when, by mistake, the wrong notes are played or the instrument produces unintended squawks, harmonics, or Wolf notes, or the conductor hums and sings audibly, or a music stand is accidentally knocked over. Other cases are more interesting because they are an inevitable byproduct of, and in that way are integral to, the process of sound production. Examples include the whirs and creaks of bellows and tracker mechanisms of organs, the audible movement of the pedals of pianos, harps, and tympanis, the rattle of keypads on wind instruments, the pneumatic sound of brass valves in motion, the breathing of singers and of wind and brass players, and pitch slides and squeaks as fingers move from note to note on guitars and other stringed instruments. Though sounds in this category count as not part of the work played, and despite the fact that musicians usually do what they can to minimize them, they are not intrusive in the way that chatty audience members and passing police sirens are. Indeed, as a quiet corollary of live playing, they can contribute positively to an atmosphere of intimacy between musician and audience. They draw attention to the practical skills that invest the bodying forth of music with human warmth.

As well as distinguishing music from non-music, the comprehending listener must be able to discriminate between overlapping but distinct musical performances or soundings. In other words, the listener must know when the given performance starts and stops and, as it sounds, separate it from other musical performances or soundings occurring at the same time. The listener must know that the melody of the *William Tell Overture* that issues from an audience member's cellphone is an interruption to, and not a part of, a performance of Igor Stravinsky's *Jeu de Cartes* (and know also that the same theme is part of the work when Stravinsky goes on to quote it). And at Balinese temple ceremonies, where different gamelans a few meters apart noisily play different pieces, the listener should be aware that distinct works are offered, not a composite one, even if she cannot separate them clearly from the joint racket.

---

[2] This last point invites consideration of John Cage's *4′33″*, since this is usually described as a silent piece or as a piece that takes as its content what otherwise would count as ambient sound. (Cage himself is never entirely clear about the difference in these accounts of the work's ontological status, though he tends to favor the second.) Though I cannot elaborate the argument here (but see Davies 2003: ch. 1), I would suggest that Cage's work is best viewed not as music but as a theatrical piece about the performance of music. For discussion of the usual aesthetic functions of silences in music, see Judkins (1997).

[3] I talk of soundings as well as performances to acknowledge that, while most musical works are for performance, not all are. For example, electronic compositions issued on disk are for playback, not performance. Such works are sounded by a decoding device and the person who activates this does not thereby perform the work. Recordings can also be of performances, of course, and in that case we might use either term. For further discussion of the ontological variety of musical works and their relations to recordings, see Davies (2001a, 2003: ch. 2).

The relevant discriminations often depend on noting the spatial distribution of the various sound sources in the environment, but this is not an inevitable guide. The offending cellphone might be in the conductor's pocket, or perhaps the soloist aims to play Tchaikovsky's First Piano Concerto and the rebellious orchestra embarks on the Grieg. Meanwhile, many works call for contributions from offstage players or from physically separated orchestras, as in works by Giovanni Gabrieli and Karlheinz Stockhausen's *Gruppen für drei Orchester*. As well, other pieces contain parts for recorded music or sounds, as is the case with Luigi Nono's *La fabbrica illuminata*, which is for soprano and a recording of electronically modified factory sounds and choral singing. Moreover, it is not always possible to separate distinct renditions by reference to the works or melodies from which they derive. Joseph Taylor was the source of the folk tune Brigg Fair that was arranged for orchestra by Frederick Delius in 1907. At the first performance, 'legend has it that on hearing "his" tune, Joseph Taylor immediately stood up and began to sing along with the orchestra' (Bird 1976: 111). Yet he could not have been performing Delius's work, because that contains no part for a singer.

So, how is it done? How does the skilled listener tell the musical performances or soundings from the non-musical sounds with which they are contiguous and how does she individuate different but simultaneous musical performances? Since most music lovers do so without a formal musical education, the relevant skills must be acquired through experience and the usual processes of musical acculturation that begin in one's earliest childhood. To the extent that what counts as music can vary from one sociohistorical location to another, the capacity to recognize music as such is not purely biological or natural. But also, because we can often identify the music of foreign cultures as music, even if we are not well situated to appreciate and follow it because we have no grasp of the principles on which it proceeds, neither is the identification of music purely or arbitrarily cultural. Similar things can be said about the individuation of distinct (but perhaps simultaneous) musical performances or soundings. To some degree, what counts as a musical performance is socially malleable and conventional, but not necessarily entirely or arbitrarily so.[4] We will obtain a clearer view of these matters by considering what it is to experience and understand music as such, which are the topics to which I now turn.

Having located the performance or sounding that is her target, the comprehending listener must experience what she hears as music. In other words, she has to hear the sound of music in the noise it makes. This capacity underpins not only her ability to understand and appreciate music for what it is but also her aptitude in discriminating music from other sounds occurring at the same time that are not part of the performance or sounding of the given work, and also in discriminating one musical performance or sounding from another. In what does it consist?

---

[4] For discussion of the elements of music, see Davies (2001a: 47–98), and of the individuation conditions for performances, see Davies (2001a: 184–96, 2003: ch. 6).

By contrast with the standard case, some music is strikingly incoherent or unpredictable, without being less good or interesting for that fact.[5] Moreover, some music does not make much sense as music—for example, because it is generated entirely by randomizing processes or indiscriminately appropriates sounds from many sources—and in those cases it counts as music on institutional, musico-historical, or other grounds, rather than in virtue of the experience it engenders in the listener. The status as music of such pieces can be considered to be parasitic on archetypical musical works that pre-date them within a continuous tradition. It is with paradigm instances that we should begin, so it is works such as Beethoven's Fifth Symphony that are considered in what follows.

In hearing music as the music it is, the comprehending listener should be aware of it as beginning and as coming to a close, so that she can tell the difference between its ending where it should and its stopping unexpectedly due to some abnormal intervention. This applies to the work as a whole, to its movements (should it have them), and to its melodies and subsections. In general, the listener should be able to judge when one melody has run its course and another has begun. As well, the listener should usually be able to recognize repeats as such, though this can be difficult if they involve long sections or if the original material is varied or elaborated as it returns. To hear repeats, the listener must be able to recognize and re-identify earlier themes or other material, even if the repetition is not exact. To understand a sonata form movement in the minor key, for instance, she has to identify the second subject when it is recapitulated as the same theme as that which was presented in the exposition, despite the differences that arise from the theme's move from major to minor. Or to mention similar examples from a different context, she has to recognize Elvis Presley's *Blue Moon of Kentucky* as a recording of Bill Monroe's bluegrass classic despite the change from 3/4 to common time, or hear the *Star Spangled Banner* in Jimi Hendrix's parody of it at Woodstock. (I consider such matters in Davies 2001a: 54–8.) Where we should draw the line between a variant of a given theme and a related but different one is not always clear, of course, and that ambiguity can be a musically significant feature of the given work, but in other pieces there often is a distinction to be made and fair agreement among experienced listeners about where it falls.

In addition, the listener should hear the waxing and waning of musical tension and movement, and the expressive character of the music, if it has one. Because of their frequent interaction—sometimes confirming and supporting and at others challenging and undermining—she will consider what is expressed in the music in relation to more obviously structural elements. In general, she has to follow the progress of the music, so that its course makes sense. This requires of the listener that she be able to predict how the music will continue at any given moment, that she is often right in her predictions, and that where she is not, she is able to distinguish between an unanticipated but

---

[5] For discussion, see Tanner (1985), Hicks (1991), Davies (1994a: 367–9), Kieran (1996).

appropriate continuation and a performance or compositional blunder.[6] Typically, she can identify performance errors as such, and she often knows what should have been played instead. She experiences the music as unfolding in a 'logical' way, with what preceded as justifying or making appropriate what follows.[7]

Does the listener need to feel the pull of tonality, the tension of a discord, the need for resolution, if she is to recognize such things? Not always. She might observe these as features of the music without feeling them from the inside, so to speak, just as she might note the music's happy or sad character without thereby mirroring these emotions within herself. But it is unlikely that she could always be unaffected by such things. We recognize music as having such properties because, other things being equal, it tends to evoke an appropriate response. They are features of the music, just as blueness belongs to the sky, but like the blueness, such properties are attributable only by creatures who can be affected by them and who are evolved to have the necessary perceptual sensitivities along with an interest in discriminating them.

Our capacity to identify and re-identify musical configurations comes 'free,' as part of the biological endowment, so long as our hearing is not defective and remains undamaged. Nevertheless, the skill can be refined through explicit practice, as occurs in ear training, or informal exposure. Moreover, what we are able to recognize and discriminate is affected by the familiarity of the kinds of items and their setting. When the listener approaches music of a type with which she is not at home, she may not be able to identify and re-identify all the musically significant elements. So, this biologically grounded skill is subject to considerable socio-cultural tweaking.

Because the flow of musical tension and resolution is a complex function of the music's tonal/modal system, genre, and style, and because these in turn are culturally malleable, the listener's ability to predict and follow the flux of musical progression is developed through practice.[8] Since comparatively few music lovers are formally educated in music theory and ear training, the relevant education is provided by exposure and non-technical commentary. We take in our mother music much as we take in our mother tongue, by osmosis at a very young age, with the result that its sense seems natural and inevitable and comprehending it is comparatively effortless. Most

---

[6] Meyer (1956), with his discussion of information theory, did much to explain the role of prediction in following music with understanding, and of the way in which composers often thwart or delay the realization of the listener's expectations. Meyer was less successful, I believe, in thinking that he could account for music's expressiveness and the listener's emotional response to this in such terms (Davies 1994a: 25–9, 287–91).

[7] Zemach (2002) suggests that music works as a proof of the rules of a musical calculus. I would not go so far as this. As well as flouting 'the rules' on occasions, musical works can contain inexplicable singularities, as I allow in Davies (1994a). Accordingly, Scruton (1987, 1997) is correct to regard such rules as there are as summing up a mutable, empirical practice. Sharpe (2000: 184) makes the interesting observation that following Bach's music is like following an argument, but following Mahler's is more like following a story.

[8] While it is sometimes suggested that some tonal systems have a special validity licensed by the natural harmonic series, this is widely rejected. All cultures seem to recognize the type-identity of notes at the octave, so they hear notes an octave apart as the same note but with different pitches, and most include a perfect fourth or fifth in their scales, but beyond that almost anything that is humanly discriminable goes. The 'grammars' of rhythmic, metric, and harmonic systems are no less flexible.

people are no more familiar with the technical terms of music analysis than they are with words such as 'gerund,' 'dative case,' or 'pluperfect tense.'

As well as absorbing the local musical conventions that inform her expectations as to how the music will continue from the given moment, the listener also takes in other important information as a result of observing how music is made. For instance, she develops a sense of the characteristics of different instruments and of the difficulties that playing them presents, which will be important when she tries to appreciate works, such as virtuosic concertos, that make a musical point of such things.[9] This can come from learning to play the violin, say, but it is also conveyed simply by paying attention to what musicians do. And with this information secure, it then is possible to listen to recordings with an appropriate sense of what one would see if one were present at the virtual performance that is sounded.

The preparation of the appreciative musical listener cannot rest alone with what she can grasp unreflectively, simply through attentive exposure to music in the raw. For the deepest understanding, she will need a sense of the various challenges posed by different genres and of the problems and difficulties composers took themselves to be addressing in their works (Davies 2003: ch. 13). If her interest spans more than one kind and period of music and she aspires to a high and refined level of understanding, she will need some idea of the course of music history—of which styles came first and of how they changed and evolved, of technical changes in musical instruments, of alterations in the conventions of performance and in the presentation of performances. She may even need to consider the development and role of musical notations, say. And above all, she must have some idea of the genealogies that relate composers to each other, so that she can recognize what is an original achievement as against established common ground and so that she can spot influences, quotations, allusions, caricatures, rebellions against, homages to, and so forth. It has been argued that, whereas a contemporary poet can write an interesting sonnet, old musical forms and styles are not usable in the same way by modern composers—they cannot say anything 'new' with them or, anyway, cannot express through them what earlier composers could—with the result that music is more historically linear and directional than is the case for narrative or depictive arts.[10] I have reservations about these claims, but I agree that the fullest appreciation of music must be historically informed. And this process must be self-conscious and reflective, because that kind of knowledge cannot be

---

[9] I disagree with those, like Scruton (1997), who regard musical works as structures of 'pure' tones, with musical instruments merely (dispensable) means to their performance, as if there is nothing to choose between giving first prize in the piano concerto competition to a human performer and to a computer pre-programmed to produce a sounding with the acoustic character of a piano. This unlikely piano competition is discussed in Godlovitch (1990). Mark (1980) argues that, in virtuosic music, comprehension of the work requires appreciation of what is involved in playing it. In Davies (2001a), I follow Levinson (1990: ch. 4) in arguing that a work's instrumentation is among its defining features, at least for works postdating 1750. The contrary view is presented in Kivy (1988a).

[10] See Cavell (1977) and for commentary, Ross (1985), Davies (1994a). Sharpe (2000) is also relevant.

gleaned merely by listening, without reference to record sleeves, program notes, musical treatises, and the like.

One other, crucial aspect of the listener's task in understanding the music she hears has yet to be mentioned. If she attends to a freely improvised performance that performance is her target, and if she listens to the playback of a purely electronic piece issued on disk that work is her focus, but frequently she has two things to consider: the work and its interpretation through the performance she hears. She will need to calculate what belongs to the work and that should therefore be credited to the composer and what belongs instead to the interpretation the performer brings to the work. To help her, she might consider what is in the score (if there is one) and how the performance legitimately goes beyond that by putting flesh on the notated bones. She could also listen to many performances of the given work by different, skilled performers, with contrasts between these to be understood usually as artifacts of the interpretations they present. More generally, she will bring to her listening a view based on prior experience of what kind of work is in question and of the limits to which interpretations of such works can be stretched without traducing it. To achieve this, she will have listened with care to many such works and many different performances of them. And because the definiteness with which musical works are specified by their creators varies from period to period and genre to genre, as does what can be expected by way of elaboration and articulation by the performer, her approach to musical works and performances must be sensitive to the place of the work and of the performance in their respective periods, styles, and traditions.

Musical works and performances are very diverse. Some are highly sophisticated, complex, and extended, as well as replete with subtle allusions, ironies, and the like. Some others, such as *Silent Night*, are short, simple, and transparent.[11] Almost all musically acculturated listeners are likely to appreciate *Silent Night* in a fashion that is immediate and effortless. They may be happy to hear it again, they may even relish the experience, but they cannot expect to learn more or appreciate the piece more profoundly than at its initial hearing. By contrast, the appreciation of works of the former kind can be the hard work of a lifetime. As the listener returns to it, she finds more in the work; sometimes there is the feeling of passing beyond the surface to new, deeper levels of meaning. The listener will be drawn to hear a variety of interpretations of such a piece, both for their own interest and for the new light they shine on its possibilities. She is likely to think about the work and the performances she knows. She may even read about it or study its score.

---

[11] I make no judgment here about the comparative merits of classical and popular music. Some classical music is very simple and straightforward; some popular music is cleverly and delicately crafted. Of course, different kinds of music can have different functions and address different musical issues and problems. The mode of appreciation appropriate to these varieties of music must be relativized accordingly. For discussion, see Gracyk (1999, 2001), Davies (1999c).

Not all listeners are equipped or sufficiently interested to probe the depths of works of the first kind. Whether they find anything to understand and enjoy about a piece of this type depends on whether it rewards merely casual acquaintance. Sometimes very great works do this nicely—witness Mozart's 'Jupiter' Symphony—though they provide much more to the connoisseur who makes the effort to achieve a more intimate understanding of the music's subtle complexity. At other times, masterpieces are difficult and unapproachable at the outset; consider Bach's *Art of Fugue*. In that case, the unskilled or uninterested listener is likely to find little to understand and enjoy. She might, nevertheless, sense herself in the presence of a greatness she cannot comprehend, or she might simply not 'get it.' Also, the comprehending listener may find that understanding does not always yield appreciation. She may learn that a work that was advertised as interesting or that at first sounded that way turns out to be not good enough to repay the effort it demands. As well, listeners differ in their tastes, so that not every listener who enjoys Haydn likes Mahler, even if they acknowledge the greatness of both.[12] Despite these caveats, it is not by coincidence that the enjoyment and rewards of appreciation go to those with the most refined understanding, because music is often highly crafted and developed, so that when understood it becomes an object of wonder and enjoyment.

As one would expect from the role that experience and exposure play in preparing the listener to follow all but the most straightforward music, musical understanding comes in degrees. And so it must, if we can enhance our abilities through unreflective practice, by bootstrapping, without resorting to a formal musical education. (Later I consider if the highest echelons of music appreciation are reserved for those with training in technical musical concepts or formal analysis.) Whether a person should cultivate her talents as an understanding listener as far as she can is another matter. Deliberately to avoid doing so would show no aesthetic or moral failing on her part. She might prefer to spend the time in refining her sensitivity to literature or helping the poor. Nevertheless, music lovers do tend to judge each other in terms of their musical tastes. Perhaps this is because these are often so fundamental in their lives that they are integral to each person's sense of their own identity and value.

Momentary listening

Earlier I emphasized that, in understanding a musical performance or sounding, the listener must identify its themes and parts, and re-identify them when they return, either in the original or in an amended version. I implied that this helps the listener grasp the work's overall articulation and structure, and that doing so is important to

---

[12] Higgins (1997) rightly complains that philosophers of music, in concentrating on the comprehension of music's 'objective' features, largely ignore what is idiosyncratic and perspectival in the listener's experience. For the listener, it may be what is personal in her relationship to it that gives the music its significance. 'Meaning-for-the-subject' is compared with various other kinds of musical meaning in Chapter 6. Meanwhile, arguments for the relativity of judgments of aesthetic value are too numerous and complex to be considered here, but an interesting consideration of the musical case is offered in Sharpe (2004).

recognizing and experiencing the closure of cadences and to hearing the work as ending and not merely as stopping. Such claims would not be regarded by many musicologists as controversial, because music appreciation frequently is approached and concerned centrally if not exclusively with 'architectonic' listening that maps the work's form. This common view has been questioned by Jerrold Levinson (1997), however, and I now review his argument.

Levinson develops and defends a position, first outlined by Edmund Gurney in 1880, that he calls 'concatenationism.' According to it, apprehension of large-scale musical structures is not relevant to the listener's full appreciation of music. She must be aware of locally perceptible effects caused by a piece's organization, but she need not cognize or be conscious of its overall form. She can understand and evaluate the music correctly if she is aware only of what she hears in the moment and of its connections to and implications for events for a few seconds prior to and subsequent to that instant. According to this view, large-scale musical form cannot be perceived directly and, insofar as we are aware of it through thought and analysis, it plays only a relatively minor role in our enjoyment and appreciation of the music. We can hear present sounds and we 'quasi-hear' immediately prior passages while anticipating those about to come. Quasi-hearing spans a minute only. We cannot perceive patterns separated by longer intervals, though we can be intellectually aware of them. The pleasure we take in that awareness is weak by comparison with, and feeds upon, that afforded by music in the moment. Moreover, either the object of such pleasure is the music's form, not the music as such, or the response involves a level of sophistication (for instance, in recognizing allusions or complex expressive properties) that goes beyond what is required for the kind of musical understanding that is fundamental and central.[13]

Levinson allows (1997: 64) that, in following a work, one usually must think something tantamount to 'this bit, or something like it, occurred earlier,' but he denies that such experiences involve structural listening because he thinks that even the experienced listener does not clearly recall when and where the theme was first encountered (1997: 65). He holds more generally that most of the relevant processing is unconscious and is not retrievable in propositional form, so that the listener need not be able to describe the music in ways that reveal her grasp of it (1997: ix–x, 72–3).

These views are questionable. The listener identified by Levinson as competent is one who can recognize a theme as having occurred earlier. Yet would this recognition suffice for understanding in a listener who did not know if she had previously encountered the theme in the present work or in another? Also, if she already has heard the piece several times, as has Levinson's listener (1997: 45), it would be surprising if she has no idea where within the piece the theme first occurred. Levinson suggests that knowing how to continue a piece one is familiar with is evidence for one's

---

[13] Though he differs from Levinson in regarding large-scale form as perceptible, Cook (1990) also defends the irrelevance of formal listening. For critical discussion of Cook's views, see Kivy (1992), Ridley (1992), Davies (1994a), Sharpe (2000).

understanding of it (1997: 26), yet it is hard to see how anyone could demonstrate this knowledge if she could not recall the order in which the main thematic ideas were introduced. In addition, the understanding listener should be able to discriminate a repetition of a theme from a variant on it and from a new tune that is similar but distinct. Yet it is doubtful that Levinson's auditor can hear such differences if she cannot describe them and is satisfied merely with 'gratifying impressions of familiarity, unity through change, and the like, [that] require no conscious reflection on where or when some musical material was previously encountered, no active appreciation of the pattern of events...as a whole' (1997: 82). Levinson trusts unconscious memory to tie things together for the listener, who does not have to be able to describe the work in a fashion that shows she makes distinctions of the kind identified above. In fact, though, the relevant concepts are so mundane—'here again is the tune that first sounded after the slow introduction, and now here's a similar but different one'— that a person who cannot express them surely cannot hear the relevant differences and patterns and thereby could not possess the degree of musical understanding that Levinson attributes to her.

My point is not simply that more cognizing must be involved in the kind of perception that produces musical understanding than Levinson acknowledges, and hence that musical understanding cannot be so inarticulate as he suggests. And neither is it solely to claim that Levinson already goes beyond concatenationism when he writes (1997: 92) of the listener's perceiving long-distance repetitions or resemblances or of hearing a theme through a variation upon it. My main claim is that, if such recognitions are truly perceptual despite lying outside the scope of quasi-hearing, I do not see why structural hearing is not also possible and relevant to musical understanding, for, on one plausible account, the listener goes a long way toward following a work's form if she perceives when earlier material is repeated, varied, re-ordered, and the like.[14]

Levinson shows not that grasping a work's overarching form is irrelevant to musical understanding but that such awareness must arise from the listening experience. Musical form should be heard as flowing from interactions between the work's materials rather than being imposed intellectually and externally via musicologist's textbook schema. I agree with this nice observation by Alan H. Goldman (1992: 38): 'the point is not to comprehend or apprehend an abstract form—one can do so more easily from score or diagram—but to have one's listening informed by an implicit grasp of structure, so that one can hear a cadence as a resolution or a development or variation as such in relation to a main theme.'

These criticisms of Levinson's account bring to attention two, crucial points. Following the music with understanding is rooted primarily in the way we experience

---

[14] For further critical discussion of Levinson's view, see McAdoo (1997), Davies (1999b), Perrett (1999), Kivy (2001), and the symposium in the journal *Music Perception* (volume 16, 1999), to which Levinson (1999) is a reply.

it as we hear it. That understanding is cognitively founded, as I have suggested above. But this is not to say that one verbalizes that understanding as one listens, supplying a commentary that runs alongside the listening experience it describes. Cognitively informed perception does not have to be accompanied by linguistic thought. The second point develops the last. Perception involves more than the mindless reception of sensory input. As noted earlier, we distinguish music from incidental noise occurring at the same time, and within music, one voice from another, and so on. Organizing the perceptual manifold in these ways does not always involve conscious processing. In recognizing the sound as of an oboe, we do not bring from memory recollections of how oboes sound, compare the current sound with those in thought, and thereby judge of what we hear that it is an oboe. Indeed, we could not do it this way. To adapt a point made about color perception by Wittgenstein, how could we check the reliability of what we remembered? Not by conjuring from memory yet another oboe sound and by then comparing this to the first two! Besides, everyday experience shows that recognition is independent of active memory. I can recognize many tunes when I hear them that I could not hum in advance, just as I may recognize an acquaintance though I cannot picture his face in my imagination when he is absent. And I can recognize a theme that is not as I remember it because it has been varied, just as I can recognize someone I have not seen in many years, despite the changes to his appearance (see Chapter 10). The cognitive process of recognition is modularized, to use the jargon of cognitive scientists. In other words, there is a perceptual input and as an output, recognition, but the neural procedure by which the output is derived from the input is 'encapsulated,' which is to say not available to consciousness.

Here is the point. Recognition is experienced as continuous with perception, as an aspect of the perceptual process. Very often we are aware not only that we recognize an individual from some earlier encounter with it, we know when that earlier event occurred and how it is ordered with respect to other events. So, we can track overall musical form.

Sometimes musical form is not large-scale—consider the binary repeated forms of Scarlatti sonatas, or the tripartite structure of da capo arias and minuets—and not difficult to keep in mind as one listens. Sometimes large-scale musical structures are very elaborate and difficult to follow, even after repeated hearings. Where they are hard to track, it is the kind of hardness that often can be answered by practice, concentration, and close attention. We can improve our listening skills should we wish to. There is not the intrinsic difficulty of comprehension that Levinson claims. Moreover, many listeners testify that the effort that goes into following the structure of long, complex pieces is well justified in terms of the enhanced appreciation that results. What is grasped seems not to be an ancillary, minor appreciation, but something that goes to the heart of the music.

We can now frame the point to show not only how Levinson goes wrong but how some of his critics do so also. Levinson emphasizes the experiential element of musical understanding over the kind of grasp that depends on conscious reflection and propositional articulation. I think he is right to do so. But he underestimates the extent to which perception is cognitively informed, even where it does not involve mental deliberation and self-commentary. In particular, he fails to appreciate the extent to which recognition typically is impregnated with awareness of temporal order and structure, so that recognizing a melody or section as repeated or varied is both a fully perceptual experience and an experience of structural relations that extend beyond the limits of quasi-hearing. Meanwhile, his critics are correct to defend the listener's awareness of extended musical structures and patterns as a precondition of her musical understanding, but they are often wrong in regarding this awareness as invoking conscious deliberation and mental processes of comparison and calculation that are not part of the phenomenology of understanding for all musically sensitive listeners. Both sides undervalue the extent to which perception is cognitively impregnated (as a result of modular processing that does not impinge on the listener's consciousness) and the extended temporal compass this furnishes to the experience of hearing the music.

Levinson draws the implication from his account that the listener's understanding can be inarticulate, simply because she need not reflect intellectually on her experience of the music in order to resonate moment by moment with its progress. It might be thought that I should endorse this view, though not for reasons like those that Levinson offers. I have stressed that the processing of some musical and other types of perception is modularized and, to that extent, cannot be introspected. It follows from the impenetrability of the relevant perceptual modules that the listener cannot describe what goes on in them. And I have also allowed that the listener need not articulate her understanding as she listens. Does any of this entail that she cannot do so, that musical understanding ultimately is ineffable?

The alleged ineffability of musical understanding

Diana Raffman (1993) is one philosopher who thinks the experience of music has ineffable aspects. She discusses structural ineffability and feeling ineffability, but it is nuance ineffability that is her main focus. In considering it, Raffman suggests that the sound of music has a texture so fine that it falls through the mesh of our conceptual categories. She also maintains that, because we cannot retain in memory the level of sensory information that we experience, we cannot invent more precise categories with which to describe our perceptual experiences.

Notice that, on this account, the ineffability of music is a result of the ineffability of all sensory experience. The sound of a performance of a Beethoven symphony is no more ineffable than that of an advertising jingle or of breaking glass, and the appearance of wallpaper is as ineffably subtle as the appearance of a painting by Rembrandt. Nuance ineffability goes with the boring and mundane, as well as with the interesting and great. The view also entails that, however exhaustive we make our descriptions of perceptual experience, there are always aspects of the detail of occurrent perception that cannot be described. It does not imply, however, that music renders us mute or that the experience of music cannot be described in great detail.

Some of those who suggest that music is ineffable may wish to claim that it conveys deep and profound but otherwise inexpressible truths. There is no warrant for this conclusion in Raffman's thesis. The very subtle shades of occurrent perception that are ineffable according to her—such as the differences in timbre between two neighboring second violins playing the same note—are unlikely to be the source of music's importance. Indeed, Raffman's view counts against their significance if she is correct, because she holds that we can keep our awareness of music's ineffable nuances in mind for only a few seconds after perceiving them. We cannot keep them in memory, she insists, because we do not have the conceptual pigeonholes in which to store them.

When he compares the ordinary, unschooled listener with one trained in music theory, Mark DeBellis (1995; see also 1999a, 2005) provides an account that implies a view of ineffable experiences of music that is more relevant to considering what understanding music involves.[15] The listening of the expert is theoretically informed. For example, when she hears a dominant seventh chord, as well as sensing its stylistically appropriate harmonic functions and tendencies, she identifies it as a dominant seventh chord. She brings it under the concept of a dominant seventh chord and, accordingly, acquires the belief that it is a dominant seventh chord. Her listening is 'theory equivalent.' The untutored but experienced listener also is aware of the harmonic function of the chord she hears, in that she recognizes it as tending to resolve to what the expert would correctly identify as the tonic, but unlike the expert, the untrained listener cannot bring the chord under the relevant concept since she lacks it. As a result, she does not acquire the belief that it is a dominant seventh that she hears, though she represents the chord to herself as involving a tendency toward a certain direction of resolution or succession. In DeBellis's terms, this listener's experience of the music is *non-conceptual* and to that extent ineffable.

If our listener studied some music theory and thereby acquired the relevant concept, she would not necessarily be able to apply it correctly to her experience of music. She might not be able to identify the dominant seventh chord as such, because her hearing is not informed by the theoretical terms she has read about. This is the case of what DeBellis calls the intermediate listener. Again, this listener does not acquire the belief that it is a dominant seventh that she hears, so her experience of the music also is *non-conceptual* and ineffable.

DeBellis argues that there is a stronger sense than that already discussed in which the hearing of ordinary and intermediate listeners is non-conceptual. The possession of perceptual concepts (as distinct from linguistic terminologies) presupposes the capacity to discriminate perceptually between their various instances (under standard perceptual conditions). I have the perceptual concepts of *red* and *orange* because I can correctly sort relevantly colored tokens into the two types. If I cannot do the same for *burgundy* and *vermilion* tokens, I lack the perceptual concepts for these colors. Now, ordinary and

---

[15] It is not DeBellis's project, as it is Raffman's, to provide an account of the ineffable in music. Here I draw out the consequences of his position in a way that reflects on the issue.

intermediate listeners cannot regularly and confidently identify dominant seventh chords and distinguish them from other chords. It follows that they lack the relevant perceptual concepts.

DeBellis goes on to suggest that theory-equivalent hearing provides a richer and better experience of music. There is a fusion between perceptual and theoretic concepts in the expert's experience of the music. It is not that she feels the achievement of closure while separately believing correctly that the music moves to the tonic, nor that she now knows the cause of the closure she experiences. It is, rather, that she feels the achievement of closure as a movement to the tonic. She knows more about an appreciable feature of the music. Because the theory bleeds into and colors her experience of the music, the trained listener finds more to understand and appreciate in it than the ordinary or intermediate listener can. The ordinary listener's experience, to the extent that it is ineffable, is deficient. And the intermediate listener, even if she knows as much 'book' theory as the expert, is no better off, because her knowledge does not infuse and enhance what she hears in the music. To make what for these listeners is a non-conceptual and therefore inchoate grasp of music into a conceptualized, belief-generating comprehension, ear training is needed, DeBellis argues.

DeBellis's central claims—that the experience of following music is ineffable for non-expert listeners and that this entails the impoverishment of their understanding by comparison with listeners who hear the music in terms of music-theoretic concepts that permeate their experience of it—runs contrary to a view widely supported by other Anglophone philosophers of music.[16] Their rival position allows that, while knowledge of music theory and the technical vocabulary that goes with it is likely to enhance the level of the listener's understanding, the ordinary listener is not debarred in principle from attaining a high degree of understanding by her lack of such knowledge. Those who hold this view do not always assume that she will be able to articulate her understanding. Nevertheless, I maintain that she must be capable of doing so, though she will not use the musicologist's terminology. As a result, I deny that the listener's musical understanding can be ineffable; it must be expressible in ways that can be evaluated for their truth. To stand by these views, I must defend them against DeBellis's argument. In doing so, I suggest that ordinary and intermediate listeners do make the musical discriminations relevant to following music with understanding. In DeBellis's terms, they do possess the relevant perceptual concepts. Moreover, they have folk-theoretic terms with which they can refer to the musical targets of their understanding, so the understanding they possess is not ineffable in principle.[17]

Considering DeBellis's favorite examples, I agree that ordinary, untrained listeners cannot usually identify and re-identify the fifth degree of the scale as it occurs throughout a tonal melody or the dominant chord whenever it appears in a harmonic sequence although, as acculturated listeners, they recognize the melodic and harmonic

---

[16] See Budd (1985), Tanner (1985), Kivy (1990), Davies (1994a), Levinson (1996a: ch. 3), for instance.
[17] For other critical discussion of DeBellis's views, see Levinson (1996b), Ridley (1997).

implications appropriate to these occurrences. And I agree that those who can make the relevant identifications possess knowledge that the ordinary listener is without. I do not think this supplementary knowledge counts much toward the level of musical understanding that is attained, however. All listeners with perfect pitch can make such identifications without training. Though they often are highly musical individuals, we do not automatically assume that they attain a superior understanding of music than those who lack perfect pitch. And there is good reason for this, I posit. Musical understanding is mainly concerned with melodic and harmonic gestalts. The capacity to individuate their constituent elements does not translate directly into a better understanding of these higher-order entities because melodies are not merely strings of pitched tones (or intervals) and chords are not merely aggregates of pitched tones.

I have already discussed the case of melody at length elsewhere (see Davies 2001a: 47–58) and will not repeat that argument here.[18] Instead, I raise related observations concerning chords. It is a nice question if G-B-D (reading from the lowest to the highest note) is the same chord as B-G-D or D-B-G. The answer is not as obvious as most musicologists would assume. And if they are the same chord, are B-D-F, G-B-F, and G-D-F also the same? Were any of these combinations to occur in a context where it is preceded by a major chord on the fourth degree of the C-major scale or a minor chord on the second degree of the scale and followed by a tonic C major chord, they would rightly be identified as the same, I think. Meanwhile, a second occurrence of B-D-F might be properly regarded as a different chord from the earlier B-D-F if it resolved unexpectedly to A-C-E. (It might be heard in terms of an unsounded E, rather than G, root.) And C-E-G might be identified as the same chord as G-B-D if the piece had modulated to F in the meantime, because these two chords are functionally equivalent. The identification of chords is not settled simply by considering the intervals or the pitch types they involve. In tonal music, we normally identify them in terms of their harmonic functions and the relative frequency with which they are preceded by certain chords and resolve to others, so if there is a reductive analysis to be effected, it is from harmonic sequence to chord succession, not the other way. If I may quote myself (2001a: 58): 'music is organized hierarchically and multi-dimensionally, with most of the higher structures not being reducible to aggregates or strings of their component elements. Musical identity and significance reach most of the way up the hierarchy. Indeed, the principles of identity and individuation that govern the "simpler" constituents of musical sound structures usually depend on higher ones. The works composers create need not be organized to the highest level, however. It is an empirical matter, then, to characterize the various elements and levels crucial to a work's identity.'

The point is that the ordinary listener does not lose much to musical understanding if she cannot consistently identify recurrences of individual pitch or chord types. The contents to be appreciated and understood are gestalts of a higher order of complexity:

---

[18] Maconie (2002: 84–5) makes a point like mine: people recall a melody as a shape or contour rather than as a succession of pitches.

themes, developments, modulations, harmonic resolutions, and so on. And the ordinary listener does have the perceptual concepts for these because she can recognize and discriminate among them.[19] For instance, many ordinary listeners can recognize the resolution and relaxation of some chord sequences and among those that tend to the tonic, can distinguish between perfect, plagal, and double-leading-note cadences, though they lack the technical terms with which to refer to the items they discriminate. Similarly, ordinary people successfully recognize many kinds of items in nature, as well as individual human faces, without always knowing what names to attach to them.

The argument so far claims that the experience of the ordinary listener is not *strongly* non-conceptual at the level where musical understanding finds traction, though it may be underpinned by modes of hearing that are strongly non-conceptual. The next step in challenging DeBellis's argument is to suggest that the ordinary listener has linguistic resources with which to characterize her discriminations. As a result, her understanding is not *weakly* non-conceptual and ineffable.

DeBellis distinguishes (1995: 40–1) between theory-equivalent hearing and theory-inequivalent hearing. He characterizes the former as typically integrated with linguistically mediated thought where the latter is not. All his examples suggest that the relevant linguistic categories are those adumbrated in an advanced musicology. The ordinary listener, who is unschooled in music theory, lacks the relevant terms. It seems to follow that her listening is theory-inequivalent and not linguistically expressible. At least, this is how DeBellis presents the case, but that conclusion is too hasty. Even if she is not formally trained, the ordinary listener possesses a 'folk' or everyday musicology and a barrage of terms that serve it. As a competent language user, she knows and uses words like *tune, rhythm, beat, volume, discord, harmony, chord, note,* and *key*. She can use these to refer to bits of the music she hears. She says: 'this is a return of the slow tune that came right near the beginning.' Or she uses a noun-phrase rather than a single noun. 'The chords that sound like "Amen" at the end of a hymn come after the silence.' She can also make the reference ostensively: 'that bit, the one that sounds like "Amen" at the end of a hymn', she says, or she hums or whistles the parts she wants to draw attention to. We pick out and characterize other things we do not know by name in the same way, by using ostension or general terms and spatiotemporal markers. 'That guy who was on the train last week was in the supermarket tonight.'

It might be thought that these comments apply only to a certain kind of music, that in which the musical results operate at some distance from the technical bases that

---

[19] DeBellis allows this and writes (1995: 65): 'most people can recognize "Happy Birthday"; therefore they have a perceptual concept of "Happy Birthday".' And again (2005: 56): 'most people have robust perceptual concepts of familiar songs and themes, as well as stylistic and generic properties of works. People can easily tell polkas from reggae, which is to say their repertoire of perceptual concepts extends to these categories. It is only at certain levels, with respect to certain properties, that the mental representation of music is nonconceptual in the present sense.' Moreover, the stern tone of DeBellis (1995) is succeeded in DeBellis (2003) by a much more positive view of the intelligent listener's capacity intuitively to grasp much that is necessary for musical understanding, and he also allows there that listening that is permeated by theory sometimes is distracting and inadequate for being so.

undergird them. For music of this kind, it is sufficient that the listener registers the aptness of the surface outcome, without observing what hidden currents and undertows produce this result. Many Romantic symphonies might be of this type. But there is another kind of music in which the technicalities are neither hidden nor easily redescribed in terms of the music's expressive or dynamic character. To follow such music is to follow the (sometimes complex) manipulation of its musical materials. Fugues, chaconnes and passacaglias, themes and variations, and virtuosic concertos are often illustrative of this variety of music.

DeBellis's defender might claim, then, that the listener must have a technical vocabulary with which to express her understanding of music of the second kind, if not of the first. I doubt this, though. Even if it is necessary for the listener to hear augmentation, stretto, inversion and retrogrades in the fugue if she is to follow it with the highest degree of understanding, she should be able to describe what such terms denote without resorting to the musicologist's vocabulary. She says: 'here the tune is turned upside down. There it is sounded backwards. Here it is slowed down. And now the voices cascade, with each statement of the tune on top of the other.'[20]

The ordinary music lover might rest content with listening and not try to describe the music or what she thinks of it, but there is no reason to suppose she lacks the resources to articulate the comprehension she has. If she can pick out the objects of understanding—and I have suggested that her ordinary linguistic training supplies her with the mastery of a folk musicology that allows her to refer to the melodies, etc. that she hears—she can go on to describe her experience of them. When she follows the music, she should be able to give an account of it that reveals this, though her descriptions may seem naive, metaphorical, or quaint to the specialist. It is not the case that only those with a background in music theory or ear training have the necessary linguistic concepts.

The argument, remember, is about degrees and levels of understanding. DeBellis might allow much of what I have argued yet maintain that a theoretically backgrounded listener almost inevitably notices and comprehends more of what is relevant to music's appreciation. Compare a listener who recognizes that a tune first heard earlier has returned with a listener who identifies this return as the beginning of the recapitulation in a sonata form movement. The first listener recognizes the tune, but that provides her with no basis for predicting the sequence of events that should follow. The second, by contrast, learns more in recognizing the melody because, in hearing it as the start of a recapitulation, she has more extensive and more refined expectations about where things can be expected to go from there. A person who informs her listening with knowledge of structural norms almost always will achieve a higher degree of understanding than one who does not.[21]

---

[20] For further discussion, see Kivy (1990), Davies (1994a: 341–56).
[21] This view has been proposed by some of Kivy's critics; see Sharpe (1982), Dempster (1991), Price (1992).

I agree with the last claim, certainly. And I allow that the study of music theory might be the fastest method for awakening one's awareness of these higher-level formal conventions and for sensitizing one to the expectations they generate. But I am not convinced that the unschooled listener cannot achieve the same understanding. Many musical forms are very obvious and familiar: ABAB (verse and chorus), ABA (da capo aria, minuet, and trio), AA'A" (theme and variations, chaconne, passacaglia, ground bass), ABACA (rondo). The experience of listening to a range of pieces that follow the pattern is sufficient to instill it in the listener's awareness. More extended or complex forms, such as fugue—supposing this is better regarded as a formal template than as a technique of treatment—or first movement sonata form, may be harder to grasp, but I see no reason to assume they will be beyond the command of the serious but untutored listener, who becomes conscious of them as patterns common to (movements of) a number of works.

I have been concerned to argue, first, that a formal education in ear training, analysis, and music theory is not essential if the listener is to become highly skilled in understanding and appreciating music and, second, that it must be possible to express this understanding in descriptions she gives of the music, though the relevant descriptions need not be technical. It remains to note that there are other potential indicators of the listener's discernment.

The listener may respond emotionally to what she hears. This can involve much more than registering the music's surface temperature, because there often is an important link between a work's formal and expressive features.[22] In any case, because emotions usually are thought-founded, her affective reactions can reveal how she tracks and views what is happening in the music. As well, the level of her appreciation of the music (or of the performance) is indicated by the explicit or implicit evaluations involved in the following: the frequency with which she returns to the work (or to recordings of the performance), both over the short and long term, evaluations she expresses about the piece or the piece's composer (or about the performance or the piece's performer), the preferences betrayed by the discriminations she makes between the creator of the target work and other composers (or between different performers playing the target work), and the predilections revealed by her preferences among different works by the same composer (or among renditions of the work given on different occasions by a particular performer).[23]

The performer's understanding

Since performers are listeners too, all that I have said about the listener applies to the performer. My concern here is with the kind of musical understanding that is specific to the performer in her role as interpreter of the music. Though she might improvise

---

[22] For elaboration, see Kivy (1990), Davies (1994a), Karl and Robinson (1995b), Robinson (2005).
[23] For critical discussion of this section, see Huovinen (2008).

freely, I concentrate on the case in which her goal is to perform a specified work, and to do so in real time.[24] And I assume that the musician has mastered her instrument, so that what she does fairly reflects her goals and intentions.

Performance interpretations

To perform and thereby interpret the composer's work, the musician must first locate it, so to speak. Composers communicate their works via sets of instructions addressed to performers. To find the work, one must understand the work-identifying instructions. Doing so requires a considerable amount of knowledge and experience.

To begin, one must know what is unmentioned because it is assumed by the composer as knowledge he shares in common with the musicians who are to perform his work. The composer does not (usually) include among the work's specifications instructions about how the instruments are to be built and played. When he indicates something for the violinist to do, he takes for granted that her instrument is appropriately constructed, that it is tuned in the standard fashion, and that she is familiar with and suitably skilled in the performance practice associated with the instrument. That way he can indicate 'Achieve this on a violin' and trust to the performer to know how to execute the instruction. It is only if something non-standard is required in the method of playing—scordatura tunings, mutes, playing with the wood of the bow—that an explicit instruction is needed. If the music is old, it may not be easy to know what in performance is necessary, tolerable, idiomatic, sophisticated, subtle, coarse but possible, idiosyncratic yet acceptable, standard but mundane, and so on. In extreme cases, we might not know what instruments are to be used or be sure how they are to be played.

In the Western classical tradition, we have a fairly secure knowledge of the performance practice that goes with church and court music of the past four hundred or more years, which is not to deny that there is controversy over many of the details. Even so, complacency would be misplaced. Recordings make us aware how much performance norms (and musical tastes) have altered over only the past one hundred years, yet these changes were gradual and largely unremarked by the musicians who perpetuated them. The player is at risk, then, of mistaking current performance practices for accurate representations of the traditions in which the pieces she plays found their homes. She is also in danger of confusing modern equivalents of musical instruments for their predecessors: the clarinet for the basset horn, the Böhm clarinet for the one for which Weber wrote, the pianoforte for the fortepiano, the modern 'cello for the ancestor that lacked a sound bar, high bridge, endpin, metal strings, sustaining bow, and so forth.

Someone might ask: 'why should we feel obliged to interpret the work according to outmoded performance practices and on antique forms of instruments?' I agree that this question deserves to be taken seriously. But it is one thing to ask sophisticated questions

---

[24] For consideration of the differences between live and studio performance, see Davies (2001a: 186–96). Detailed discussion of performance can be found in Thom (1993), Godlovitch (1998). For discussion of rock music, see Gracyk (1996).

about our interpretative options once we have located the work we are trying to perform and quite another to misidentify that work out of ignorance. It is the latter I am warning against here. The player might decide later that she is justified in departing from the performance practice or instrumentation in which her target work had its genesis, but first she must be sure to find the work she represents herself as giving.

As well as taking for granted the performance practice of his time, the composer also adopts the notational conventions of the day when he records his work-determinative instructions. The score does not usually spell out the vocabulary of signs and the grammar it employs because it is addressed to musicians who are supposed to be already literate in the notation. The musician has to know notational rules, such as that an accidental applies to all notes of the given pitch in a measure until otherwise cancelled or that a dot above or below a note indicates that it is to be played staccato. She also needs to know how the performance practice affects the reading of the notation so that, for instance, some rhythms are to be double-dotted, the melody is to be decorated when it is repeated, and a cadenza is to be interpolated where a caesura is written.

As just indicated, not everything that is notated is to be read literally, nor is every notational indication work-determinative. Scores can contain suggestions or recommendations—for example, regarding fingerings, pedaling, or cadenzas—that the performance practice treats as falling within the performer's prerogative. Sometimes scores specify alternatives (e.g., ossia) or indicate note types rather than the tokens that will be played (e.g., figured bass).

We have a fairly secure knowledge of the notational practices of the West of the past four hundred or more years, which is not to deny that there is controversy over many of the details. Nevertheless, musicians are at risk of mistaking current notational practices for accurate representations of the traditions in which the original score was created. Pierre Monteux, who (in 1949) wanted to give an absolutely authentic performance of J. S. Bach's Brandenburg Concerto No.5, apparently remonstrated with the continuo player, Putnam Aldrich, 'What are those chords you're playing? Bach wrote no chords here! . . . If Bach wanted chords he would have written chords. This is to be an authentic performance. We shall play only what Bach wrote!' (Troeger 2003: 218).

The musician also needs an accurate copy of the composer's notation or, if she works from an editor's modern performance version in which there has been a 'translation' (and probably also an expansion of detail) into current notation, a clear account of what was indicated by the composer and what added or amended by the editor. What is crucial is not that a single Ur-text exists, but that relevant differences between various sources or versions are shown as such, along with a footnoting of their sources, reliability, plausibility, and so on.

Suppose all these initial conditions are met. As a result, the musician has located the composer's work and identified what is required in delivering it faithfully. Already the first acts of interpretation have been completed, namely, those involved in interpreting (reading) the score in the light of appropriate notational conventions and relevant performance practices. What comes next?

Whose interpretation is to be given?

A first question asks who is to do the interpreting. In a string quartet, the group might share in the task of generating the interpretation and hopefully they coordinate their efforts so that the interpretation produced is internally consistent. More often, one person takes overall responsibility. Where there is a conductor, she has the job of shaping the performance's interpretation (provided there is the usual time for rehearsal and explanation). But conductors mainly control pace, balance, expressive highlights, and dynamics. Important though these are, they leave many subtleties of attack, phrasing, and the rest for the interpretation of the individual musicians (or section leaders).

For the sake of simplicity, assume the work is for a single player. She might continue to ask whose interpretation is to be used if her goal is to emulate some great player of the past. Will she ape Brendel or Rubinstein, copy Du Pré or Rostropovitch? But again to avoid irrelevant complications, let it be the case that she intends to offer her own interpretation.

Authenticity and interpretation

A crucial choice for this stage is one about the degree of authenticity that will be pursued in the performance. I am reluctant to call this an interpretative decision, having previously written (Davies 2001a: 207) that 'authenticity is an ontological requirement, not an interpretative option.' This principle is entailed by the performer's commitment to playing the composer's work.[25] To play the work, she must, at the minimum, follow sufficient of the composer's work-determinative instructions to make the work recognizable in her performance. Deliberately and systematically to disregard the majority of those instructions is to fail to perform the work in question, not to interpret it.

Also, it is as well to bear in mind that faithfully following *all* of the composer's public, work-determinative instructions leaves open the possibility of many different interpretations, including ones offering contrasting, even opposed, visions of the piece. Not all authentic performances are good ones or provide a convincing account of the work, but even among those that are very good there can be great variety and disagreement. This is because the work-determinative instructions underdetermine much of what goes into any actual performance, including the conception of its overall organization. Even where the tradition allows the composer to be as explicit and detailed in specifying his work as is Mahler, for example, considerable interpretative freedom remains to the performer.

Nevertheless, works can survive in performances that accidentally or deliberately mistreat them. And there can be good reasons for aiming at a degree of authenticity

---

[25] That commitment was assumed in this discussion as an initial premise. If it does not obtain, the story will be different. But whatever new story is most appropriate, it could not be one about the performance of the composer's piece as such.

that falls short of what is ideally possible: simply, it can be too difficult, or inconvenient, or aesthetically unattractive, given the circumstances of performance.

Only prissy puritans could hold that inauthenticity in musical performance is always egregious. It is disappointing, therefore, that so many musicians spuriously claim authenticity for their performances and thereby distort what is meant by that useful and important notion. They say their performances are authentic because through them they express their heartfelt feelings, or because the composer would have wanted his work done as they do it if only he could have lived to the present, or because they seek out the spirit of the music rather than mechanically following the letter of the score. It would be better and more honest were they to admit that they have chosen to ignore some of the composer's work-determinative indications or to make changes in what would usually be work-determinative features in pieces of the kind in question. If we would admit to performing the Prague version of 1787 as against the Vienna one of 1788 (see Chapter 12), why not also allow, if appropriate, that we are giving the slightly re-modeled version of 2011?

Any performance in which the work remains recognizable could be said to meet the minimum standard for its authentic performance. Because musical works can be recognized in performances in which they are seriously abused, a competent musician who targeted only the minimum would deliberately have to play wrongly many notes she could easily play correctly. Competent musicians, to be accepted as such, must aim higher than the minimum, then. But there is a considerable gap between the minimum and the ideal, and settling for something less than the ideal typically will take the performer far past the minimum. The performer can (and often does) choose to aim lower than the ideal in pursuing authenticity in her performance. And her choices in this regard may turn out to be relevant to the interpretation she offers. For instance, if she chooses to play on the pianoforte a work clearly indicated as for the harpsichord, she will not be able to exploit the interpretative possibilities offered by stops, octave couplings, and multiple keyboards, but she may be able to give the piece a weightier and perhaps therefore a more noble character than would be possible on most harpsichords.

Creativity in performance

Suppose the performer aims to perform the work authentically and that it is has a detailed score. Even within such constraints, she cannot offer a thoughtful, original interpretation of the work without exercising considerable creative freedom and imagination. Indeed, interpretation is creative all the way down, so to speak. For instance, the performer's control of microstructural nuances has a very considerable impact on the expressive character and other interpretationally significant features of the performance. For example, millisecond differences in the timing of beats and rhythms have expressive implications and are responsive to the work's structural features (Repp 1998, 1999, 2000). Nor is the performer's control confined to fine-grained details. She also shapes the macrostructural pattern of the performance. For example, rather than giving each climax its undiluted weight, she might build the series of peaks to climax on one that is structurally pivotal. As well, by the way in which she brings out or represses relations between themes, sections, and movements, she sculpts the performance to present the work's structure from a particular perspective. The performer has extensive control over what is made salient, the highlighting or downplaying of similarities and contrast, and how she handles these matters affects what aspects of the work's character, mood, and form are presented in her rendition of it.[26]

What is a performance interpretation?

How is a performance interpretation to be characterized? I suggest the following: the performance interpretation of a work, W, is the overall expressive and structural vision of W that emerges from W's complete performance.[27] A given interpretation can be repeated in different performances, including ones by different performers—so, interpretations are performance *types* that can have multiple *tokens*—and a given performer can offer distinct interpretations of the same work on different occasions.

I claim that a vision of the work emerges from every performance and, hence, that every performance embodies an interpretation. Some of these interpretations will be inchoate and silly, however. In other words, as I use it, 'to interpret' is not a success-entailing verb. (In this it is unlike, 'to marry,' to take one example.) Also, the vision that emerges is not always projected or even intended by the performer, because performance interpretations are not necessarily intended by the people who make them, as I now explain.

Performance necessarily is intentional, but not always to the highest level. In other words, work performance requires the low-level intention to follow some set of work-determinative instructions, but need not depend on the high-level intention to play a given work by a given composer, because the high-level intention can be defeated though a performance takes place. This is what happens when musicians intending to play a trumpet voluntary by Henry Purcell end up performing a piece by Jeremiah Clarke.[28] Interpretation also is intentional at the low, but not necessarily the high, level. Interpretational choices are inescapably involved in the most basic performance decisions regarding what and how to play. To play the notes at all, the performer must settle issues of attack, decay, dynamics, vibrato, phrasing, balance, melodic nuance, intonation, harmonic texture, timbre, rhythmic inflection, etc., all at a level of subtlety that goes beyond what is determinatively instructed, with the result that interpretation penetrates to the deepest, most elemental level of the performance. But on the other hand, the performer might make these decisions in real time, without prior

---

[26] For further consideration, see Levinson (1996a: ch. 5), Davies (2001b, 2003: ch. 15).

[27] Here I differ from Levinson (1996a: ch. 5), who requires in his definition of performance interpretations that they have been considered, by which I take him to mean that the performer who gives the interpretation must have thought about it in advance.

[28] For further discussion of the nature of and conditions on performance, see Thom (1993), Godlovitch (1998), Davies (2001a: ch. 4).

consideration or concern for the total effect. She might play in the moment, leaving the overall vision to emerge as it will. If she does so, the interpretation that is generated derives from her intentional acts but is not intended by her as such. When that happens, she cannot take credit for the overall expressive and structural vision of the work present in the complete performance and, at the same time, she may leave herself open to criticism concerning the performance's interpretative failings, given that musicians *ought* to plan for and interest themselves in the large-scale interpretations that result from their performances.

For the sake of this discussion, however, suppose that the player does calculate and consider the accumulative effect of her local decisions on the view presented of the work through its complete performance, as well as focusing on what she will do in the moment. The interpretation projected in her performance will be intended and owned by her in the fullest sense. How she will shape her interpretation now will depend on how she conceives the *raison d'être* of performance interpretations. Several models are worth considering.

Models of interpretation

According to the first model, performance is equivalent to quotation and the interpretation should aim to communicate the composer's 'utterance' by repeating it with his inflection, intention, and feeling (see Chapter 5). The player subjugates herself and directs her interpretation to voicing the work as its composer would do. With 'utterances' as complicated and multi-layered as musical works are, it remains likely that many different interpretations—some placing the emphasis here, others there— will be consistent with interpreting the work in this fashion. After all, when composers conduct or play their own pieces on different occasions, they frequently vary the interpretation. The quotation model need not lead to interpretational univocity. Nevertheless, this approach is more self-effacing and restrictive than is required.

One way the performer could inject more of herself into her interpretation without abandoning the quotation model is by affirming, not merely repeating, the composer's utterance as she conceives it to be. If a person agrees with and asserts what she takes from another as she quotes it, she can make those sentiments expressive of her own thoughts and feelings, not merely a neutral report of theirs. She says: 'to thine own self be true' and *means* it. Performers who feel a close affinity with the character, mood, or attitude of a musical piece probably can personalize their interpretations in the way just described. They appropriate for themselves the significance of what they quote and thereby express themselves (Mark 1981).

A third model accords yet more autonomy and freedom to the performer by comparing interpretation with translation.[29] (Note that those who orally translate languages are called 'interpreters.') Translation is bound to be more creative than

---

[29] For a different comparison, between composers' various versions of their works and translations, see Chapter 12.

quotation because it can succeed only by adapting what it communicates. So, comparing performance interpretations to translations seems like an improvement, because planned performance interpretations undeniably involve a high degree of skill, judgment, and creativity. Counting against the usefulness of this comparison, however, is the fact that translation involves adapting the original utterance to a different medium or language, whereas the composer and performer work in the same medium, even if the composer does so at a more abstract level.

The models of what is involved in work interpretation considered so far have a literary flavor. The initial attractiveness of these models lies in their capturing two central ideas: that the performer mediates between the composer and his audience and that the performer can deliver the composer's work only by interpreting it. These basic intuitions seem right. No decent account of the sort of interpretation being discussed here can forget that it is the composer's work that is interpreted and that it is only through the performer's interpretation that the work is delivered to its audience.[30] Nevertheless, while these models could inform and account for some types of musical interpretations, they are not perfectly apt. One difficulty is that of knowing how to parse the metaphor of musical works as composers' 'utterances' standing in need of quotation or translation. And while the model of performance interpretation as quotation underplays the creativity brought by the musician to the act of interpretation, that of interpretation as translation seems to invoke a kind of creativity that does not easily correspond with what the musician does.

Here is a new suggestion. It construes performances on the model of... well, performances!

Many musical works (and plays) are created *for* performance. Among other things, this means that they are issued via instructions about what is to be done or achieved. As described earlier, these work specifications, even when conjoined with the notational conventions and performance practices they take for granted, significantly underdetermine the concrete detail of any actual performance. Though performers undertake the job of instancing the work, they must go beyond the work's boundaries to do this. 'To be or not to be' is integral to *Hamlet*, but Shakespeare leaves to the actor decisions about the specific inflection, pitch, phrasing, timing, and stress to be used. The words cannot be spoken without being uttered in some specific manner, but it is the words only, not the further qualities displayed whenever the words are spoken, that belong to the play. The melody notated on the opening pages of Beethoven's score for his Sixth Symphony must be shaped and articulated in every actual sounding of the work with a detail that goes far beyond what is notationally specified (or *could* be

---

[30] I assume that performances are made for audiences, whether actual or imagined, and in this differ from rehearsals, practice, exercises, doodling, and so on. Not all musical playings are performances. (And not all performances are of works, of course, though this discussion was restricted at the outset to those that are.) I also suppose that only a tiny minority of listeners can generate virtual performances in their minds' ears simply by reading the work's score.

specified, in the kind of notation used). In consequence, its performances display many qualities that are not part of the work as such. Because the work can be embodied or instanced only in the performances that are of it, its presentations always and inevitably have a richness that it does not itself possess. Unlike the work, they are saturated with the sensuous opulence that marks everything that can be immediately perceived via the unaided senses. In its turn, the performance depends crucially for its identity on the work it is of. An attempted work performance fails as a performance unless it recognizably presents the work it aims to be of. To say such works are created *for* performance is to indicate the symbiotic character of the relation between the work and its performances.

It is the performer who brings the work to life. She does this not by delivering it along with some extraneous filigree that comes as a bonus but by producing a surface that is available to perception and within or through which the work can be apprehended. In other words, she speaks or acts the play or sounds the music. Composers and playwrights know they are licensing the performers to exercise their creative talents by going beyond what has been specified as work-determinative. Their works could not be concretely instanced otherwise. Audiences are similarly aware of the importance of the performer's contribution. Indeed, we sometimes recognize individual performances as 'works of art' in their own right. We acknowledge as much when we call the best performers artists and distinguish them from others, such as those who print novels or who screen movies. These latter make artworks available via mechanical processes but are not performers of the works they transmit.

Interpretation lies at the very heart of performance. Interpretation penetrates every aspect of the generation of a concrete instance of the work. It constructs the ground of the performance, the figure of the work, and the fashion in which the figure emerges against the ground.[31] Interpretation is not something added after the delivery of the work has been secured. The work is bodied forth through acts of interpretation that infuse it with flesh and breath, blood and muscle. The performer's low- and high-level interpretative decisions generate the electricity needed both to galvanize the work into life and to energize the ecosystem that sustains its being.

There is no instance of the work without a performance and no performance without an interpretation. Interpretation (and hence performance) is creative because it must go beyond what the composer supplies in order to bring the work alive for the performance's duration. We value musical works and their creators, but we have no less respect and affection for performance interpretations and for the musicians who exercise inventive, inspired talent in making them.

---

[31] Whether the listener is more interested in the figure, the ground, or the symbiotic relation between the two can vary. Some works are very thin and the audience is liable to attend more to the detail of the performance. Or again, it may be that the work is already very familiar, so the focus falls on what is unusual about its interpretation.

Contexual factors as relevant to performance interpretations

So far I have concentrated on the relation of the interpretation to the work it is of. In particular, I have described its purpose as the presentation of an overall vision of the work's structure and expressive character. Though interpretations must be work focused, factors outside the work can be highly relevant to its interpretation on any given occasion.

Among the most obvious of such considerations is the skill of the performer. A musician may be competent to play a work to a standard that results in its (perhaps even faultless) performance, yet not be capable of bringing off all possible ways of playing it. Her technique might be deficient or it could be limitations in her talent, imagination, experience, nerve, or personality that constrain what she can achieve with the given work. Obviously, she would do well to recognize her boundaries and to pursue only those interpretations she has the ability to realize successfully.

Also to be considered are the proclivities of the particular instrument that is to be played. These might recommend some interpretative options and restrict others. What is interpretationally effective on a particular organ or harpsichord might not work so well on other organs or harpsichords. Even among more or less standardized instruments, such as the violin or pianoforte, there can be significant differences between the instruments produced by different makers and even between individual instruments. One can be warm sounding where another is brighter and more metallic. This can be relevant to deciding what interpretative selections will promote the preferred overall vision of the work or will be convincing and desirable at a more local level.

Another issue is the performance's venue. An interpretation that succeeds in the dry acoustic of a salon might be turned to slush in the reverberating interior of a church. The dry acoustic allows the performer to highlight the piece's intricate details along with the expressive subtleties these permit, whereas the church musician interpreting the same work may be forced to emphasize its broader contours and overall mood.

In addition, whether the performance takes place as part of an examination, a competition, or a recital tour can affect the style of interpretation that is appropriate. A musician whose aim is to demonstrate that she meets some level of technical efficiency should highlight her handling of difficult passages. A competitor, as well as doing this, is likely to aim at an interpretation that is powerful and distinctive. A less exaggerated (which is not to say a less interesting or engaging) mode of interpretation is suitable for a public concert, especially if the musician is to play the same piece frequently over a short period.

As well, the agenda of a given performance is set by its audience. If the musician is playing only for herself, she can afford to be introspective or eccentric. If she is playing for a large audience in a hall, she needs to project her account of the work. If the audience is comprised of school children, a straightforward, unsubtle interpretation would be apt, whereas a more exotic, risky, or extreme interpretation might be better appreciated by an audience of experienced listeners who are already familiar with the piece. If the work is new, however, a conservative approach to its interpretation is wanted.

Live concerts and the recording studio lend themselves to different stances as regards interpretation (Davies 2001a: ch. 7). Intimate, reflective, fastidious, and polished interpretations are better on recordings. Because recordings can be repeated and are to be lived with, they do not readily tolerate bizarre or hyper-charged interpretations. By contrast, styles of interpretation that grab the audience's attention and buoy them along succeed well in the live concert. Meanwhile, rough edges, risky maneuvers, and blemishes need not disfigure the live interpretation as they would the recorded one.

A further consideration concerns the work's place in the concert's program and the other pieces with which it is surrounded. The first piece should energize the audience while the remainder should progressively build the intensity of the listeners' involvement and reaction. One would expect a more over-the-top account of Beethoven's *Leonore* No. 3 overture if it ended the concert, than if it opened it. And if nineteenth-century warhorses flank Béla Bartók's *Divertimento*, it might stand out more effectively and provide a desirable contrast if its twentieth-century dissonances and rhythms are accented. By contrast, its warmth, charm, and melodic fluidity deserve attention if the remainder of the program consists of works by Anton Webern and Pierre Boulez.

Performance interpretations and descriptive interpretations

The musician interprets the work in performance through her manner of playing it. If she plans the interpretation, she might use trial and error, with final decisions based on gut reactions about what comes off or feels right and what does not. She designs her interpretation on the basis of intuitions and feelings, without bothering to articulate the reasons behind them. And if it is not planned, the interpretation that emerges from the performance is not intended as such. These facts indicate that there is no reason to believe the performer always will be able to give a verbal account of the overall vision of the work presented in her performance.

The same is true of the performer's low-level interpretative acts. Though these must be intended, it does not follow that they must be intended under a description of what they involve. If the playing of musical instruments becomes automatic, then the player aims directly at the output without concerning herself with the mechanics by which she achieves it, as I explain further below. She can intend to produce a sound with a distinctive quality yet have no conception of how to provide a verbal account of what that quality is. She might rely on musical intuitions honed through careful practice and repeated playings of the piece; that is, she might choose what feels right, or what works, or what is interesting without bothering to verbally articulate what about it is so. Moreover, she might do this without considering the work's overall form, trusting to the composer to have written a piece that functions as a whole so long as she, as performer, gives a fair treatment of the parts.

In other words, the musician might not be able to offer a *descriptive* interpretation that matches her *performance* interpretation or the low-level, local interpretative acts from which her performance interpretation emerges. A performance interpretation shows the work in a certain light, but without describing it. Indeed, different performance interpretations might be equally consistent with and illustrative of a given descriptive interpretation of the work, and different descriptive interpretations might be compatible with and exemplify a single performance interpretation (Levinson 1996a).

Nevertheless, musicians often can supply eloquent descriptive interpretations of their efforts, though this involves skills additional to or apart from those required to create a performance interpretation. There is much to think about, both in trying to understand a musical work and to devise a way of playing it that presents it in a plausible and interesting fashion. Though some of this thinking is likely to involve the aural imagination, it is unlikely that successful interpretation only involves mental rehearsal. Discursive thought inevitably plays a part in considering how things are to be structured or expressed, and languages have impressively large vocabularies with which to represent issues and concepts of form, action, and emotion.

Performance as practical knowledge

Musicians *make* music; that is, the performance of music involves applied knowledge or know-how. How does practical knowledge differ from discursive knowledge?

Consider acquired practical knowledge or 'knowing how' more generally.[32] It involves a learned skill or capacity to do something—typically, to perform an action—as in 'I know how to ride a unicycle.'[33] 'Knowing how' can be subdivided into types. A first variety is always conscious. For most people, mental arithmetic is of this kind. It is not mental arithmetic they are doing if they do not follow an appropriate rule, algorithm, procedure, or principle, even if they fluke the right answer. Many practical skills are of this sort. I know how to fill in tax forms, immigration documents, and hire purchase agreements. In all these cases, the working of the skill and the steps through which it is exercised are held inevitably before my mind. A second type of 'knowing how' might be termed 'retrievable.' I know how to drive a car. Most of the time, I am not aware of the processes, judgments, and procedures that are involved. I do not have to think about my driving as I drive. Nevertheless, if I reflect on what I do, I can describe the steps or routines I go through. A third type of 'knowing how' is cognitively impenetrable. Cognitively impenetrable processes are opaque to introspection. Some bit of neurological hardware receives an input, processes it, and outputs some result, but the nature of that processing is not recoverable by consciousness. The skill is learned but the many computational, muscular, kinesthetic, or other activities involved in the skill's application or execution are not available to the agent's

---

[32] I skip over the discussion of innate practical knowledge. Even if great musicians are born rather than made, they still have to learn how to play the violin, the piano, or whatever. Perhaps musicianship builds on a special genetic inheritance so that not everyone can attain it, but even the most naturally gifted must nurture her talent if it is to ripen to fruition.

[33] One can know how many times the postman rings, but that is not the sort of know-how covered here, which is always followed by a verbal infinitive. In fact, knowing how many times the postman rings is an example of 'knowing that,' that is, of propositional rather than practical knowledge.

awareness. From my own case, typical examples are of knowing how to walk, how to pick up a glass, and how to speak English.[34] When a person intends to perform an action of this kind, he aims at it directly, as it were. He intends to turn his skateboard to the left, say, not to flex this muscle here and so. He can intend to produce a certain action as output, but the intermediate steps and movements involved in this, to the extent that they are controlled in an irretrievable fashion, are not what he can intend. Similarly, where 'knowing how' is retrievable but automatic, the action is intended directly. The intermediary steps and movements are not what are intended so long as the action remains automatic.

In what ways is practical knowledge acquired? In some cases it can be learned from verbal descriptions of the appropriate basic actions and their sequences—'put the left leg in and shake it all about'—or of the relevant rules or algorithms—'multiply by πr^2.' In others, learning is by example, copying, or experimenting. Some procedures work better for some skills than others. Generally speaking, when we encourage children and stroke victims to walk we do not provide them with examples. By contrast, language skills are often conveyed via paradigm instances. And while it may be possible to learn to fly a plane from an instruction manual alone, one is more likely to be successful by following and being assisted by an instructor. Always conscious skills are often acquired by memorizing the procedure or rule that must be kept in mind, whereas automatic but retrievable skills, because their application is unconscious, are usually acquired through physical repetition until the routine becomes unthinking. Nevertheless, even cognitively impenetrable skills might be learned by first following written instructions. What makes the skill impenetrable is not the method by which it is acquired but the inability to recall or describe the relevant steps, rules, or procedures when the skill is entrenched.[35]

A given skill might be cognitively impenetrable for one person, retrievable for another, and always conscious for a third. Some people can tie their shoelaces but cannot describe the sequence of actions by which they do so; some can provide the description if asked, though they tie their laces unthinkingly; and yet others—I have in mind some stroke victims, for instance—can tie their laces only by reciting the steps to themselves as they go through the process. Actions that are always conscious for most

---

[34] Even if it is true that basic neuro-structures of deep, transformational grammar are innate and universal, one's language is learned. Had I been raised differently, it would not have been English I learned as my mother tongue. For discussion of differences between explicit and implicit knowledge and between accessible and inaccessible memory as these affect language use and acquisition, see Ellis (1994). A comparison with songbirds (passerines) might be relevant here. Some species, such as the Chaffinch, sing when raised in isolation from their kind, but what they sing is a crude caricature, a kind of Ur-version, of the Chaffinch song, which in practice is much more detailed and is inflected by many local dialects. The song of the Chaffinch may be based on the innate, proto-version, but goes far beyond this in ways that depend on learning by imitation. In my terms, the Chaffinch song involves acquired and cognitively impenetrable know-how.

[35] My distinction between retrievable and non-retrievable practical knowledge does not presuppose the existence of independent explicit and implicit learning systems. Within the psychology literature, there is controversy over whether there is an implicit learning system (see French and Cleeremans 2002).

people may be retrievable or even cognitively impenetrable for others. Autistic or 'fast' calculators, as depicted in the film *Rain Man*, calculate unconsciously and might not even be able to retrieve the procedures or algorithms they use. Where an action requires grace or fluency, it is likely to go better if it has become automatic and thereby unconscious. A person who knows how to waltz but can do so only in an always conscious fashion—counting 'one, two, three, one, two, three' and mentally anticipating each step—is unlikely to move like Fred Astaire or Ginger Rogers.

Let us return to the musician. Her skills are practical but what varieties of know-how are involved? All of them, of course! Sight-reading, like all forms of reading, involves always conscious know-how. One does not read a score except by following it and 'following' of this kind must be deliberate and, therefore, self-conscious. The same surely goes for planned, high-level interpretative or expressive effects. A great deal of what goes on, though, is unselfconscious or automatic. The musician simply targets the output. She sounds the relevant notes or matches her efforts to those of others in the ensemble without intending or thinking of any of the micro-processes involved *en route*. Much of the performer's know-how is retrievable, though. Indeed, almost all instrumentalists are capable of teaching tyros how to play their given instrument—'for this note, place the finger just so and the hand at this angle.' Other aspects of performance will be cognitively impenetrable, for some individuals at least.

To generalize, the better the musician, the more automatic is the ordinary business of performance; that is, playing all the notes in the right sequence, in tune, at the right speed, with the appropriate dynamics, phrasing, attack, and decay, from beginning to end. Indeed, this is implicit in the manner by which musical skills are taught, which relies more on example than on verbal instruction and emphasizes repetition and practice to an extraordinary degree. The goal, obviously, is to ingrain the skill, to make it physical and unselfconscious. There are two reasons why this is important. To be convincing musical performance must be effortlessly seamless, though an extraordinarily large number of complex physical processes are involved. The more the musician is aware of the mechanics, the less likely she is to achieve the required fluency. A second consideration is this. If the musician's concentration must be devoted to dealing exclusively with the technical demands of the moment, she is left with no time or ability to shape a wider vision of the piece. The emphasis in musical training on achieving involuntary perfection does not indicate, therefore, that performance should be brainless; the reverse, it acknowledges the need to free the player's mind from the mechanics of performance so that she might achieve something more appealing and revealing than technical proficiency.

What is the relation between the performer's know-how and her ability to describe in language what she does? To what extent is the musician's know-how recoverable by her as propositional knowledge and, if it is, what is the cost of doing so? Some musicians fear that, by retrieving and verbalizing their practical knowledge, they may damage or inhibit the skill they have and thereby become alienated from their hard-won abilities. (For discussion of a variety of cases, see Dreyfus and Dreyfus 1986.)

A person may have had to think through what he was doing as he was learning to drive but now, as an accomplished motorist, if he retrieves that same detail and tries to allow it to control his actions, he is likely to drive very much worse. And, as any golfer knows, there is a phenomenon that might be called 'paralysis by analysis.' Self-conscious concentration on the minutiae of technique can fatally inhibit the smooth naturalness that is an essential element in a successful exercise of the skills involved. Musical performance is similar, observes the musician.

I am skeptical about this dread. There is an important difference between keeping in mind an analysis of what one does as one tries to do that very thing and providing a description of what was done after the event. It is the latter that is invited, not the former. And there is no reason to think that, having recovered the relevant information for the sake of providing a subsequent description, one cannot then banish it from consciousness when one next attempts to exercise the given skill. After all, among golfers it is the amateurs, not the professionals who teach them, who are most subject to 'paralysis by analysis.' As I noted previously, very many musicians are gifted teachers and some, at least, can offer detailed and informative descriptions of what they do without endangering their ability to perform. If she dreads breaking the spell simply by speaking, the musician's worries are exaggerated.

There are, however, two reasons why we should not expect much by way of explanation or analysis from musicians' accounts of the nature of musicianship. Where the skill is cognitively impenetrable, they do not know what they do, though they may be able to name the output at which they aim. They may speculate about what goes on, of course, but they are less well placed than are scientists to work out what happens in the 'black box' of the relevant neuro-processor. And where the skill is retrievable, they may be able, on reflection, to describe the steps and processes they go through, but the result may be less informative than we would hope. When a complex action is analyzed in terms of more elementary subroutines, the account comes to an end with ordered lists of basic actions. For driving a car, the basic actions would be such things as depressing the pedal, turning the wheel, and looking in the rear vision mirror.[36] Now, how 'deep' the reductive analysis of an action can go depends on how quickly we run up against such basic actions. I suspect that, in the case of music, this happens quite soon, which is why description in this realm gives way so quickly to humming and hand waving, that is, to ostension and example. Despite the complexity and sophistication of musical performances, there might not be that much to say by way of describing the actions that go into making them.

Joseph Kerman (1985: 196) writes: 'a musical community does not maintain its "life" or continuity by means of books and book-learning. It is transmitted at private lessons not so much by words as by body language, and not so much by precept as by

---

[36] My use of the term 'basic action' is deliberately vague. With reference to the competent musician, playing a trill might be an example of a basic action. For the beginner, the basic actions might be better thought of as finger and hand movements.

example.... The arcane sign-gesture-and-grunt system by which professionals communicate about interpretation at rehearsals is even less reducible to words or writing. It is not that there is any lack of thought about performance on the part of musicians in the central tradition, then. There is a great deal, but it is not thought of a kind that is readily articulated in words.' If Kerman's point is that words soon run out when it comes to the description of the actions that go into performing, I agree. There may be much more to be said, though, about the thoughts and judgments that lead the musician to one interpretation or way of playing as against another. Some musicians are able to talk fluently and intelligently about their interpretations, even if they grunt at each other in rehearsal.

The music analyst's understanding

The music analyst might have many goals. Three are of special importance: to analyze (a) the basis of effects (such as unity, closure, instability, etc.) experienced in the music, (b) how the music is (or might have been) put together, and (c) the process of composition. On some occasions, one process of analysis simultaneously satisfies all three goals. This would be the case where there is a neat correspondence between all that takes place in the background and the audible effects that supervene on that background, and given also that this correspondence is achieved self-consciously by the composer without any redundant effort. Frequently, however, these analytical tasks lead in different directions. The process of composition may involve dead ends and rejected experiments that later found no place in the finished composition, and there might be aspects of the music's organization that produce no audible effects.

As well as these central undertakings, the analyst might be interested in relations between different works (either within the composer's oeuvre or across many sources), with stylistic or structural trends or norms for the works of a genre or period, and so on. Alternatively, the analyst's goal might be to aid the performer, not to address the audience (DeBellis 2003). Some kinds of analysis shade into the study of musical sociology, editing, history, ideological deconstruction, or criticism. In this brief discussion, I ignore these possibilities in order to concentrate on the primary ones listed above, all of which are aimed at understanding an individual piece; at understanding how it goes, how it works, and how it got to be as it is.

There is a voluminous literature within musicology discussing and disputing the alleged merits of different schools of analysis and the ideologies they presuppose. I do not have the space here to engage with those debates. But there is an issue frequently raised by philosophers of music in their discussion of music analysis that I wish to consider. It concerns the hearability of the relations analysts characterize as significant.

We have already seen that Levinson downplays the importance of large-scale structural accounts of music on the grounds that such structures cannot be directly heard. Many who would dispute his claims about the limits of aural perception nevertheless share the view that the value of music analysis resides almost entirely in its drawing to attention, and thereby making audible, relationships or structures that might not be noticed otherwise. Kivy, for instance, argues as follows against Rudolph Reti's analysis (1961) of the underlying melodic basis for the unity of Beethoven's Ninth Symphony: Reti's analysis clearly assumes 'that we do not perceive this understructure as part of our aesthetic experience of the work even *after* the musical "atomist" has revealed its presence' (Kivy 1990: 133). He continues (1990: 136–7): 'this is not science; this is astrology. It is the well-known fallacy of finding what you want to find by putting on your "finding" technique no restraints at all except the restraint of never allowing it to fail to "find" what is wanted.'[37] 'We see [the relationships] when we perform Reti's operations on the notes. We do not hear them thereafter in future listenings of the work—that, at least, is my experience' (1990: 139). Scruton is more positive about Reti's analyses (see 1997: 406–11), but challenges (1987, 1997) the claims of Schenkerian analysis (see Schenker 1925–30) because it does not provide an account of what we can hear.[38] He writes (1997: 319–20): 'the test of Schenkerian theory is that the structure generated by the theory coincides with that which is heard in the music, by the person who hears with understanding.' In a detailed critique, Scruton argues (1997: 313–29, 416–26) that Schenker's theory fails this test, along with others.

I have argued (Davies 2003: 243) in similar terms when reviewing the idea that music analysis can account for our experience of a work's unity in terms of the transformation into surface variety of a limited set of underlying motivic ideas: 'the relationships exposed by analysis could have the significance claimed for them only if they were audible relationships. . . . The analyst who sees in the score relationships that cannot be heard by anyone will not convince us that he has exposed the source of the work's unity. But the analyst whose analysis allows us to hear relationships of which we were previously unaware may well convince us.'

I now believe these views are wrong as they stand. The error becomes quickly apparent when we consider how Scruton extends his objection from the analyst to the composer who employs compositional techniques that cannot be heard to do their work. A favorite target is the dodecaphonic serialism of the second Viennese School, at least to the extent that it negates all tonal implications (Scruton 1987, 1997: 281–5,

---

[37] In a similar vein, DeBellis (1999b) asks about the falsifiability of the generative tonal grammar described by Lerdahl and Jackendoff (1983). He argues that it is falsifiable only to the extent that the perception of background structure is not as unconscious, and hence not as cognitively modular, as they describe.

[38] Kivy describes (1990: 126) Schenkerian analysis as having the 'aura of a cult' but does not know or inquire if it is guilty of the faults he finds in Reti's approach. DeBellis (2003) suspects that Reti stands proxy for Schenker in Kivy's account. When he considers if Schenkerian theory would hold up better to Kivy's criticism, he denies that it is unfalsifiable but agrees that one need not hear a piece in Schenkerian terms in order to achieve an intuitive understanding of what is achieved. Scruton distinguishes (1997: 393) between Reti and Schenker. Reti seeks to show how the musical surface is derived from common thematic motives, which is a worthwhile undertaking because it 'bears on our aesthetic attention.' By contrast, Schenker's approach goes in the opposite direction by reducing the surface variety to a universal, underlying prolongation of the major triad. Here I am inclined to side with Scruton against Kivy. I can see that Schenkerian analysis can be done, but I doubt some of the claims made about the aesthetic satisfaction this yields and about what the analyses allegedly prove about what makes the best music great.

294–305). 'The score of [Berg's] *Lulu*—one of the great masterpieces of modern music—shows vividly what I mean. Each section of music is introduced by a title, in gothic script, which presents it as an instance of some classical archetype (canon, passacaglia, etc.). And yet there seems to be no way in which the music can be heard as exemplifying those classical forms. To discover the justification for the titles is to discover details of the music that escape the educated ear.... At crucial moments, Berg uses the concepts of the Schoenbergian system, not in order to create something that can be heard in the music but in order to provide intellectual justification for the written notes' (1987: 171).

This charge is unwarranted, even if Scruton is correct that the form cannot be followed. The composer faces the blankness of the empty page and must do something to mobilize the music that is to cover it. It is not uncommon for composers to resort to arbitrary codes and processes or to adopt rigid systems in order to energize and challenge their creative powers. They have used letters from their names or solmizations of texts to dictate crucial notes; they have thrown dice or employed other randomizing procedures; they have applied complex mathematical functions to determine what to write; they have serialized the various elements of music, such as pitch and rhythm. And it always has been so. In the thirteenth century, modal rhythmic sequences were serialized and this process became more elaborate in the isorhythmic motets of the Ars Nova, which sometimes also repeated the melodic scheme in a way that did not coincide with the rhythmic one. Riddle canons in the fifteenth century employed retrograde, inversion, mirroring, different mensurations, and a panoply of other devices. For instance, the tenor in the Agnus Dei of Dufay's *Missa L'homme armé* is to be read backwards with full note values, then forward in half note values. Josquin adopted a common practice in deriving the theme (re, ut, re, ut, re, fa) for his *Missa Hercules Dux Ferrarie* from the vowels of the title. Parody masses of the sixteenth century paraphrased and disguised music from other sources, sometimes in an aurally undetectable fashion. Mozart wrote a treatise on how to compose minuets with dice.

While a number of these operations are, and were intended to be, audible—the mirror fugues in Bach's *Art of Fugue* are a case in point—many cannot be detected, even by expert listeners aware of their presence, and were not intended by the composer to be audible to the audience. They are, so to speak, her business. Bits of technical craft, self-amusement, intellectual challenge, or whatever, that are not offered for the audience's delectation (Davies 1994a: 356–60). And what is wrong with that? It would be absurd to pretend that we can dictate to composers that every aspect of the musical organization and the process of composition should leave its mark on the work's outward face. So, Scruton's criticism of Berg surely is out of place, especially given his concession that *Lulu* is one of the great masterpieces of modern music. And Kivy's response (1990: 143–4) to the issue—that what cannot be heard is not part of the work—looks no better than an attempt to legislate the problem away.

Once we have allowed that the score can contain aspects of organization that are not separately apparent in the sound of the music it encodes, and that principles of composition need not always be obvious, it is a small step to allow that the analyst can legitimately interest herself in these features of the work. I suggested earlier that the analyst can consider how the music is (or might have been) put together and the process of composition. I do not see any reason to suppose she must confine herself to structures and technicalities that always are potentially audible in their operation and effects.

When we recall also that the process of composition is sometimes extended, complex, and revisable, we are directed to the same conclusion. Suppose the composer records her labor on a particular composition in sketchbook fragments. These may show, for instance, that one theme derived historically from another, though it was elaborated and refined to such an extent before it was incorporated into the work that it bears no audible relation to its source. As well, the composer may try out and reject many ideas. The analyst can record and study all of this, it seems to me. If the work is a good one, there is much of interest in learning how the material was generated and, subsequently, how it was put together, altered, and revised, even where the manner of this is not audibly present in the finished piece.

Kivy and Scruton might point out that my discussion here deals with intended but inaudible procedures. Perhaps their goal is to exclude searching for hidden factors that were *not* intended. This would be too quick, though. An unreflective or naive composer might rely on her intuitions for what sounds right when making her compositional choices, without bothering about, or intending, the substructural bases for these outward results (Davies 2003: ch. 14). In other words, many of the factors Kivy and Scruton would have the analyst attend to may not have been explicitly intended by the work's composer. In such cases, the analyst can reasonably ignore the composer as she probes beneath the music's surface in search of the underlying causes of what is heard.

More likely, as we have seen, Kivy and Scruton reject the relevance of Retian or Schenkerian analyses by denying not only that what is detected by analysis is intended but also that the analysis uncovers a basis for the music's aesthetically important features. Background relationships, for example, could not explain the unity we sense in a work if expert listeners cannot detect the contribution they make to that unity. So, Retian or Schenkerian analyses are irrelevant to understanding the work's features.

Obviously, their arguments are meant to score against these analytical approaches in general, not against particular, questionable analyses. Kivy (1990: 140) argues, for instance, that the 'relationships' to which Reti attaches significance are an inevitable result of Beethoven's composing his Ninth Symphony within a tonal tradition. They are, he thinks, too easily demonstrable; too common and too cheap to explain why one work is unified where another is not. But it is not plain that Retian methods inevitably guarantee results that have no explanatory usefulness. For instance, it could be that rather simple, tonally common elements do indeed unify a given work, and this result is not undermined by the fact that it shares some of these in common with other works or that other works featuring some of these elements are not also unified (Davies 2003: ch. 14). Besides, the Retian approach might identify more complex motivic foundations than those listed for Beethoven's Ninth as underpinning a work's unity. It does not presuppose that the unifying function is always or only met by simple elements that are inevitably widespread in tonal music.

In the end, the key assumption is that only *hearable* relationships could have the explanatory power the analyst attributes to them. That intuition is shared by a number of music theorists who otherwise hold different views about the nature of music analysis. Douglas Dempster and Matthew Brown favor a 'scientific' model according to which analyses uncover objective facts about the work and are to be evaluated in terms of truth. They write (1990: 249): 'in some sense, music analyses/theories should present relations that are audible, or at least confirmable by what suitably qualified listeners are capable of hearing. What is to be avoided at all costs is a picture of music theory that renders analyses as adventitious and untestable impositions on the musical facts... [Our image of music analysis] places a premium on the aural testability and confirmation of theories and their related analyses.' By contrast, Nicholas Cook regards (1987a, 1987b) analysis as a mode of interpretation and as subjective in part, but he also places great store on the hearability of what the analyst discusses. He stresses that few ordinary listeners listen for structure or hear Schenkerian prolongations, but he also allows that Schenker created the possibility of a new way of *hearing* music, a way that some people can follow, and he rejects (1987a: 220–7) the value of music analyses that point to features that cannot be heard at all, partly because he spurns certain models of unconscious perception. (For a philosopher's defense of a similar view, see Sharpe 1993.) Schenker was elitist and racist, according to Cook, in setting the minimum standard for musical comprehension at that achievable only by the ideal listener and by assuming the superiority of paradigms of Western eighteenth- and nineteenth-century classical music. Unlike Schenker, Cook does not think the inability of the ordinary listener to hear Schenkerian structural elaboration and prolongation amounts to a fatal failure in her musical understanding, though she is denied access to the experience of structural hearing the Schenkerian expert can achieve.

The opinions listed above generally allow that aspects of the listener's experience of the music—of closure, unity, overall coherence, balance, and the like—might depend on underlying musical causes that she does not hear as generating the effects she experiences. In at least one sense of the term, she is unconscious of some musically significant elements that, nevertheless, influence what she does perceive in the music. These views also insist that it must be possible for some listeners aurally to detect the working of these underlying causes. If no one can do so, there can be no genuine test of the analyst's hypothesis and no reason, therefore, to attach credence to the explanatory power claimed for the analysis.

All this may sound reasonable, but I regard the position as unnecessarily strong.

The idea of unconscious perception can be saved from the aura of psychological quackery by resort to contemporary linguistic and philosophical theories emphasizing the modularity of some cognitive systems, including perceptual ones. Modules usually are understood to be introspectively impenetrable. Some music theorists, such as Fred Lerdahl and Ray Jackendoff (1983) and Eugene Narmour (1990, 1991) refer explicitly to modular perceptual systems in explaining why the relationships they account for are not usually perceived, and DeBellis (1991, 2002, 2003) characterizes Schenker's theory in such terms.

There is a problem, though. Music theorists like Narmour, Schenker, and Lerdahl and Jackendoff do claim to chart processes that they can hear, but if these are processed in neurological modules, they should not be able to do so. DeBellis (1999b) sees this as a significant problem for Lerdahl and Jackendoff's theory. Naomi Cumming (1993) observes that the fact that Schenkerian analyses can affect how the listener hears the music might be thought to count against the modularity of the processes involved. She responds that accepting the modularity of input systems does not preclude the recognition of learning as an influence on how input is interpreted at a higher level, however. And to return to the discussion of the performer's know-how, we can note that processes that are not retrievable to consciousness by some individuals may operate through routes of cognitive awareness or calculation for others. Besides, nothing requires us to follow every aspect of the account of cognitive architecture that is popular in the philosophy of current cognitive science. Perhaps some forms of perceptual modularity are not entirely closed off from other cognitive systems.[39]

Rather than tinkering with the cognitive science, however, let us cleave to the notion of modular perception according to which some subterranean musical processes cannot be aurally experienced by anyone as generating important surface consequences, though in fact they do so (via the workings of the cognitively impenetrable neuro-perceptual module that takes them as input). We could deal with the problem identified above by acknowledging that the analyses are intellectual rather than perceptual, with the result that they cannot be tested against the way expert analysts and others hear the music. This strategy looks unappealing because it immediately returns us to a difficulty highlighted earlier. If they cannot be tested against perception, the analyses appear to be unfalsifiable and lack any convincing empirical basis. Remember, that was the crucial issue for Kivy and Scruton, as well as for Dempster and Brown.

This is where the argument goes wrong, though. It is true that, if the music analysis is to be testable for veracity—or, if this is too strong, for plausibility, insight, coherence, and the rest—it must be subject to some empirical standard. But why assume the relevant test must be one of audibility? If modular processing is involved, this might be detectable through neurological or other physiological measures. Scientists, at some future date, may be able to probe the workings of some of our modular systems, so that they can test the counterfactual dependency of kinds of outputs on kinds of inputs, and in that way confirm or disprove claims made by music analysts about unhearable connections between background musical processes and hearable surface effects.

---

[39] In a personal communication, DeBellis makes this intriguing observation: 'about modular processing, I wonder why it is that certain analyses seem more plausible to us than others. One explanation would be that they "translate" the listener's awareness into the language of conscious deliberation. In that case, the processes wouldn't be fully modular in the sense of being isolated from the rest of cognition.'

Some music theorists express their views in ways that are open to the possibility just described, even if elsewhere they insist on hearability as the only satisfactory test. For example, Dempster and Brown write (1990: 248): 'although we insist that analyses/theories should fit with reality, we do not imply that the theoretical entities and structures themselves need be directly audible; all we claim is that, sooner or later, the theoretical entities postulated by an analysis have empiric consequence.' (Compare this with the earlier quotation from 249.)

We remain with these possibilities: there can be forms of organization in the musical background that produce no effects on the surface of the music. There can be forms of organization in the musical background that produce hearable effects on the surface of the music and that can be heard to bring this about, at least by some expert listeners. There can be forms of organization in the musical background that produce hearable effects on the surface of the music and that cannot be heard to bring this audible effect about, even by expert listeners. The existence of these causal ties is testable in principle, though introspection and close listening are not reliable measures because the relevant ties are forged by cognitively impenetrable neuro-perceptual modules. The analyst can legitimately interest herself in all of these forms of organization and can present empirical hypotheses about if and where they connect to hearable features of the musical foreground. But given that we currently lack reliable empirical techniques for testing relations between inputs and outputs of the relevant modular systems, the analyst's theories and claims about connections established within cognitively impenetrable neuro-perceptual modules must be regarded as speculative, though not thereby as illegitimate.

The composer's understanding

The composer has already often been mentioned, so the comments in this section will be brief.

Composition, like performance, is a practical skill. It is possible that the composer simply selects among the ideas that come to her, without bothering to consider why her preferred choices are superior to the alternatives that she rejects. Some Baroque composers produced so much music that it is hard to believe they could afford to labor over their work. It is also possible that the composer knows nothing of musical notations or music theory. She may operate in an aural culture that conveys its works via exemplary performances rather than scores, or she might rely on the assistance of an amanuensis. In addition, she may be able to compose at her instruments without a grounding in the technical terms of music theory. Some pop music composers, such as John Lennon and Paul McCartney, were apparently ignorant of musical notations and, though they could no doubt refer to chords after the manner of guitar tablatures, they knew little of music theory.

Because composition is practical in these ways, the composer's understanding of what she does and of the works she produces could be less knowledgeable and refined than that of an analyst or performer. Nevertheless, the process of composition can be so complex that one would expect it to be frequently self-conscious, and hence, that the composer often has a deep understanding of what she does and why. Also, the skills are not always practical. A composer who writes idiomatically for a large orchestra must have considerable propositional knowledge about what is involved in playing various instruments, about their strengths and weaknesses, and about their special characteristics, but is unlikely to have a practical mastery of more than a few of them.

Of course, the composer cannot be ignorant of the music of her culture (or at least of the genres that interest her) and the stylistic, structural, tonal, harmonic, and other conventions that govern it. She must have a working knowledge of such matters if what she produces can be recognized as music. (She can have her own opinions on this, but in the end this is a matter of public judgment, since the label, 'music,' is a word in the public language.) It is true that the music she creates may set out to challenge, repudiate, or subvert the default norms of her culture's music; she need not be a musical conservative. But again, if she is to produce revolutionary *music*, she must cling to much that characterizes that notion even as she rejects other of its conventions and practices. Over time, all the 'rules' of some previous period of music can be eroded or overthrown, so that the contemporary music sounds little like earlier music and could not have been recognized as music by those who were at home with the ancestral kind. This process must be piecemeal, though, so that, with each change, what emerges retains sufficient of what went before that it reasonably can be counted as music. If we have reached a time when silence, factory noise, and much else can qualify as music, this shows not that the concept is empty but that the history of the concept's evolution is central to its identity.

Can the understanding required of the composer be taught? Certainly. An aspiring composer can be taught notation, acoustics, musicology, and whatever other aspects of music theory would be appropriate. She can study the history of music and changes in the principles that govern music's construction. She can read composers' accounts of what they were trying to do and why, and analysts' descriptions of what they find in musical works and what this is supposed to show about those works and how they operate. She can also be trained in the skills that are involved; for instance, by orchestrating piano transcriptions of orchestral pieces and then comparing her efforts with those of the original composer, or by writing exercises in counterpoint, or by analyzing styles and works.

As regards the process by which the composer comes by her original ideas, the only reliable generalizations concern its variability. Creative individuals come from many backgrounds and can have very different personalities. A wide assortment of *modus operandi* is used by creative people. Moreover, a given individual might employ different methods on different occasions, sometimes grinding painstakingly over her work and at other times guided by inspiration or intuition.[40]

Though composition is a human action and as such is intentional, it is not the case that all that finds its way into the music is explicitly intended. The intention might be

---

[40] For recent discussion of artistic creativity by philosophers, see Gaut and Livingston (2003).

to relinquish control through the adoption of chance procedures for selecting the succession of musical events. Or the intention might not run down all the levels of the process, so that, for example, the composer aims successfully to write a suspenseful ending but does not calculate how what she writes achieves the desired effect. She targets the higher-level outcome and opts for what brings it off, but at a more basic level she does not intend the causal workings that underpin the result because she does not concern herself with them. Or her intentional choices might have unintended (but perhaps musically interesting) side effects that she did not predict and remained oblivious of as she composed. As with all complex works of art, there often are layers of significance for the interpreter or analyst to explore that go beyond what the work's creator intended or calculated. This is one reason why composers are not always the best or most revealing performers of their own works. Finally, composers can fail in some of their intentions, with the result that what they had in mind is not always to be found in the work. The composer might intend the bassoon line to stand out against the orchestra, but, through her incompetent treatment of the trombones, muddy the texture so that it cannot do so.

Nevertheless, where we know them, reference to the composer's intentions is almost always useful in indicating how her work is best to be approached, how it functions, and what is in it. They provide an ideal introduction, if not the last word, to understanding the music. Similarly, a composer's performance of her work is almost always of interest as indicating a revealing view of it via the interpretation that is offered. No matter how good that interpretation is, however, it does not preclude other, very different, interpretative strategies, so long as these remain sufficiently faithful to the composer's work-determinative specifications (Davies 2003: chs 5, 15). The composer spells out that of which her work is comprised, but as I explained earlier in discussing the performer's role, this underdetermines the detail of any actual performance, both as regards the aspect under which the work is presented and the respects in which the performer must go beyond what constitutes the work. When the composer performs her own music, she presents an interpretation as well as her work. That interpretation can have a recommendatory force, but it counts ultimately as only one among many possible interpretations, and leaves other performers free to shape their own visions of the piece.

8

The Experience of Music

The composer and the performer have their own experiences of music. I ignore them, though, in order to concentrate on the person who hears music without having written or played it. More particularly, I will focus on the person who listens to music. She gives it her attention and does so because she hopes to find in it something to understand and appreciate.

To understand and appreciate the music, the listener must be suitably prepared for what she hears. In light of her recognition of its style, syntax, genre, instrumentation, etc., she is able to follow the progress of the music. She is aware of where bits begin and end, of prominent melodies and motifs, of repeats, variations, and developments, of the waxing and waning of musical tension (whether tonal, harmonic, or rhythmic), and, where appropriate, of the music's expressive tone, its symbolic character, and its referential or quotational nature. She can sense what is likely to come next, what is normal and what unusual, when one major structural part has come to a close and another has begun, and when material is entirely new, or related to what has gone before, or repeated from a previous statement.

Such matters have been considered by philosophers—see Chapter 7, Kivy (1990), Davies (1994a), Levinson (1996a: ch. 3)—as well as by musicologists. And for an illuminating account of the phenomenological aspect of following music with understanding, see Levinson (1997). Rather than revisiting these familiar discussions, I will take them as read. In this chapter I develop my comments in a series of loosely connected sections. Some of my observations supplement and expand on matters that have been widely debated. A few introduce topics not previously considered under the heading of the experience of music.

Does the experience of music carry with it an awareness of ineffable truths?

The auditor just described obviously brings to her experience of music a great deal of background knowledge. This is not to say that she requires formal training or an understanding of music theory and technicalities. The kind of knowledge that is

First published in A. C. Sukla (ed.), *Art and Experience*. Westport: Praeger (2003): 109–20.

relevant can be acquired over time by exposure to music in all its variety.[1] Because it is practical rather than bookish, the accomplished listener often cannot articulate what she knows, especially when asked to present this information systematically in abstract terms. Nevertheless, I doubt that the auditor's comprehension could always be inexpressible. As implied above, she should be able to indicate that the melody begins here and ends there, that what is happening now is an exact repetition of what happened a few moments ago, that one passage is more energetic and happy than another that is sad and lethargic, and so on. Even if she does not share the specialized vocabulary of the musicologist, composer, or musician, the musically literate listener can describe what she hears in terms that reveal her as capable of following the music's progress.

Sometimes it is held that music conveys to the listener important truths that are special in not being expressible in language (for instance, see Langer 1942, Scruton 1997). In other words, music is held to be a source of ineffable knowledge. I reject the extreme form of this view. The experience of music is ineffable in the way that all perceptual experiences, including those of the most mundane kind, are (Raffman 1993). There is a plenitude to perceptual experience that language does not capture. Indeed, language could not perform its central function of abstracting and summarizing how things are, or seem to be, if it did replicate all the abundance of experience. But there is no more reason to think that the rich texture presented by music to the senses somehow contains the meaning of the universe than there is to think the same about the indescribably complex and subtle play of sunlight on a leaf's surface. Music is infused with the human intellect that lies behind its creation and performance, admittedly, and is scented and spiced by the emotions expressed in it, undoubtedly, but it does not communicate deeply important truths about such things beyond what it wears on its face and can be described as showing. This is not to deny that music is important sometimes as a source of knowledge; instead, it is to deny that what is conveyed by music is indescribable or inexpressible.

The composer Felix Mendelssohn said that what is expressed by each musical work is unique to it. For the reason that it can be hard to put into words how the emotions expressed in different works are qualitatively distinct, this thought lies behind the idea that music is ineffable in its expressiveness. My own view is that what is unique to the musical work is not, as just claimed, the emotion expressed, but rather the means of expression. Music usually expresses rather general emotions and two different works can express the same quality of sadness. What is highly specific to each work is the detail of the means—the actual notes, harmonies, and so on—by which the emotion is expressed. These differences are describable and, therefore, are not ineffable. If we cannot put into words how the sadness of the slow movement of Beethoven's *Eroica*

---

[1] Most people probably underestimate the extent to which music pervades their environment or the quantity of information that can be gathered and stored by the very young. Children seem to pick up their culture's tonal system with the same natural facility as they show in learning a language, and first show an initial practical grasp of both at much the same age.

differs from the sadness of Chopin's funeral march that is not because there is some subtle contrast that evades description. Instead, their sadness is of the same general character, with the relevant differences between the pieces lying not in what is expressed but in the musical means—means that are linguistically describable—by which this sadness is given its embodiments.

Can we experience music as the composer's contemporaries did?

Returning to the music lover described previously, notice that her listening is what I call 'historically contextualized.' Musical genres, styles, and grammar change over time. To locate the piece that is the object of her attention, the music lover must hear the music in terms of the genre, style, and grammar that apply to it, which requires that her listening be informed by a familiarity with the musical ideals, goals, types, conventions, practices, instruments, and techniques presupposed by the composer as the musical heritage he shared with the performers and audiences he addressed. The sophisticated listener will also be aware of the composer's oeuvre, of influences on his development and thinking, and of music in the same genre written by others.

Yet, however much she tries to 'contextualize' her listening, will not the experience of the modern music lover differ from that of the composer's contemporaries? For instance, a Baroque composer's contemporaries rightly believed they were hearing the latest music in the most avant-garde style and they had no idea of what would follow in fifty or a hundred years. They were shocked by the discords they heard, startled by innovations in performance technique, impressed by the virtuosic demands made on the performers, and so on. When the present-day listener hears the same music, she believes that it is in an old style that was eclipsed by the Classical sensibilities of Mozart, Haydn, and Beethoven. The discords are tame by comparison with what followed, the instrumental techniques are all too familiar, and she is used to a much higher standard of virtuosity. Given that a person's beliefs affect what she perceives, these differences suggest that the present-day music lover cannot experience the music as the composer's contemporaries did.

I agree that there are bound to be discrepancies between the experiences of the two listeners. Some of these give an advantage to the music lover of the present time. She can assess the place of the given piece within a broader span of musical history and thereby is better situated than the composer's contemporaries to weigh its significance. The important issue, though, is whether her modern beliefs prevent the present-day listener from experiencing the waxing and waning of musical tension, the music's melodic and tonal telos and closure, and so on. If she cannot, then what is alive, dynamic, and organic to the composer's contemporaries must be hollow, bloodless, and academic to her. A significant corollary is that the pursuit of 'authentic' performance is without point if the present-day listener cannot experience such renditions as bringing the work to life.

Fortunately, however, the different beliefs of the listener from our own time need not prevent her from experiencing older music as full of movement, tension, expressiveness. So long as her listening is conditioned by expectations tailored to the music that is her focus, rather than to the most familiar types of her own age, she can experience it appropriately. And the majority of listeners do seem to be capable of making the relevant adjustments, as is apparent from the ease with which they move between styles, genres, and periods of music. Just as the jazz fan is not precluded from listening to rock with appreciation and enjoyment, so the listener of the present day is not debarred from hearing and experiencing the flux of energy within older varieties of music. When she does so, she puts her knowledge of the different 'grammar' of later music 'off line.' While it is true, then, that the present-day listener will not experience the music exactly as the composer's contemporaries did, she is not thereby debarred from a full engagement with and deep appreciation of the music of the past.

Pleasure and the experience of music

Why do people listen to music? What do they get out of it? The answer seems obvious: pleasure. They do not listen as a matter of duty owed to others or as an exercise in self-discipline but for pleasure taken in the music understood and appreciated for its own sake. Accordingly, the discussion of aesthetic pleasure (and how it differs from other species of pleasure) has occupied a central place within aesthetics and the philosophy of art (Levinson 1996a: ch. 1).

One common objection to this view is badly conceived. It maintains that we value music as an end in itself, for its own sake, and not merely as a means to other things. The conclusion drawn is that the person who seeks pleasure from music uses it as a mere means and is not, therefore, a true music lover. The objection is misconceived because it wrongly assumes that the pleasure taken in music somehow is separable from the process of following and appreciating that music. For instance, it wrongly thinks of the pleasure as a bodily sensation that could possibly be caused by things other than the music. The pleasure and the music are not separable in this way, however. The music is the unique means to the pleasure. The pleasure has to be described with reference to the music that is its object. The pleasure depends on an active perceptual and cognitive engagement with music recognized and appreciated in its particularity. The music is not merely a dispensable means to the pleasure because the pleasure is not something that comes unbidden when one is exposed to the music, whether one notices it or not. It is bound up with an active involvement with the music and, as such, is taken in the music, not incidentally derived from it. (For discussion, see Levinson 1996a: chs 1, 2, Stecker 1997, Davies 2003: ch. 12.)

It is obvious, I have suggested, that we listen to music for the pleasure we derive from the experience it affords us. The number and variety of apparent counterexamples might give one pause, though. We listen to sad music, even knowing that we may be moved to feelings that are negative in mirroring what is expressed in the music. Also, a fair amount of music turns out, when understood, to be banal and uninteresting, not a source of pleasure at all. (For that matter, not all music that is pleasing on a first encounter turns out to be enjoyable in the longer run.) Besides, a person might attend concerts of the latest avant-garde music though she accurately predicts she will not enjoy them. She goes, nonetheless, because she likes to keep abreast of the latest trends and developments.

Several lines of reply are available. We might sort higher, cognitive levels of enjoyment from lower, emotionally negative ones they encompass. We might hold that it is the anticipation of pleasure that draws us to music, even if that anticipation sometimes is thwarted; when it comes to choosing which music to listen to for a second or third time, it is the music that gave us pleasure formerly to which we are attracted. Or we might distinguish the pleasure taken in music as a whole from that taken (or not) in particular works. Or we might distinguish aesthetic pleasure from other pleasures that could be derived from art, and among aesthetic pleasure, we might sort genuine from immature, uninformed, or otherwise inferior varieties. As for the conscientious listener who subjects herself to music she predicts rightly that she will not enjoy, we might suggest that she is motivated by pleasure after all, that is, by the pleasure she takes in riding on music's cutting edge, if not in the pieces as such.

There are people who argue that all human action is motivated by self-interest. Each apparent counterexample is met by an appeal to a subtler or higher or longer-term self-interest, so that, for instance, the anonymous donor to charity is driven ultimately by his need to feel morally worthy, or superior, or whatever. In the end, the notion of self-interest becomes empty of explanatory power, because it turns out that the complete stranger who gives his life so that others can fill the lifeboats is as self-interested as another who tramples over women and children with no care except for saving himself. In the process, the concept of self-interest moves far from the moral notions of selfishness, callousness, hubris, and the other vices, with which it is initially associated. As a result, the claim that self-interest inevitably dominates no longer has the morally significant implications that seemed to lie behind its introduction.

Now, the idea that we are motivated by pleasure (when we are not driven by duty or self-discipline) is similar in being vulnerable to over-extension, with a corresponding dilution in its explanatory power. With a bit of ingenuity, we could respond to any counterexample by identifying some kind of pleasure, connected directly or indirectly to the music, lurking in the background. But the temptation to take the account in that direction should be resisted out of respect for what stands in need of explanation. For instance, it might be more honest and more convincing to allow that we can be motivated to listen to music for its own sake out of curiosity, or habit, or for many other reasons that pay no regard at all to a pleasurable pay off. In other words, there can be many reasons for acting other than the pursuit of pleasure. Even if my trips to the dentist are self-motivated and self-regarding, it certainly does not follow that those visits must be a source of direct or indirect pleasure to me or that they take pleasure as their goal.

Despite the caveats just registered, someone might reasonably maintain that, though pleasure is not always forthcoming when its pursuit is the main reason for listening to music, and though there may be many other reasons why a person would aim to understand and appreciate music, nevertheless, the primary motivator for music lovers is the pursuit of pleasure. Some could be driven to listen to music by curiosity, or to pass the exams in their music appreciation classes, or for the knowledge (of music, its history, its interpretation, instrumental technique, etc.) they obtain, and the experiences of all these people might be pleasure-free yet thoroughly satisfactory from their point of view, but in fact they would be in the minority. Fancy arguments aside, most music gives pleasure in being understood and appreciated and if particular pieces do not, this is a reason for not seeking them out in the future. Most people enjoy and value music, importantly if not exclusively, for the pleasure it gives them.

It is surprising, then, when a philosopher argues that the pursuit of pleasure has little to do with our interest in appreciating music for its own sake. R. A. Sharpe writes (2000: 32–3): 'I go to many concerts. Do I enjoy them? Well, it is hard to say. Sometimes I am dissatisfied with the performance.... The occasions on which the music is brought to life are relatively few ... I am prepared to try [new music], even though I know the likelihood is that it will be incomprehensible or boring. I don't expect to like it, because I realize that only a tiny proportion of music is deeply moving and affecting.... The natural rejoinder from an advocate of pleasure as the end motive will be that I listen on the off-chance that it will give me pleasure. But when the chances are so remote, is that a reasonable account? The fact is that I love music, and I am very interested in it. Life without music would be, I am inclined to guess, very nearly intolerable.... The focus of my interest is the music. That is the object. I don't pursue it because of what I can get out of it; that would be a travesty. My interest in music is, in the proper sense, disinterested.'

I have two, brief, critical comments to make. Sharpe diagnoses (2000: 37) the emphasis on pleasure as a 'corrosive effect of utilitarianism,' but one does not have to agree with the utilitarian that pleasure is the only or ultimate value in order to acknowledge its importance in the experience of music. Pleasure can provide a very good reason for acting even if other reasons can be as powerful and even if some (such as the demands of justice) are overriding when they obtain. Secondly, Sharpe thinks that valuing music intrinsically excludes the possibility that we value it instrumentally, as a means to pleasure. But either it makes no sense to say we value it intrinsically (Stecker 1997: 251–8) or our valuing it intrinsically is compatible with its being valued as the unique source of the pleasurable experiences that are inseparable from its appreciation (Davies 2003: ch. 12).

My interest, though, is not in criticizing Sharpe's view but in teasing out the crucial insight it contains, which is that hedonic rewards are far too puny and one-dimensional to measure music's human significance. Sharpe says he loves music, and contrasts this with enjoying it. This brings to mind the image of a mother who, when accused of taking an interest in her child mainly for the pleasure she obtains as a result, replies that, to the contrary, she is devoted to the child because she loves it for its own sake. The music lover, in other words, is like any lover—not out for himself but devoted to the object of his passion, which may be frustrating or irritating as often as it is delightful.[2] And even if pleasure is taken in the object of love and also in the relationship of love, that hardly begins to account for the passion with which the object of love is desired or for the way that the interests of the lover become absorbed and subsumed within a larger unit that encompasses his love's target.

Consuming love is an over-heated condition that is not sustainable in the long term. To that extent, it is not an apt model for the relationship between the music lover and music. Nor is that of unrequited love, even if the music never reciprocates the listener's feelings. A better analogy is with the kind of love that sustains and fructifies an ongoing, developing relationship.

The relevant point is this: under the influence of love, the subject's sense of her own identity changes and expands, so that the relationship becomes focal to the subject's conception of herself as a being. For music lovers, music is that central. For them (to quote from Davies 1994a: 276), 'music is yet more than an important element in the fabric of life; it is integrated into their personal being and becomes part of what gives meaning and identity to their lives. Without music, the members of this group would no longer be the same individuals, for music shapes their conception of themselves no less importantly than do their relations with family, friends, lovers, and work. Listening to or performing music is for such a person a mode of existence and self-realization.'

By now, I hope Sharpe's point is clear. To suggest that we listen to music for the pleasure we get from the experience is odd in the same way that saying we eat food for the pleasure we get from the experience is odd. Though this might be the reason given for eating a particular food on a particular occasion, and though the consumption of food is regularly pleasurable, the claim is peculiar because it so badly fails to understand that eating is a necessity, not something we choose to do for its instrumental value. It would be similarly strange to ask a person if she is the way she is because of the pleasure she gets from being like that. Even people who are comfortable with themselves are not the way they are for the enjoyment they take in being that way. If listening to music has become part of one's identity and selfhood, the suggestion that one listens for the sake of pleasure, even if often true, does not come near to indicating the role of music in one's life.

The claim that a love of music can contribute to one's sense of oneself as a person can easily be misunderstood as sensationalizing or over-dramatizing the place of music. Music's assuming this importance can come through a moment of transcendent revelation and transformation, a kind of epiphany, as when one hears a particular work and feels that one's life and outlook cannot remain the same thereafter. More often, though, it occurs in the most everyday fashion, as repetition turns to habit. Music

---

[2] Many families are such that, while bonds of love and history link them together, their members might wonder what that tie is supposed to have to do with pleasure.

can creep up on a person, just by being around all the time, and the same applies to a particular work if it is repeated often enough.

Play it Sam, play it again: repetition and the experience of music

The repetition of musical works has not been much discussed, except in the context of trying to explain how an effect can be surprising the second time around.[3] This neglect may reflect the fact that, in Western classical music, it is not common to listen over and again to the same work.[4] There is something odd, then, in the behavior of Philip V of Spain, who employed the most famous singer of his time, the castrato Farinelli, to sing the same four songs every night for nine (some sources say ten, others nearly fifteen) years.[5] Good classical works are supposed to be worth re-hearing throughout a lifetime, but undue repetition over the short term can be expected to kill the listener's appetite for the work. Nevertheless, not all groups of music listeners oppose frequently repeated hearings of a single piece. Devoted fans of pop sometimes will play the latest single ceaselessly for weeks at a time. In many folk traditions, particular songs have a long history of regular performance. The same is true also for parts of the musical repertoire of some non-Western cultures. The effect of repetition on the experience of music deserves closer attention, especially as repeated exposure to music can help make music central to the life and self-image of the individual.

Performers often spend hours with a piece, playing it over and over to learn and master it. Many girls in Bali begin dancing from about the age of six. Usually, the piece they are taught is *Legong Lasem*. Those who are good enough to perform publicly do so from about nine years of age. My guess is that performers of *Legong Lasem* may dance it about once each day for the best part of a decade. That surely is guaranteed to secure it a significant place in their lives! But I promised at the outset to concentrate on the listener, not the performer. In doing so, I will stay with the example just introduced, that of Balinese legong.

Many Balinese do not seem to tire of *Legong Lasem* and other pieces that are played very frequently. In previous years, a number of princes bankrupted themselves through their obsessive devotion to legong. I can now see the source of this fascination, though it has taken some years for me to do so. I had to learn how to follow the music and how the dance fits with it. I needed a working knowledge of techniques, themes, and symbols in Balinese dance in general, as well as of the specific stories and their stylized expression in individual dances. My appreciation was sharpened through

---

[3] This has been viewed as a problem for Information Theoretic approaches to musical significance; see Meyer (1961).

[4] And in music improvised or performed live, it was not possible to re-hear what was played until the invention of recording devices. Brown (2000) has argued that, because they can be replayed, recordings of jazz kill what they capture.

[5] For Philip, the songs were therapy for his pathological depression.

watching lessons and rehearsals, and by becoming aware of subtle differences in the choreography and music that distinguish local variants.[6] And bit by bit, as if by osmosis, the dance and music came to occupy a place alongside other musical works that I love and cannot imagine living without. (For further discussion of the dance, see Davies 2006.)

Where is the interest in seeing *Legong Lasem* done again and again? For me it has two aspects. The first is a sense of satisfaction that comes from witnessing how a living performance tradition is continued, sustained, and extended. Though exceptional legong dancers can perform and teach to a great age, a gap of only three or four years separates each generation of dancers, so it is possible to see a group trained and groomed for public performance, appear for the first time before a tourist audience or in the temple, achieve maturity as performers, and close their careers or graduate to new dances, all within less than a decade. The second thing that holds my attention is the relentless passion for beautiful perfection that drives the whole enterprise. This is not to imply that there is some single, ideal performance to which all others aspire. Because the individual personalities of the dancers and musicians inevitably and quite properly emerge through their mutual interaction, what counts as perfection differs from group to group and time to time. So, the point is not that repetitions can be interesting because each rendition holds out the possibility that, finally, the ideal might be realized. It is, rather, that repetition makes possible a perfection that varies from instance to instance and that thereby facilitates the audience's focus on fine details of any rendition. Perfection in this dance is as complex and multi-dimensional as the facets of a cluster of crystals. It can be achieved often, but never in a complete or exhaustive fashion, so each new performance offers the hope of adding something unique to a precious store.

Recordings, functional listening, and idiosyncratic perspectives

One way music can be repeated and reheard is via recordings. Most of the music encountered by the listener (or hearer) is on disk, even if the work that is played was created and intended for live performance, as is so for most classical music (but not most rock music). To the extent that listening to a disk is not like hearing music played live, this means that much music is not experienced as it was intended to be. What would pass in a live performance as minor slips and as an excitingly original interpretation might be rightly perceived on a re-playable disk recorded in a studio as unforgivable blunders and as an irritatingly eccentric interpretation (Davies 2001a: ch. 7). Performers of and listeners to classical music take account of the special conditions offered by the studio and of the comparative permanence of recordings in crafting and assessing recorded performances,

---

[6] It is possible to see *Legong Lasem* every night in tourist shows, with performances by six or more different troupes. When presented for tourists, the piece is abridged to less than half its full length, but even then runs to fifteen to twenty minutes.

which must therefore meet different, and sometimes higher, standards than are required in live performances. For instance, a recording probably should aim for a more intimate, painstakingly careful rendition than a live performance, which by contrast, must be projected to its audience and must grab their attention from the beginning but need not sustain repeated hearings. Yet, even if the experience of recordings and live performances differ in the ways just indicated, as well as in the obvious respect that one can usually see what is involved in eliciting the music from the instruments at a live performance, it seems reasonable to acknowledge recordings as providing access to works intended for live performance, which is how we consider them in fact. The reasons for this are not difficult to discern: although the piece is not played in real time when it is recorded in the studio, we can know that the musicians who tape it are capable of playing the same music live; although we do not see the instruments played as we listen to a recording, the experienced auditor knows what she would see if she were present at the performance the recording simulates; and although the interpretation that works best on the disk would be less satisfactory in the concert hall, and vice versa, both kinds of interpretation can be faithful to and consistent with the work.

This discussion of recordings brings another issue to mind: while we might often choose to listen to music, we are also likely to hear a great deal of (broadcast) music that has the function of creating an appropriate ambience. The experience of this music can be subliminal; it creates a complementary background mood to whatever is the main idea, event, or activity. At other times, music is very conspicuous in performing its functional role. For instance, thunderous, noble fanfares herald the king's arrival, or the congregation joins together in singing a prayer or hymn. Even when it is prominent, music often serves to accompany some other idea, event, or activity, and as such is functional. It is to be danced to, or to be married to, or to be buried to.

Philosophers of music tend to focus on music that has been designed to be appreciated for its own sake. This is understandable, I think, but it would be foolish to overlook the extent to which music functions as a handmaiden to other activities. Acknowledging its functionality does not entail undervaluing its importance to us. The reverse is true. It is precisely because music can stir the passions, can focus our attention, can quicken our responses so that we want to sing or dance along, and can generate a sense of involvement and community as well as of occasion, that it is resorted to so often. Its power to heighten the significance of any occasion is accepted and confirmed whenever music is harnessed to the promotion of some functional purpose. Accordingly, a crucial aspect of the experience of music often will involve a sense of its contributing to a wider social event.

The potency of music not only suits it for exploitation in the public arena, as just described, but also for a comparable, perhaps idiosyncratic, use in the private sphere. For instance, a ballad playing when we met might become 'our song.' It becomes emblematic of our relationship not merely by its contiguity and association with it but also because it exemplifies features pertinent to or possessed by that relationship; it is serious but warm, tender but firm, and so on. Philosophers do not normally discuss what is personal in the listener's experience of music (for an exception, see Higgins 1997). This is because they are interested in what is intersubjective, and thereby generalizable or even universalizable, about our connection to music. This is as it should be. The very personal interest and value that music can have for us is significant more as autobiography than as philosophy. But from the inside, writing as a listener rather than as a philosopher, that inescapably intimate dimension to the individual's experience of music is usually as or more important than the rest.

9

Così's Canon Quartet

The *opera buffa, Così fan tutte*, followed *The Marriage of Figaro* and *Don Giovanni* and was composed about two years before Mozart's death. The plot concerns a wager between Don Alfonso, a 'cynical philosopher,' and two men, Ferrando and Gugliemo, confident of the faithfulness of their fiancées, Dorabella and Fiordiligi. Under Alfonso's direction, and with help from Despina, the ladies' maid, the men are disguised and court each other's former lover with such success that the bet is lost. When all is revealed, mutual forgiveness prevails and the couples marry.[1] These events supposedly take place within the span of twenty-four hours.

The opera was dismissed in the nineteenth century as immoral and in the twentieth as irretrievably silly. Perhaps it is because he shares this latter view that Peter Kivy attempts to save the music by treating it as separable from the dramatic context when he declares the work to be a *sinfonia concertante* for voices. He writes (1988b: 259): 'its "characters" therefore are not Fiordiligi, Dorabella, Gugliemo, Ferrando; they are *the* soprano, *the* mezzo-soprano, *the* heroic tenor, etc. They are instruments in a *sinfonia concertante*, instruments with proper names.... Like the characters of *opera seria*, the characters of *Così fan tutte* are as close to being character types as they can be without ceasing to be characters at all.' Mozart did write *The Impresario* [*Der Schauspiel-Director*] for characters identified in the way Kivy describes, because in that *Singspiel* he was satirizing the singers and conventions of the day. *Così* is quite different, however, or so I maintain. I argue that the work is no less dramatically interesting or successful than its predecessors. The key to understanding the dramatic theme of this *opera buffa* is revealed in Mozart's treatment of the work's enigmatic canon quartet.

Così's quartet

In the finale of the last act of *Così* there is a magical moment of divinely beautiful music when the action freezes. The four main protagonists sing a canon or round in A-flat major to words proposing a toast. Or, at least, Fiordiligi, Ferrando, and Dorabella take

---

First published in Garry Hagberg (ed.), *Art and Ethical Criticism*. Oxford: Wiley-Blackwell (2008): 245–58.

[1] The stage directions do not make clear who marries whom, though. (I think it is important that this uncertainty is preserved in performance.) One might speculate about the source of the plot's attraction for Mozart, who seems to have loved the sister of his wife.

their turns with the melody but, when it comes to Gugliemo's, the theme is passed again to Fiordiligi while Gugliemo mutters discontentedly.

Why does Gugliemo not take his turn? Mozart's operatic music almost always serves or creates a dramatic point, so it is in this direction that one most naturally seeks an answer. Gugliemo's confident trust in Fiordiligi has only recently been betrayed. Ferrando, Fiordiligi, and Dorabella have had longer to acknowledge and accept the reversal of affections on which the opera's plot hinges. The music indicates that Gugliemo has yet to accommodate himself to the new situation. Were one to look for a precedent, it might be found in the last act finale of *Abduction from the Seraglio*. There the main characters one by one sing the verse of a strophic song (with short chorus) praising Pasha Selim. Osmin, who is unhappy with the outcome, begins the verse but breaks off in a fit of pique. (Mozart quotes here Osmin's aria in Act I, which he famously discusses in the letter of 26 September 1781 addressed to his father.)

This account is perhaps not entirely convincing as it applies to *Così*, however. It is apparent in *Seraglio* that Osmin will not be reconciled to his failure to gain the love of Blonde, Constanze's maid, so it is appropriate that the opera closes as it does. By contrast, Gugliemo soon is to accept Fiordiligi's apparent betrayal of their earlier love. And the canon, which the audience cannot fail to recognize as such, so plainly is it presented, is a form calling for single-mindedness, both musically and dramatically. Gugliemo's subversion of the structure is amusing and effective in its way, but one might wonder why Mozart did not reserve the canon for later, when Gugliemo might have shared both the sentiments and the melody with the others. If the canon is to be highlighted, as it is here, it might seem that it would be located more appropriately in the happy dénouement that is to come.

Inevitably, Mozart's canon quartet is compared to 'Mir ist so wunderbar,' the canon quartet in Beethoven's *Fidelio*. In Beethoven's quartet, the characters' thoughts differ considerably, with the result that the musical and dramatic forms do not match. He is attracted to large, abstract themes, such as the redeeming power of love and the value of political liberty. His characters are props, rather than people. The musicologist, Edward T. Cone compares (1974: 37–9) the two quartets in these terms: 'what is the dramatic relevance of [Beethoven's canon quartet]? Beautiful though it is, it attaches identical music to diverse words sung by a motley quartet. But this is no ordinary ensemble. It is not a conversation but a fourfold soliloquy in which each character comments on a situation that three of them misinterpret. Only Leonora knows the truth, and she must conceal it. Thus the conscious thoughts of the characters—their words—are various. Yet the canonic device implies, through the identity of the melodic lines, that the intuitions of the deceived ones have somehow led them to a subconscious appreciation of the real state of affairs—perhaps not to the truth about Leonora's disguise, but at least of the truth about her character.... It is interesting to contrast Beethoven's canon with that of Mozart in *Così fan tutte*. As has often been pointed out, Gugliemo's inability to carry his imitative part in 'È nel tuo, nel mio bicchiero' reflects his rage, which makes it impossible for him to mask his true feelings by accepting the words and music of the canon.... One has the suspicion that Ferrando has enjoyed the whole charade and might not be averse to the change of fiancées! Is this really the case? The answer is not easy. It depends on how successfully music can seem to mask as well as explore a character's true attitudes—and on how one can tell which it is doing. In depicting a character consciously playing a deceptive role, the composer may choose to emphasize either his real subconscious nature or that of his assumed role. Mozart's solution to the problem throughout *Così fan tutte* is typically subtle and ambiguous.' I take up and develop the idea Cone intimates: there is a dramatic point that explains Mozart's quartet, whereas no such justification for Beethoven's wonderful canon can be found.

Gugliemo and Benucci

Why does Gugliemo's fail to join with the others? There is one unobvious reason. He does not take his turn with the melody because 'he' cannot. Francesco Benucci is not able to take the tune because it lies beyond his vocal range. Benucci is the singer who took Gugliemo's part in the original production; he is the singer for whom Mozart composed.[2]

It is important not to lose sight of the fact that Mozart penned his operas for particular companies and performers. On 26 September 1781 he wrote to his father about *Seraglio* as follows: 'in working out the aria I have ... allowed Fischer's beautiful deep notes to glow.... Let me turn now to Belmonte's aria in A major ... I wrote it expressly to suit Adamberger's voice ... I have sacrificed Constanze's aria a little to the flexible throat of Mlle Cavalieri.' And even if Mozart's own inclinations had not led him to take account of the special talents and predilections of those for whom he wrote, so self-important were the singers of the day that they would have demanded nothing less of him. *Don Giovanni* was written for the company in Prague, following the earlier success of *Figaro* in that city. When, seven months later, *Don Giovanni* was produced in Vienna, the performers were not satisfied to accept music written for a company they regarded as provincial. Mozart had to compose additional arias for Don Ottavio and Donna Elvira, and a duet for Leporello and Zerlina, to satisfy the singers' demands.

What resources could Mozart use in accommodating Benucci's compass to the music of the quartet in *Così*? Could he meet the difficulty by using octave transpositions within the tune? No. While octave transpositions work well enough when sequential passages are involved, they would ruin the distinctive character of a melody such as this one. Would the problem be removed if the key were other than A-flat major? No. With the melodic spread of a major eleventh, a change in register would be bound to take the tune out of the range of one of the singers. Besides, so carefully does Mozart treat the tonal centers in the act finales of his late operas that it is doubtful that

---

[2] Benucci was also the singer for whom Mozart wrote the part of Figaro and he took the part of Leporello in the Vienna production of *Don Giovanni*. Benucci is mentioned only once in Mozart's letters—on 7 May 1783 he wrote to this father: 'well, the Italian opera buffa has started again here and is very popular. The buffo is particularly good—his name is Benucci.' All quotations from Mozart's letters are in Emily Anderson's translations.

many alternative keys could have been integrated into the structure at this juncture. Could the difficulty be avoided by writing the canon at the interval of a fifth instead of the octave? No. The problem then arises with respect to the range of the singer playing the part of Ferrando.

Such questions may be of technical interest but they overlook the obvious. Mozart could have written a different canon, one that would have allowed Benucci to join with the others. (Probably, he could have written ten such canons before breakfast.) Ultimately then, this second attempt to explain the course of the canon quartet is no more satisfying than the first. To progress further, we need to understand Mozart's approach as an opera dramatist.

Drama, plot, and structure

The plots of the *opera buffa*, while not so fixed as those of *opera seria*, follow well-established patterns; for example, there is a confused jumble of mistaken identities, neatly unraveled at the end. In the middle of the opera, and at its end, more and more characters are brought on stage, with the sympathetic protagonists in trouble on the first occasion and winning out on the second. Such themes derive from the *commedia dell'arte* tradition, as do many of the stock characters, such as the simple, rough, greedy, but basically good-hearted male servant.

This dramatic structure inevitably generates a bipartite musical one. Both the middle and the close of the opera see a rise in tension and complexity, as well as a quickening of the pace, as more musical voices are added to the mêlée. In the final scene, this tension is resolved, as the forces of good win the day. Other aspects of the musical setting draw on established forms. For instance, the typical aria is in da capo form—an ABA structure (both for text and music). Dialogue that takes place between arias and ensembles is presented in secco recitatives (a stylized representation of speech accompanied by the harpsichord and bass instruments) or, less commonly, in accompanied recitatives (in which the orchestra supports the singer in a style allowing more freedom of rhythm and tempo than is usual in the 'numbers'). And the central and closing sections are given over to finales, consisting of continuous music uninterrupted by recitatives.

Meanwhile, the composer and librettist must also conform to other practices and conventions associated with the performance practice. For instance, major characters are each to receive two arias at the close of which they exit the stage, and those with lesser solo roles should be given one such piece. The point in such cases is to provide the singers with vehicles for their skill (in singing, acting, or both) and a chance to milk the audience's applause.[3]

---

[3] I draw attention (Davies 2003: ch. 13) to the way such requirements operate against the overall musico-dramatic structure in the last act of *Figaro*. Marcellina and Basilio are there provided with arias, as is their due, but this happens at the expense of the dramatic development. The progress of the plot is halted and the acceleration of musical tension is dissipated. If these arias are cut for the sake of preserving the drama's pace, however, the structural balance between the second and fourth acts is upset.

Mozart worked within this framework but did much to transform it. This is apparent, for instance, in his treatment of solos. The aria is effective for dramatically static reflection on a character's inner state and, in the repeated section of the da capo form, for vocal display through melodic elaboration. In *Seraglio*, Constanze (or, rather, Caterina Cavalieri, the singer) is indulged with an aria of nearly 300 measures (No. 11), including an instrumental introduction of 60 measures. The mature Mozart might have conceded that this contains 'an awful lot of notes' (as Joseph II notoriously complained of *Seraglio*), given the way he treats the form in the later *opera buffa*. There the arias are much shorter. For instance, K. 584 was written originally for Guglielmo, but finding it too long, Mozart rejected it in favor of No. 15 in *Così*. In some cases the aria is integrated into an ensemble: for example, Nos 3 and 15 in *Don Giovanni*. Meanwhile, there is a tightening up of the introductions. The accompanied recitative becomes more prominent and often is merged with a following aria. This device, adopted from *opera seria*, plays an important role in establishing the seriousness of many of the female characters—Anna and Elvira in *Don Giovanni*, Dorabella and Fiordiligi in *Così*. In the case of the most dominant characters—those who control the action and command the stage for much of the opera—the arias are sometimes downplayed, as is so with those for the Don in *Don Giovanni* and Susanna in *Figaro*. Mozart did not abandon long da capo arias, but he reserved them either for characters, such as Don Ottavio in *Don Giovanni*, who do not develop and who contribute little to the advancement of the action, or for situations where the dramatic context invites self-consideration, as in Fiordiligi's solos in *Così*. Meanwhile, ensembles increasingly became the focus of attention, both in their number and length.[4] The finales are considerably expanded. This new focus on large-scale numbers brings problems in generating musically integrated structures. The use of quasi-sonata forms in the first act trio and third act sextet of *Figaro*, for example, show Mozart's skill in meeting these demands, but it is in the operas' finales, with their spiraling patterns of modulation and with the controlled inevitability with which pace and breadth accumulate, that his command of musico-dramatic structure is displayed at its most virtuosic.

The point of all this, obviously, is for the composer to take charge of character and dramatic development. Mozart's goal was to create rounded, human characters, revealed mainly through their interactions with others, so that the stories would come to life. And, in achieving this, it is necessary to meld music and drama in a marriage that produces an integrated form responsive to the themes underlying the formulaic narratives on which the plots of such works draw. Already, in quotations offered above, Mozart's awareness of the difficulties posed by this reconciliation are acknowledged. As his letters testify, Mozart charges the librettist with furnishing a book that can be transformed by the composer into music-drama.

For example, when writing *Idomeneo*, Mozart demanded many cuts and alterations in the libretto, always looking to the dramatic effect to be obtained. (See the letters of

---

[4] The ratio of ensembles, excluding finales, to arias reveals this. In *Figaro* it is 9:14, in *Don Giovanni* 10:14, and in *Così* 15:13.

8, 13, 15, 24, and 29 November; 9 December 1780 and 3 and 18 January 1781.) The following quotations are typical: 'the second duet is to be omitted altogether—and indeed with more profit than loss to the opera. For when you read through the scene, you will see that it obviously becomes limp and cold by the addition of an aria or a duet, and very genant for the other actors who must stand by doing nothing; and, besides, the noble struggle between Ilia and Idamante would be too long and thus lose its whole force.' 'In the last scene of Act II, Idomeneo has an aria or rather a sort of cavatina between the choruses. Here it will be *better* to have a mere recitative, well supported by the instruments. For in this scene which will be the finest in the whole opera ... there will be such noise and confusion on the stage that an aria at this particular point would cut a poor figure—and moreover there is the thunderstorm, which is not likely to subside during Herr Raaff's aria, is it?' More of Mozart's attitude to the librettist's role is offered in a letter to his father dated 13 October 1781. On 5 July 1783, Mozart writes: 'an Italian poet here has now brought me a libretto which I shall perhaps adopt, if he agrees to trim and adjust it in accordance with my wishes.' The correspondence with Varesco, via Mozart's father, finds Mozart demanding many changes and suggesting how they should be written. (See the letters of 6, 10, and 24 December 1783 and of 10 February 1784.) Though we have little by way of written commentary regarding Mozart's collaboration with Lorenzo da Ponte, the librettist of *Figaro*, *Don Giovanni*, and *Così*, no doubt he too was often subject to Mozart's direction.

So far I have suggested that Mozart, as opera composer, worked with conventions of the day—practical conventions of performance practice and musical tradition—and that a consideration of this fact is important to a fuller grasp of those works and the composer's achievement in writing them. I have claimed that he was concerned primarily with creating a dramatic whole, populated by believable characters. This is achieved within the limits allowed by the conventions of the genre, sometimes by exploiting their potential and sometimes by working against and overcoming limitations inherent to them. Even if all this is true, it does not yet explain why so majestic a composer as Haydn would write (Deutsch 1966: 358) to Franz Rott, Chief of Commissariat in Prague, December 1787, as he did about Mozart's operatic exploits: 'you ask an *opera buffa* of me. With the greatest pleasure, if you have the desire to possess some vocal composition of mine all for yourself. But if it is to be performed on the stage in Prague, I cannot oblige in that case, since all my operas are too closely bound up with our personnel, and moreover would never produce the effect which I calculated according to local conditions. It would be quite another matter if I had the incalculable felicity of composing an entirely new libretto for the theatre there. But even in that event I should be taking a great risk, since the *great Mozart* can scarcely have his equal. For if I were able to impress the soul of every music-lover, and more especially the great ones, with my own understanding of and feeling for Mozart's incomparable works, *so profound* and so full of *musical intelligence*, as my own *strong sentiment* dictates, then the nations would vie with each other to possess such a jewel within their encircling walls. Let Prague hold fast to the precious man.... It makes me angry to think that this *unique* Mozart has not yet found an appointment.... Forgive me if I stray from my path. I love the man too much.'

What has been said so far sets the stage for a new story. Mozart plays off the outward, conventional structure in his *opera buffa* against a less obvious musical structure that shapes their dramatic character.

Internal dramatic structure and external form

Don Giovanni begins, after Leporello's first aria, with a frenetic twenty minutes of action the tension of which is electrifying. The Commendatore, Donna Anna's father, dies in defending his daughter's honor, killed reluctantly by Don Giovanni.[5] Anna and Don Ottavio swear vengeance. Then, for the next two hours, nothing much happens. Of course, all sorts of events occur—the Don attempts more seductions, Leporello is beaten, Donna Elvira joins with the avengers but cannot shake free of her infatuation, and so forth—but, although the Don is identified as the murderer before the end of Act One, retribution never is carried through. Finally, when the Commendatore's statue in the graveyard accepts the invitation to dinner, the dénouement is set in motion, proceeding from that point with the irrevocability of a massive door's closing. As a result, the opera has an inverted bow/arch structure that is set off and played against the surface form in which each act builds to a climax at its close. That dramatic structure is built in the music, not only by its generating the pace and pressure of action but also by returning to the brooding menace of the overture's introduction in the final scene. Here, as ever with Mozart's late operas, the underlying dramatic structure tracks the musical structure, so closely does the one control and shape the other.

Why is the lack of dramatic development through the middle parts of the opera not a fault, as is the dramatic hiatus in the last act of *Figaro*? Because that lack of development is a crucial element in the work's structure; it underlines the point that gives the opera its very power. Don Giovanni, as evil personified, is no merely mortal sinner. There is something supernatural about the power he exercises, which renders not only the women but also the men powerless against him. Indeed, Don Giovanni is a vessel through which this force is exercised, since he is as much victim as author of his appetites. This character calls not only on the legends of Don Juan and the Stone Guest but also on that of Faust. Despite the passionate vows of his earthly victims, the Don is immune from their retaliation. Only a force from beyond the grave, the avenging, murdered father, can bring him down.[6] It is this dimension acknowledged in the structure created by Mozart, and it is this dimension that gives extraordinary force to the tale.

[5] Whether Donna Anna has retained her virtue never is entirely clear. This topic has inspired at least one novel—Brigid Brophy's *The Snow Ball* (1974).

[6] It is difficult to resist speculating about Mozart's psychological state in being attracted to the story. The opera was written immediately following the death of Mozart's father (28 May 1787—the first performance took place on 29 October), the father who fostered his gifts, but was a stern master. Peter Shaffer's play *Amadeus* makes much of the connection.

If the theme of *Don Giovanni* is cosmic, that of *Figaro* is domestic and political. The plot concerns the attempt to counter obstacles to the happy marriage of Susanna and Figaro, especially by preventing Count Almaviva from exercising the *droit du seigneur* that he has officially renounced.[7] Beaumarchais's play, adapted by da Ponte for the opera, was banned for its political content, for its indirect criticism of the aristocracy. While Mozart's music explicitly acknowledges the conflict between master and valet, the concern, as revealed in the work's underlying structure, is focused more centrally on sexual politics—and Mozart's vote goes to the women. Susanna may not command the stage in her arias but she dominates the action throughout, as is apparent in the ensembles. She is revealed mainly through duets shared with Figaro, Marcellina, Cherubino, Rosina, and the Count; she appears in all the work's ensembles. The opening duet sets the pattern for the opera's development in that her melody eclipses Figaro's.

Susanna's part draws attention to the division between the sexes, not distinctions of class. As well as mocking Figaro with his own vengeance music ('Di qua non muovo il passo' in the Finale of Act IV), she amuses herself at the Count's expense with feigned slips of the tongue (No. 16). Meanwhile, she cooperates as an equal with the Countess. If class conflict is highlighted in the dramatic foreground, it is the strains of sexual politics that create the deeper dramatic form. This dramatic form is generated not by the text of the libretto but by Mozart's treatment, through the musical development of character and the control of pace and emphasis. The manipulative woman who gets her way by clandestine machination is a common stereotype. This, though, is not how Susanna is portrayed. Whereas the woman who fits the stereotype derives her enjoyment from meddling simply for the sake of the exercise of power involved, Susanna is revealed acting as she does in order to retain her autonomy and, hence, control over her own life. Her status and circumstances dictate that she pursues her plans by indirection. For her, scheming is a necessary means and not an end in itself. She emerges from the opera as its most sympathetic character. As such, she is the composer's creation.

Here there is a complex interplay between two structures. The foreground plan is governed by conventions and traditions (social, as well as dramatic and musical); the background structure places Susanna at the opera's heart and provides a dimension that takes the work to a different level. This *musical* form, I have been arguing, is no less a *dramatic* form, created by Mozart. The success of the opera depends on Mozart's breathing life into the work's characters, for there could be no formal alternative to the surface formula—that is, to the mechanical unfolding of the narrative along boring because predictable lines.

Così revealed

Given what has been argued above, it might be expected that *Così* continues the trend established in *Don Giovanni* and *Figaro*, with Mozart achieving a musico-dramatic form

---

[7] For a more detailed analysis than I offer here, see Davies (2003: ch. 13).

through the development of character and action, thereby going beyond the surface of stock characters and formulaic plot. Indeed, this is what I will now argue.

In effect, *Così* is a chamber opera with only six characters. The symmetry between the three pairs of men and women allows for a nicely balanced number of duets. Everything *seems* to happen on the surface and it is easy to view the lovers as mirror-image pairs gavotting through the obvious permutations. *Così* offers nothing so throat rattling as is found in *Don Giovanni* nor so politically pointed as occurs in *Figaro*. It has a delicacy and subtlety, easily mistaken for effete refinement and fatuousness, which befits its subject, that being human character and relationships rather than the supernatural or blunt sexual politics.

As I hear it, *Così* is about nothing more complicated (and about nothing less important) than difference and similarity, individuality and community, among people.[8] On the surface, it is about couples (men, women, men and women) that mirror each other's images, so that members of the pair might be interchangeable. Despina vies with Alfonso in her cynicism about the other sex; Fiordiligi and Gugliemo match the depth of their love against that of Dorabella and Ferrando; Gugliemo competes with Ferrando as a seducer; Fiordiligi rivals Dorabella in her attraction for her new, honey-tongued suitor; Ferrando is not to be outdone by the complacent arrogance of Gugliemo in assuming the undying commitment of his love's faithfulness; and so on. Yet at this level, the characters can be no more than cartoon-like. They become more than that, though, and the opera is more than a collection of clichés, because each individual is distinctively characterized by Mozart. The opera really would be silly if we could not take seriously the love the couples share for each other at the beginning, and we could not take those loves seriously if there could be no sense of each person's difference from the others. Mozart is at pains to make these characters separate while, at the same time, conceding and playing on their many similarities. Dorabella is more adventurous, more flighty, more easily led, more 'romantic' than Fiordiligi, and when Fiordiligi commits herself she does so with a depth and seriousness Dorabella lacks. Gugliemo is the more bitter in betrayal; Ferrando the more superficial. Ferrando is as much like Dorabella, and Gugliemo as much like Fiordiligi, as either is like the other. While Alfonso and Despina might both be cynics, Despina has a cheerful warm-heartedness contrasting with Alfonso's world-weariness. All this, and more, is established primarily by Mozart's musical treatment, I claim. In their arias (especially) and in the duets, each character receives a distinctive musical personality.

The surface reveals a difference between the sexes—it is the men who are betrayed in their affections by the women. But not far below the surface is the message that the betrayal, if such it is, is mutual, for the men play their lovers false in regarding affections as gifts that might be trifled with, and in risking for the sake of their self-esteem the

---

[8] A psychologically more complex characterization might be developed, for the opera is equally about the interplay between reason and sentiment, and the balance between the two necessary in a person's character if that person is to be capable of achieving happiness through interpersonal relations.

relationships they had achieved. If women are thus—'così fan tutte'—then men are so, and all have been shown wanting but as no less deserving of love for that fact. If women have a capacity for serious love, they might also love more than one man. If men take conceited pride in being loved, they might also endanger the love they receive. And if such features of human psychology are identified and accepted for what they are, a happy union between the sexes is possible. Their recognition depends on awareness not only of the potential faults of the other and forgiving acceptance of these but as well, on an acknowledgment of one's own weaknesses. What is needed is knowledge of others as they are, of oneself, and of the human frailty all share.

Earlier I mentioned that the finale coming in the middle of the *opera buffa* pits the protagonists against the antagonists, with the former in danger of succumbing to the latter. In *Figaro*, Susanna, Rosina, and Figaro are opposed by the Count, Marcellina, Bartolo, and Basilio. In *Don Giovanni*, the Don, as anti-hero, and Leporello, by association, are under attack from Anna, Elvira, Zerlina, Ottavio, and Masetto. The situation in *Così* is instructively different. Alfonso and Despina function as catalysts, not as the lovers' enemies. Instead, Dorabella and Fiordiligi are torn between holding to their pledges and offering comfort to the attractive strangers who (apparently) have taken poison because their affections have not been returned. Meanwhile, Gugliemo and Ferrando devalue the women's seriousness both with their inner light-heartedness, born of misplaced confidence and arrogance, and their outer histrionics. As revealed here, the enemy lies within, not without.

There could be no clearer indication that the danger to be confronted follows from the absence of self-awareness and mutual comprehension. Insofar as *Così* has a deep structure underlying and informing the patina of public action and dramatic form, as I have claimed is true for *Don Giovanni* and *Figaro*, it is one echoing and reflecting on, while transforming, that surface. The public display of love, disguise, rejection, deception, defeat, exposure, forgiveness, and reconciliation is matched by a psychological journey through which each learns of the desires, attitudes, capacities, and potential present within themselves as well as others. They respond ultimately to these revelations with acceptance and mutual forbearance. The opera ends not with protagonists triumphing over antagonists but with the four main characters coming to appreciate their own virtues and vices, as well as those of others, thereby laying a more secure foundation for rewarding, mutually appreciative, and informed interpersonal relationships. The wheel turns full circle, so that, on the surface, one returns to the point at which the work begins, but the psychological drama created and forwarded in Mozart's music reveals, by contrast, just how far the protagonists have traveled and grown in their understanding of themselves and others.

The point of the quartet

How do the above reflections provide an insight into the apparently anomalous treatment of the canon quartet in *Così*? Pace and action is not all. As I wrote earlier, the action freezes for the sake of the quartet. Similar moments are found also in *Figaro*—the trio ('Da questo momento') in the finale of Act II—and *Don Giovanni*—the trio ('Protegga il giusto cielo') in the finale of Act I. Such passages are the more striking for the fact that their occurrence suspends the inexorable dramatic drive established previously. They transcend the context of the moment. They go beyond the platitudinous moral presented by tradition at the *opera buffa*'s conclusion. These quiescent passages are reserved for statements that are oblique and personal, I think. They serve as pointers, I claim, to the dramatic significance of the works' underlying musical structures.

In 'Da questo momento' in *Figaro*, the Count, Rosina and Susanna sing of the importance of the Count's learning to appreciate his wife's love. The general theme of the need for, and appropriateness of, respect for the integrity of others as individuals informs the work's structure. 'Protegga il giusto cielo,' in *Don Giovanni*, involves a prayer to powers above, implying that protection from the evil abroad in the world can be afforded only by forces of good not available to earthly characters. This encapsulates the theme that underpins and generates the overall bow structure of the opera, as described earlier.

The canon quartet in *Così* is to be appreciated in a similar fashion, I hold. The proposed toast advocates one's leaving behind the sorrow and regrets of the past. That thought, shared by Fiordiligi, Dorabella, and Ferrando, sets the emotional tone for the disentangling of the plot that follows, yet Gugliemo, who is as much a member of the quartet as the others, remains irreducibly an individual within the structure. How better to reveal in microcosm the subject animating the opera, which sets against the inescapable autonomy of the individual the common need for mutual acceptance and recognition? Had Gugliemo's part been assimilated to the rest, such as might have occurred in a strict canon introduced later when he also comes to accept the situation, that message would have been lost.

To return to the beginning: the suggestion that the dramatic context explains why Gugliemo does not take his part in presenting the canon's theme turns out to be correct, after all, but the route to this conclusion, if its significance is to be grasped, is a much longer one than normally is supposed. This is because the quartet draws attention to the structure that brings life to the stock characters and formulaic patterns in terms of which the particular work conforms to the general type. That structure, which is at the one time both musical and dramatic as a result of the composer's control of action and character in the music, lies below the apparent surface. If that deeper structure is harder to discern in *Così* than are its equivalents in *Figaro* and *Don Giovanni*, this is because it more obviously imitates the surface pattern, the better to point up the moral and social significance of the tale when it is enacted by individuals invested by the musical treatment with genuine feeling and rounded characters.

10

Perceiving Melodies

In this chapter I draw comparisons between the visual perception of objects and events and the audible perception of music. I consider the fact that observers can identify objects presented at different orientations and that they can frequently identify an item as the same despite changes in its appearance, for example by ageing. I argue that these cases are paralleled in music listening. Thematic ideas can (sometimes, but not inevitably) be recognized when they are inverted or played backwards. In addition, within music it is crucial that various musical statements, including ones that differ in their intervallic sequence, are sometimes recognized as versions of a single theme.

Retrogrades and inversions

We are capable of recognizing items when they are presented to us at different orientations and distances. At least, we can do so unless their three-dimensional shape is highly irregular. If I can identify a paperclip in one orientation, I can probably also identify it when it is turned through 90°. If I can recognize you in full face, chances are that I can do the same when you are in profile.[1] Apparently we are similarly skilled with temporally extended events or processes, though this is unexpected given that the opportunity to apply this talent did not exist before the invention of visual playback technologies (such as flipcards or motion cameras). It is amusingly strange to see the runners sprint energetically backward to arrive together with extraordinary precision at their starting blocks, yet the scene is visually coherent. And having seen the race the one way, it is likely one can re-identify it when it is shown the other.

These initial claims should be qualified, of course. Many things have a top and a bottom, as it were, and when they are presented the wrong way up, they can be harder to identify or details of their appearance can be harder to register. This applies to things such as horses and trees, and, with more importance, also to faces. Note that facial recognition employs parts of the brain—in particular, the fusiform gyrus in the

---

First published as part of 'Perceiving Melodies and Perceiving Musical Colors,' *Review of Philosophy and Psychology*, 1 (2010): 19–39.

[1] For discussion of psychological models of visual recognition, see Tarr and Bülthoff 1998. Pinker (1998: 274–84) considers the mental rotation of objects in perception, along with issues such as handedness and mirroring.

occipitemporal cortex—not activated when other objects are visually located and identified. The face inversion effect (also known as expressional transfiguration or the Thatcher illusion), in which inverted faces with non-inverted eyes are not regarded as distorted until turned the right way up, possibly arises because inverted faces are processed by the object-recognition neural system, not by the facial-recognition one (Rothstein et al. 2001, Solso 2003). Another, similar case is that of printing or writing, which becomes unreadable for most people when presented in mirror image.[2]

Music is an art of time, both in that the temporal order of events is specified (which distinguishes it from paintings, parts of which can be inspected in any order) and that the rate of progression is specified (which distinguishes it from novels).[3]

Can musical items, such as melodies, be recognized when played backward, inverted, or both?

Before addressing this question, I need to specify what is involved in backward playing. When a tape of music is reversed, the result often is very alien. This outcome is as much to do with the reversal of each note as the reversal of the note sequence. Notes have an attack and a decay that is usually characteristic of the musical instrument that sounds them. A note played on a piano has a sharp, percussive onset and the sound rapidly dies, whereas the same note on an organ has a more sibilant onset and is sustained at the same strength for as long as the note lasts. Because of this, when a tape of a piano is played backward, it sounds more peculiar than a reversed tape of an organ playing the same piece.[4] As well as the note sequence, timbral features are reversed as well. To take this effect out of the equation, the question about backward playing is best understood as asking about the case in which the note order of a melodic line is reversed and these notes then are played forward, in the normal manner.[5]

Material in musical works is frequently treated in retrograde (backward), inversion (mirror image), or retrograde inversion.[6] An early instance is in the thirteenth-century *clausula, Nusmido*, the tenor of which has the liturgical melody 'Dominus' in retrograde motion (Apel 1966). Another famous example is Guillaume de Machaut's fourteenth-century riddle canon *My end is my beginning*. Mozart wrote jest canons where two players simultaneously read from opposite sides of the same sheet of music, with the result that one part is the retrograde inversion of the other.

---

[2] Obviously this skill can be acquired, however. Typesetters from the era of movable type had to read reverse lettering. Etching and engraving also is done in mirror image.

[3] For further discussion, see Alperson (1980), Levinson and Alperson (1991).

[4] In a personal communication, Robin Maconie offers this description of the sound of the reversed note: 'the reversed sound of course consists of an initial radiance that is room resonance that condenses into a more structured and dynamic body of sound that races back and is guillotined with a sense of physical violence at the speaker.'

[5] I ignore other factors counting against the musical sense of backwardly directed music; for instance, that rhythms do not always retrograde in a perceptually predictable manner (see Gjerdingen 1993).

[6] The term 'cancrizan' is also used for retrograde, but more often refers to a canon where the *comes* is the *dux* played backward.

Inversion of thematic material is even more common than retrogrades. Inversion is employed in all kinds of music, including in the development sections of Classical and Romantic sonata-form movements. Arnold Schoenberg drew attention to the enduring use of such techniques in justifying the important role they play in the twelve-tone (also known as dodecaphonic) system of musical composition he developed in the 1920s.

We should be careful how we interpret the ubiquity of such compositional devices, however. Frequently, these are bits of technical craft, self-amusement, or intellectual challenge that are not intended to be audible (see Chapter 7 and Davies 1994a: 356–60). It is not uncommon for composers to labor under self-imposed constraints that motivate how the work is to proceed, without the operation of these constraints being, or being intended to be, audible in the music that results. Consider Anton Webern's Symphony, Op. 21 of 1928. The twelve-note row has a palindromic structure, with a tritone between the sixth and seventh note. As a result, the retrograde of the row is equivalent to its inversion. The first movement proceeds by inverted canon, with the second half of the movement a retrograde of the first. The second and final movement is a double canon by retrograde motion. The tight integration of the row's structure and of the movements' overall mirror forms may explain the listener's awareness of the work's unity, if that is how she experiences the piece (Davies 2003: ch. 14). Few if any listeners, however, can follow the music's unfolding in terms of its overarching canons and mirror structures, as Nicholas Cook (1987b), who describes the work as a 'hall of mirrors,' demonstrated with his Cambridge music students.[7]

Nevertheless, it is plain that sometimes composers do intend their listeners to follow inversions and retrogrades and that most listeners can do so where this is the case. If they are to be subject to audible inversion and retrograde treatments, usually comparatively short motives or themes with a distinctive character are used. Of the two practices, most people find inversions easier to recognize than retrogrades and retrogrades easier than retrograde inversions (Dowling 1972). Probably the most famous examples of more or less audible piece-length inversion are the mirror fugues in J. S. Bach's *Art of Fugue*. Number Twelve is a fugue for four voices of 56 measures. Within the fugue, the main theme and its accompaniments are frequently inverted, but the miracle is that the entire fugue is designed to be also playable in inversion. The same applies to the three-voice fugue that follows. Large-scale, academic, twentieth-century studies featuring similar techniques include Paul Hindemith's *Ludus Tonalis* and Dmitri Shostakovitch's Twenty-four Preludes and Fugues, Op. 87.

---

[7] Krumhansl et al. (1987) show that some musically trained listeners can follow the row's transformation in two chamber pieces by Schoenberg. This need not invalidate Cook's findings, however, because Webern's treatment of the material is deliberately less traditionally melodic than Schoenberg's. Interestingly, rhesus monkeys recognize diatonic melodies when these are transposed at the octave (but not at the fifth), yet do not recognize atonal melodies transposed at the octave (Wright et al. 2000). Also, human babies react positively to diatonic melodies and turn away from atonal ones (Trehub et al. 1990). Such experiments suggest that neural encodings of tonal and atonal melodies are fundamentally different.

So, the visual capacity that allows us to recognize an object in different spatial orientations is sometimes paralleled by the (limited) aural capacity to hear inversions and retrogrades in musical events.

Melodic transformation

A second dimension of visual recognition is the capacity to recognize individuals despite changes to their appearances. An observer might identify a house as the same though it has undergone an extensive restoration. (Assume it is not re-identified in terms of its location, but only in terms of its appearance.) In the most dramatic case, a person might recognize a friend she has not seen for many years, though he has aged in his appearance in the meantime. Note that children as young as three years of age realize that modification to the appearance of a living thing does not indicate a change in its kind (Humphrey 1976, Keil 1994).

The aural equivalent of this phenomenon is of the utmost importance to the way music is created and followed. A theme can retain its identity despite undergoing various changes. Among the most common manipulations are alterations to the instrumentation, accompaniment, tempo, and rhythmic articulation of the theme. The *Ode to Joy* melody undergoes each of these modifications in the last movement of Beethoven's Ninth Symphony. Other regularly used options include elaboration by decoration, alteration of harmonies, and changes in meter.

Now, it might be thought that the melody survives such changes because they do not modify what is crucial to its identity, which is the pattern of the interval sequence that shapes it. But, surprisingly, this too can be amended or interrupted without loss of identity. The sardonic rendition of the *Star Spangled Banner* given by Jimi Henrix at Woodstock would have had no point were listeners unable to identify the anthem as such, which of course they can, despite Hendrix's interpolations.[8] Meanwhile, the melody for Richard Rodgers' *Climb Ev'ry Mountain* appears to have an *AABA* structure. Though rhythmically the same, the last statement of the *A* part is very different from the first two, however. It begins in the dominant (unlike the first two statements, which begin in the tonic) and the third phrase is modified significantly to ensure a return to the tonic. The re-identification of this closing passage as a version of the opening *A*s seems foundational to an appreciation of the song's structure. And in fact, many listeners who identify the last *A* as such are probably unaware that it differs from the earlier ones.[9] To take another case, Gustav Mahler achieves a similar result in the slow movement of his Symphony No. 1, when he renders the nursery round *Bruder Martin* in a funereal minor, apparently in reference to the childhood death of his brother. In fact, the survival of a melody's identity in shifts from the major to minor

---

[8] I consider this case in Davies (2001a: 57–8). Clarke (2005: ch. 2) offers a detailed discussion and transcription of Hendrix's performance.

[9] Jonathan McKeown-Green drew my attention to the form of this song.

is crucial to the structural integrity of sonata-form movements in the minor key. In them, the second subject appears in the relative major in the exposition and in the tonic minor in the recapitulation, which almost inevitably involves alteration to the pattern of intervals. The structure would be turned to nonsense if listeners could not detect the same theme in these tonally contrasting versions. And it is not only in Western music that the identity of a melody can display this kind of intervallic flexibility. Simha Arom (1997) observes that several central African cultures recognize a melody as the same despite changes in interval sizes from the original.

The generation of structure in music depends no less on melodies that remain recognizable as they are elaborated than on contrast between different melodies. Consider the structural types that make a feature of preserving a theme's identity through processes transforming its surface: theme and variation, chaconne, passacaglia, along with da capo and simple binary forms in which the material is decorated when repeated. Almost all kinds of prolonged musical structures involve aurally appreciable thematic alteration or development as well as repetition and contrast. Melodic inversion, for example, is rarely strict (or 'real'), since this is likely to destroy tonality; inversion usually is 'tonal,' which is to say that not all the intervals are preserved when inverted. Similarly, sequential passages—for example, in which a melodic figuration is repeated on successive steps of the scale—are also usually 'tonal.' In other words, the scale acts as a constraint on how the intervals are preserved (or not), because the major and minor scales themselves are neither evenly stepped nor symmetrical.

Described in the broadest terms, the mechanism of recognition must be like this: some representation of a musical item is stored with links to processing rules, frames, or grammars that are subsequently applied to new sensory inputs to determine if they count as the same, which they may do even if they deviate in some respects from the sensible features of earlier statements. This process of comparing what is stored with current inputs need not be accessible to consciousness. Perhaps we are aware only of its outcome, which is a feeling of recognition or a disposition to judge what is heard as the same as something encountered previously. Some of the processing rules that come into play will be relevant to all kinds of music (Higgins 2006). These may include organizational principles that apply equally to melodies in, say, British and Chinese musics (Schellenberg 1996). Others will be local to the style or genre (see Dowling and Harwood 1986). Yet others may reveal the distinctive fingerprint of the composer or be confined even to individual works.

As just implied, the inputs to the process of comparison involve more than the melodies that are heard. They include awareness of contextual features—concerning the work's style and genre, say—that should affect what processing rules are to be applied. The provenance of the music is also relevant. For instance, within a work we might properly judge melody B to be a variant of an earlier melody, A, whereas if B occurred in a quite distinct work, we would acknowledge only a superficial resemblance between B and A. Or again, knowing that one composer was influenced by or referred to the work of another, we might rightly find melodic variants of the one work in the other where otherwise we would not do so. That is, the persistence of melodic identity through alteration is not determined solely in terms of absolute measures of similarity. What kinds or degrees of matching should be given salience in the judgment of melodic sameness and, hence, what processing rules should be applied, requires sensitivity to the character and genesis of the music in question.

We know quite a lot about the processing rules in terms of which we track and make sense of music's progress. We perceive the unfolding of music through a framework of expectations (for continuation, closure, direction of movement, and so on) that comprise a generative grammar (Lerdahl and Jackendoff 1983), or rules for gestalt processing (Meyer 1956, Narmour 1990, 1992, Schellenberg 1997), or general principles of auditory organization (Bregman 1990), as well as through stylistic and other invariant features (Dowling and Harwood 1986).

There is less certainty, however, about the mode of mental representation of musical items such as melodies, and how we get from such representations to judgments of similarity or identity when melodies display different pitch sequences. The absolute pitch of a tone is apparently held in a specialized memory store, and interference takes place between pitches inside this store (Deutsch 1999). In that case, perhaps we cannot remember closely enough what has gone before to make melodic identifications more precise. And something similar may apply when we recall not absolute pitches but sequences of intervals. If, as speculated earlier, many listeners are not aware of any differences when they identify the last part of the melody of *Climb Ev'ry Mountain* as the same as the first two, it appears that they cannot accurately recall the interval sequence heard earlier. Still, the recollection of interval sequences of many musical listeners often seems to be robust—they do hear differences between the opening phrases and the final phrase of *Climb Ev'ry Mountain*, though they rightly identify these as different versions of the same phrase—so memory failure is an unlikely basis for all our judgments of melodic sameness.

Perhaps what is stored is a mental representation of some melodic abstraction that is more vague, inexplicit, and gappy than any of its instances. It records some common core in terms of which different instances are recognized as the same. In this vein, J. B. Davies (1979) argues that listeners abstract from interval sequences to a more general configuration, and this explains, he says, how they can recognize melodies in which the interval sequence is not accurately preserved. Similarly, Emmanuel Bigand (1990) demonstrates that listeners successfully group melodies by abstracting to underlying melodic structures.

If this theory is plausible, the abstract Ur-melody must be less explicitly articulated than any of the various, concrete soundings co-identified as instancing it, yet it must be distinctive enough in its invariant features to reflect the huge diversity of non-identical melodies that we acknowledge. While any individual theme—*Happy Birthday*, say, or the melody of Bach's *Musical Offering*—can be presented and recognized in many guises, still there is a vast number of non-identical, individual themes, and if these are represented mentally in terms of Ur-melodies, there would have to be as many of these as there are distinguishable (families of) themes.[10]

For vision, an equivalent theory would hold that the visual recognition of objects involves detecting their invariant features (see Gibson 1968).

An alternative to the theory just discussed describes the mental representation that is stored as being of a detailed melody. Depending on one's view, what is stored could be the representation of an actually heard instance, with the melody's first unequivocal statement the most likely candidate, or what is stored could be the representation of a prototype that is derived from the instance or instances that are encountered. This prototype is no less detailed than its heard instances.[11] Alternatively, the prototype might differ from all the instances that are presented.[12] In either case, the judgment that a new tune is a variant of a previously heard melody involves, rather than abstraction to what they share in common, the application of rules for detecting equivalence that compare the sensory input with the stored melody (or melodic prototype). These rules spell out the kinds and degrees of transformation that are consistent with identity preservation. In this vein, Lawrence Zbikowski (2002), who applies prototype-based theories of recognition to music, suggests that we recognize the sameness of the varied statements of, for example, a Wagnerian leitmotiv, because we conceive them under a single 'cognitive category' that spells out the patterns and weightings of the relationships that unite them.

For vision, an equivalent theory would hold that the experience of appearance identity depends on the closeness of the relation between what is seen and its mentally represented prototype (Rosch 1975, Barsalou 1992).

These two models have different implications concerning both the mode of mental representation for musical items and the kinds of processing to which such representations are subject when recognition occurs.[13] Which of them is correct for the case of melodic recognition? Notice that neither leaves room for consideration of contextual

---

[10] Narmour (1992) identifies sixteen melodic archetypes that can combine to form some 200 complex structures that, in turn, can chain together in a theoretically infinite number of ways. Just as the archetypes are higher-level abstractions than the 200 complex structures, the 200 complex structures must be higher-level abstractions than the Ur-melodies I am describing.

[11] Indeed, the prototype could be more detailed if it is stored in tempo and pitch space as a rich and complex structure, so that when we identify an instance of the melody we find that it is equivalent to a slice of the prototype through tempo and pitch space. Such a prototype is far more detailed than any of the slices that intersect with it.

[12] The need to consider this possibility is suggested by an experiment in which listeners were presented with a number of variants based on an unsounded theme. When later asked to identify, from a series of themes they had not heard previously, their degree of relatedness to the set they had heard, listeners picked the unsounded theme as the most closely related (Welker 1982). A similar result for facial recognition was earlier demonstrated in Solso and McCarthy (1981). Their subjects mistakenly identified the prototype face as having been seen previously and were more confident of this than they were for any of the derivative faces that were actually shown. See also Franks and Bransford (1971).

[13] For discussion of some relevant factors, see Schulkind et al. (2003) and for reviews of brain imagining studies of musical memory and familiarity, see Platel et al. (2004), along with Platel et al. (1997), Peretz and Zatorre (2005).

factors that I earlier mentioned as relevant, such as whether the comparison of melodies is within or between works, and for the latter case, whether there is reason to take resemblances merely as coincidental or as deliberately contrived. In empirical studies, it is common to factor out the influence of situational and historically conditioned features, either by presenting melodic fragments acontextually or by assuming contextual factors are invariant. By shelving consideration of such issues, neither theory can be entirely adequate.

There are empirical data favoring the first theory, according to which listeners abstract from the shape of melodic details to broad contours. For instance, W. Jay Dowling (1972) found no evidence that his experimental subjects distinguished between melodic transformations that preserve the exact interval relationships and those that preserve only the relevant melodic contour. Dowling and Dane Harwood (1986) regard melodic perception and memory as relying on schemata and invariants. And Robin Maconie (2002: 84) describes a thematic catalog invented by Denys Parsons based on contour alone: 'remarkably, he found that it is possible to identify the start or incipit of a famous tune or theme (the part people remember best) by the changes of direction encoded in a relatively short sequence, with an asterisk for the first note. For example, Burt Bacharach's song 'Raindrops Keep Falling on my Head' is expressed as the sequence: *RRUDD DUDUR RUDD.' Likewise, Mark Schmuckler (1999) established that listeners rely on global shape information when identifying melodic shapes as similar.

Equally, though, when the full gamut of melodic features—not just contour but also phrasal, scalar, and tonal context, coupled with stress, duration, rhythm, timbre, and meter—are taken into account, recognition becomes faster and more accurate (Huron 2001). Albert Bregman acknowledges (1990: 467) the relevance of all such factors, not contour alone, when he suggests: 'we may mentally encode any sequence by the nature of the transformations that take place in it. When a succession of tones are all of the same type (for example, periodic sounds with similar timbres), we may encode it not by a categorization of the individual sounds but by an encoding of the changes or movements that take us from one sound to the next.' Alexandra Lamont and Nicola Dibben (2001) found that similarities recognized between different parts of a musical work are based on dynamics, articulation, and texture, as well as contour. The fact that the addition of detail speeds recognition and makes it more accurate should favor the second theory over the first, because one would expect the addition of potentially relevant detail to slow and distract reductive or abstractive modes of processing.

Perhaps the question about which theory is correct should be put aside, however, because they need not be exclusive. Modes of representation and processing that match both theories could take place. Stephen McAdams and Daniel Matzkin (2001) identify three kinds of similarity perceived between musical ideas—in the statistical distribution of surface values and their derivatives, in specific patterns of attributes, and in structural invariants. The first and third of these suggest that abstraction is involved whereas the second comes closer to the idea that what is represented is a detailed instance or prototype. And other studies emphasize the relevance for melodic recognition both of global melodic contour and of specific details of accent, phrase location, and so on (for example, see Schulkind et al. 2003).

In any case, the visual capacity to recognize persisting identities through changes in visual appearance is matched by an aural equivalent in the musical case. Indeed, the very existence of all but the shortest musical pieces seems to be predicated on this ability.

11
Musical Colors and Timbral Sonicism

In this chapter I compare instrumental timbre with visual colors and explain that timbres are experienced as properties of the instruments from which they issue. We hear in and through musical sounds the actions that go into their making. We conceive of music in terms of the actions of the performer, who bodies forth sound from the instrument, and of the listener, as she is entrained by the music, and even of the music, as we experience its internal, purely musical progress as analogous to human action or narrative construction. This counts against the position in musical ontology known as 'timbral sonicism,' according to which all that is necessary for the faithful rendition of a work with definitively specified instrumentation is a sounding as of the indicated instruments, which may be synthesized without using any of the specified instruments.

Timbre and the production of sound

In this section I consider the comparison between timbre and color. I argue against the view that timbre is solely a property of sounds and for an alternative that regards timbres as properties of musical sound-makers.

Timbre is that property of sound that makes the difference between the phenomenological character of the auditory experience of two different instruments, a trumpet and violin say, when they are sustaining a note of the same pitch at the same volume (amplitude). When a note of fixed pitch is sounded, as well as the fundamental (the pitch that is heard), overtones sound. They derive from the natural harmonic series, though additional overtone 'noise' can also occur. The pitch distribution of the overtones of the natural harmonic series is fixed relative to the pitch of the fundamental, but the comparative strength of the individual overtones is variable. It is differences in which of the overtones are included and in their relative strengths that are experienced by the listener as the sound's timbre. For example, non-vibrato unforced tones in the flute's midrange lack practically all but the first overtone (which sounds at the octave).

The material amalgamated in this chapter was first published as part of 'Perceiving Melodies and Perceiving Musical Colors,' *Review of Philosophy and Psychology*, 1 (2010): 19–39 and 'Musical Works and Orchestral Colour,' *British Journal of Aesthetics*, 48 (2008): 363–75. For a response, see Dodd (2010).

As with all musical instruments, however, the relative weight of the flute's overtones varies characteristically with the pitch of the fundamental across the instrument's range, the note's volume, and other factors.[1] Only the even-numbered overtones are prominent in the clarinet in its lowest few notes, but other registers of the instrument display a different acoustic profile, yet one that is equally characteristic of the clarinet. All the overtones, with the third, fourth, and fifth prominent, give low notes on the oboe their pungent tone. And the violin is unusual in that the fundamental is very weak in relation to the strongest overtones. In general, the stronger the first overtone relative to others, the more warm, soft, and mellow is the timbre, while if mid overtones are strong, the timbre is correspondingly bright, hard, and strident.

Fundamentals without overtones do not occur normally, though tuning forks and the stopped diapason of the organ come very close. Such fundamentals can be produced electronically, however. The waveform for such a tone is represented on an oscilloscope as a pure sine wave, whereas that of a tone mixed with overtones has a more complex and irregular structure. One might make the case for describing the 'pure' tone as without a timbre. I prefer to describe it as having its own timbre, however, because it has a distinctive phenomenal character. The debate, should one pursue it, might be reminiscent of that concerning whether black is to be classed as a color. In any case, one of the most common synesthetic designations for timbre is that of color. Works have an instrumental color according to their orchestration.[2]

The timbre of a tone can be affected by the medium of transmission—water as against air, for instance—and by the environment—curtains absorb relatively more of higher than lower frequency harmonics. (Also relevant are the relative distance and direction of the sound source and, if it is in motion, the pace and direction of this.) In the case of musical instruments, timbre can be controlled to some extent by the player. For example, there are subtle differences in timbre for string instruments between bowing over the fingerboard or close to the bridge, and playing open as opposed to stopped strings. As well, there are not-so-subtle differences, such as those between stopped notes and harmonics (where the string is touched at a node without being depressed to the fingerboard), between bowed and plucked notes, or between the standard and muted modes. (A stringed instrument is muted by having a clamp placed on its bridge.) Of course, singers can modulate the timbre of their voices by controlling the body as resonator: for example, by 'moving' the sound forward or backward in the

---

[1] For technical discussion of these and other considerations with respect to timbre, see Cogan and Escot (1976: 326–401), Meyer (1978), Handel (1995), Risset and Wessel (1999). For a more general introduction, see Dowling and Harwood (1986: ch. 3).

[2] Some individuals have synesthetic color experiences of sounds, a phenomenon sometimes called psychochromasthesia. In other words, they experience sound as colored. (Olivier Messiaen claimed to be a color-sound synesthete and Alexander Scriabin is widely but probably erroneously identified as a color-sound synesthete.) The sounds in question may be phonemes or musical keys, as well as the timbres of instruments. For neuro-physiological accounts of synesthesia, see Critchley (1977), Cytowic (1989, 1993), Marks et al. (1987). For detailed discussion of synesthesia with respect to music, see Merriam (1964: ch. 5), Wiseman and Zilczer (2005), Higgins (2012: ch. 5).

throat. Indeed, opera singers make their voices stand out over the orchestral texture by producing what is called the 'singing formant,' which they achieve by enlarging the pharynx cavity and lowering the glottis to alter the vocal spectrum so as to emphasize overtones in the range 2,500–3,500 Hertz (Sunberg 1977, Bregman 1990: 491). As well, there are differences between individual instruments of the same type: not only between an unmodified eighteenth-century cello and its modern counterpart, say, but also between different modern cellos. Finally, instrumental timbres can be mimicked by electronic sound synthesizers (or by a modern speaker through which a recording of the instruments is played).

Despite the observations just listed—namely, an instrument's timbre can vary according to how it is used, different instruments of the same kind can display discernibly different timbres, and an instrument's timbre can be mimicked electronically or in other ways—we seem to regard timbres as properties of musical instrument types and of voices, not merely as properties of sounds taken apart from the kinds of resonators from which they originate.[3] No doubt this tendency reflects the long historical association between timbres and the activation of particular types of sound sources. Until very recently, the only way of hearing notes with the unique sound quality of a nightingale, including the inimitable timbral distinctions by pitch bands across the range of its song, was by listening to a nightingale. And we are not indifferent to the fact that singing issues from an opening in a person's head.

Where the instruments in question are the human singing voice or other humanly made musical instruments, the connection becomes normative, not merely associative (Davies 2001a: 64–5). In other words, the connection is not simply ingrained; rather, we conceive of the sound in terms of its source and vice versa. It is not that the cor anglais just happens to make a sound with a certain timbre, but instead that that sound is the sound of a cor anglais, is what it should and is intended to produce, is integral, for instance, to the kind of expressiveness of which the cor anglais is capable. Instruments of these kinds are intended to display the timbral qualities associated with their types, and employing them to do so is part of the regulative ideal that informs their use.

Even if timbres are conceived in terms of the singing voice and of kinds of musical instruments in the manner that was just suggested, what is their connection to music and its works? If we return to the comparison with color and then consider the role of color in pictorial depiction, we might develop an analogy with paintings according to which, while timbre might be a work-constitutive property in some musical works, in many it is not. For the latter cases, the work's instrumentation is incidental to its

---

[3] I allow that the notion of a musical instrument here must be taken broadly; for instance to include, as well as the sirens of police cars, the New Guinea tribe that use their mouths as resonators for the tone of the drone beetle they insert there (Fisher 1994). And I include among the voiced creatures non-human animals, such as birds and whales, that often produce clearly pitched tones and glissandi, and have voices with distinctive timbres.

identity. Later I will challenge these conclusions, but let us first see how the argument works.

Traditionally, colors have been regarded as accidents that do not contribute to the identity of the items that bear them. If I paint my house yellow where before it was blue, it remains the same house, though now differently colored. This view might be extended even to pictorial representations. Supposing what is essential to the identities of pictorial representations is their depictive content, or more generally their formal structure, if these would remain discernible were the picture's paints transformed from color to black, white, and shades of gray, then the work's colors cannot be regarded as relevant to its identity.

We might challenge the initial assumption, that only content and form are relevant to a painting's identity. It is arguable that other factors, such as the work's art-historical provenance and genre, are no less important. Among these other factors is the work's medium and, where pigmented paint is used, color is an element in that.

And even if the initial assumption is tolerated, there is reason to hesitate before accepting the conditional. There are a number of paintings in which color does play a structural role or otherwise affects the depicted content. Many impressionist and pointillist works fall in the former category. The depictive character and formal structures of Claude Monet's water lilies and Georges Seurat's *La Grande Jatte* would suffer from the works' decolorization. Secondly, colors play an important iconographic role, especially in religious paintings where they are associated with particular people or characteristics. Blue for example was reserved for the gown of the Virgin, because apart from any symbolism it was also very expensive to make out of lapis lazuli.

Though these first two points perhaps apply only to a minority of paintings, two further considerations suggest color is far from irrelevant to a painting's depictive or formal character. Color often is vitally involved in organizing the represented space. For instance, artists have long known that distant items are not only smaller and less distinct than near replicas but also bluer; the shorter wavelengths at the blue end of the spectrum penetrate the atmosphere to greater distances than the longer red wavelength. Colors interact according to their area, contrast, complementarity, saturation, hue, and brightness to produce spatial and other effects, such as mixing or scintillation. For example, reds and oranges advance whereas violets and blues recede, areas of high and low brightness are respectively brighter and darker when juxtaposed, larger areas appear brighter and more saturated than otherwise identical smaller patches, and so on. Finally, where they produce realistic appearances, colors contribute to a painting's representational verisimilitude. And where they depart from realistic appearances, as in works by Vincent Van Gogh or André Derain, colors often make an expressive contribution to the work.[4] One would expect the degree of its verisimilitude and its expressive qualities to count among a depiction's identifying features.

---

[4] Unrealistic colors (red grass) in paintings do not stimulate the color region of the brain the same way as do realistic colors (red blood) (Zeki 1999).

Color can also contribute symbolic and other associations relevant to recognizing and appreciating the work's content. For example, consider Garry Neill Kennedy's *Figure Paintings* (1984), a wall painting of five gray-colored regions labeled, 'Fig. 1,' 'Fig. 2,' etc. The grays in Figures 2, 4, and 5 are indistinguishable.

Kennedy's notes for the work, which are posted nearby, read:

> *Fig. 1* paint used to cover ships of the Canadian Navy.
> *Fig. 2* paint used to cover ships of the USA Navy.
> *Fig. 3* paint used to cover ships of the Mexican Navy.
> *Fig. 4* mixture of *Figures 1* and *2* in quantities proportional to the amounts required to paint the fleets of Canada and USA.
> *Fig. 5* mixture of *Figures 2* and *3* in quantities proportional to the amounts required to paint the fleets of Mexico and USA.[5]

Despite its apparent implausibility for the case of paintings, the equivalent view, that musical works are 'pure' sound structures—colorless patterns of pitches or intervals—and that their instrumentation is redundant to their identities, is widely held by philosophers. For example, William Webster maintains (1974) that Bach's Violin Concerto in E Major would be legitimately instanced if played on any instrument, so long as the note relationships were preserved. Peter Kivy claims (1988a: 55): 'Performing a Bach fugue with a choir of kazoos...cannot, of itself, make the performance a performance of something else.' Roger Scruton observes (1997: 442): 'There is nothing in the concept of a pitch pattern that determines the timbre that will most perspicuously realise it. Hence performances of the *Well-Tempered Clavier* on a piano, on a harpsichord, by a quartet of brass or woodwind, or by the Swingle Singers are all performances of the *Well-Tempered Clavier*.'[6] He contends that we attend to the sounds of music solely as sounds, without regard to their origins.

Proponents of musical formalism point to the fact that some works have no specified instrumentation—Bach's *Art of Fugue* is usually cited here—and others are indicated as for any instruments—such as John Cage's *4'33"*, a piece in which the participating instruments are not actually played, as well as some works by Percy Grainger, such as *Spoon River* and *Irish Tune from County Derry*, in which they are. Formalists can also note that it is common for works to be transcribed for other instruments, such as the piano or lute, or to exist in different orchestral arrangements or versions, all apparently without loss of identity. In the past, a relaxed attitude to the use of specified instruments prevailed—contemporary, 'improved' instruments were used in nineteenth-century revivals of Bach, for instance—and in yet earlier periods much music was played by the instruments that happened to be available.

Earlier I listed some replies to the view that colors are irrelevant to the form and identifying contents of paintings. Do similar responses apply to the idea that a musical

---

[5] For further discussion, see Irvin (2003).
[6] Scruton develops the thesis at 1997: 2–3, 19–20. For discussion of Scruton's view, see Hamilton (2007).

work's timbre and instrumentation are not relevant to its identity, this being established exclusively by its note structure? There are some pieces by Anton Webern and Edgard Varèse that use instrumental color as the primary structural feature and Schoenberg's technique of *Klangfarbenmelodie* created structural links between timbre and harmony (Cramer 2002). In others, there are symbolic associations between musical instruments and narrative or programmatic elements that are offered as central to the work's identity. Brass and snare drums have a military flavor; horns are associated with the hunt and the oboe or cor anglais with bucolic ease (Francès 1988).

These points have a restricted application, however, and it is not easy to develop analogues to the stronger arguments for the centrality of color in painting. Orchestration can be used to help the delineation of form, for example, or to highlight a line buried within a complex texture, but opponents of the idea that a work's instrumentation is essential to its identity deny that this contribution is significant. The work's note structure survives pretty much intact when the work is (competently) transcribed for different instruments or is programmed into a synthesizer. Meanwhile, the instrumentation of musical works has little to do with their verisimilitude. Most do not aim at representation and where they do, sonic realism is not valued over musicality, as is apparent from the fact that much that is purportedly represented—clouds, the great gate of Kiev, the shimmer of a silver rose—is not sonic or dynamic in character.[7] It is plausible to suggest that a work's instrumentation can contribute to its expressive character—the nobility of the French horn, the searing passion of soaring violins in close harmony (Levinson 1990: ch. 10)—but again, the formalist can counter. He might argue that expressiveness is not a work-identifying property. Alternatively, he can maintain that the music's expressiveness depends mainly on its note structure. The French horn does not sound noble unless its melody does, and it is the high pitch and close harmonies that convey passion.

The ontological formalist usually argues as follows: if the work is recognizable in a performance that lacks some musical feature or parameter—in this case the orchestral color specified by the composer—then that musical feature or parameter cannot be an identity-conferring element of the work. Only the work's intervallic structure, rhythm, and general tempo are likely to survive this test, so the formalist reduces the work to the sound structure comprising these elements. This form of argument is inadequate, however. Musical works should be viewed as norm kinds (Wolterstorff 1975), that is, as allowing for malformed, deficient, or incomplete instances. A performance with wrong notes can be recognizably of the work, but this does not show that the wrong notes are part of the work or that the ones that should have been played instead are not. The question should not be whether the work is recognizable in

---

[7] Music may be able to represent the sources of distinctive non-musical dynamic processes, however, such as steam trains (Arthur Honegger's *Pacific 231*) or storms at sea (Felix Mendelssohn's *Fingal's Cave*). And it can also represent music, as do onstage bands in opera. For discussion, see Davies (1994a: ch. 2).

a performance that alters its instrumentation but whether such a performance is thereby less than fully faithful to the work.

In addition, the formalist's assumption that nothing outside the work is relevant to its identity should be questioned. Aspects of the art-historical context and tradition in which the work was created affect its contents and its identity (Levinson 1990: chs 4, 10, 16, Davies 2001a). For instance, a work's genre determines which of its properties are standard, contra-standard, and variable, and thereby affects its work-identifying contents (Walton 1970). Meanwhile, what genre it belongs to depends both on the composer's intentions and on the work's matching the established genres of the time.

Recognizing what is achieved in the work involves consideration of the constraints its media impose. In the musical case, the medium is not that of pure sound, but of sounds elicited by human musicians from their own body or from devices made of wood, metal, bone, gut, horsehair, and so on. In other words, the musical medium is the voice or musical instruments the use of which is specified by the work's composer. Typically, the work's instrumentation is not an incidental means to the sounding of the work. Rather, the use of those instruments is integral to the production of properly formed instances of the work. Even if a work is recognizable when performed in ways that alter or ignore its intended orchestration, such a performance is not properly formed or fully authentic. Meanwhile, transcriptions are distinct though derivative works or, in other cases, works can have more than one version, with each being instrument-specific (see Chapter 12 and Davies 2003: ch. 3).

Colorful formalism

A formalist might be persuaded that instrumental color contributes essentially to the work's identity without accepting that the relevant timbres must be elicited from the voices or the instruments specified by the work's composer. This formalist maintains that nothing beyond its timbrally inflected sound determines the work's identity and he therefore suggests that the use of the specified musical instruments is not required in producing a fully authentic instance of the work. I have called (Davies 2001a: 64) this position 'timbral sonicism.' The timbral sonicist develops his view as follows: for a long time, we associated the sounds with the instruments that produced them because there was no practical alternative to employing those instruments if we wanted to generate the specified sounds with the indicated timbral qualities. Now, though, we have the technology not only to record and replay such sounds but also to synthesize them electronically. An electronically generated rendition of a work would be fully accurate and authentic provided it matches the appropriate note pattern and invests this with the relevant timbral qualities—the sounds *as of* the instruments specified by the composer—despite the fact that the rendition is not performed by singers or by musicians playing the indicated instruments in the usual fashion.

Even if it escapes some of the objections raised earlier against pure formalism, timbral sonicism faces others. Composers write for instruments, not just for sounds. As Stan

Godlovitch (1998: 66–71) explains, musical instruments are tools of a trade with guilds that set standards for the mastery of the instrument. Though instruments can change and evolve, as is apparent in the move from acoustic to electric guitars, crucial skill elements must be retained if the practice is to remain musically kosher. Synthesizers, by contrast, are replacement, not development, technologies, when they are used to ape acoustic instruments. Moreover, despite the difficulties presented to the person who uses a computer to program a synthesizer so that it can give forth a commanding performance of a piano concerto, they cannot be such as to merit victory to the synthesizer in a piano concerto competition. The importance attached to the process of eliciting sounds from instruments is reflected in the high number of instrument-specific notational symbols, many of which indicate something about how the instrument is to be used or handled.[8]

The thought of music as the auditory bodying forth of human action is deeply ingrained, not merely as a matter of association but more significantly in how we conceive of the musical significance of the sounds produced. We are likely to feel uneasy on learning that what we took for a soprano performing a Schubert song, accompanied by a piano, was instead produced manually by programming a synthesizer. This unease stems from our recognizing that the instrument or voice, unlike the synthesizer, becomes an extension of the musician's body and thereby a mode of personal expression. Moreover, where there is no act of singing there are no words uttered: what is one to make now of the 'words' and the human narrative they seemed to convey? Meanwhile, the pulse and flow of the music is no longer suggestive, as usually it is, of the human actions and feelings that go into its generation.[9]

Of course, today's technology makes it possible for us to hear recordings of musical instruments with which we are not at all familiar. Occasionally, it is difficult to be sure how the instrument is structured and how it is used. Moreover, where the music is electronically synthesized, as in much pop of the 1980s, few of us have the slightest idea how the timbral result is achieved. In these cases, we might experience the sound as 'pure' or disembodied. And perhaps (though I doubt it) the fact that most people access much of the music they listen to via CDs or MP3 files leads them frequently to experience music this way. But if so, this is an artifact of contemporary culture. Through our long pre-history—the earliest uncontestable musical instrument, a flute, is dated to more than 35,000 years before the present[10] and we can surmise that singing and chanting long proceeded this—and up to the end of the nineteenth century, music was made live by people near the listener and it was normal to see the instruments they used and how these were employed.

---

[8] See Chapter 13 and Davies (2001a: 62–3).
[9] See Davies (1994a, 2003: ch. 9). Levinson (1990: chs 4, 10, 16, 2002) defends a position like mine, though I do not share his view that the action that goes into playing music is always apparent in the music made (see Davies 2001a: 66–8) or his theory (Levinson 2006) that we conceive of gestures heard in music as those of an imaginary persona (see Chapter 1).
[10] Described in Conard et al. (2009). Other flutes that may be as old are discussed in Conard (2005).

Dodd's timbral sonicism

Timbral sonicism has been defended recently by Julian Dodd (2007a, 2007b). He states (2007a: 25) its thesis as follows: 'a work's normative properties comprise merely acoustic properties and not, in addition to these, *performance-means properties*: properties concerning how a performance's constituent sounds are produced.' Dodd begins by laying claim to the conceptual high ground: timbral sonicism is the theory we should accept unless it is defeated. And he suggests that the arguments of those he calls 'instrumentalists'—that is, those who regard the composer's specification of the performance-means as normative and thereby as indicating what is required for a fully authentic performance—as insufficient to defeat timbral sonicism.

In defense of the first claim, Dodd holds (2007a: 26-7): 'there is something deeply intuitive about the idea that works of music are pure types of sound-event: in other words, that what makes a certain work *that* work is simply that its performances should sound like *that*. ... Someone unencumbered by developments in analytical aesthetics will most likely accept that a performance of the *Hammerklavier* on a Perfect Timbral Synthesiser, indistinguishable to the ears from a performance on a piano, would be a no less satisfactory presentation of the piece.' He affirms that the way we experience music is as connected sounds, not in terms of their sources, even if we typically refer to those sources as a way of indicating the precise timbral quality that we experience.

Turning to his rejection of arguments against timbral sonicism, Dodd notes that we cannot infer from the composer's specification of the work's instrumentation and her use of instrument-specific notations, such as *pizzicato*, that it is the use of those instruments, as against a sonic profile as of those instruments, that is normative for her work. And even if composers think in terms of the instruments to be used and take their work-establishing intentions to target those instruments, not merely their sounds, they would be wrong in believing that they thereby mandate the use of those instruments in faithful performances. Moreover, the musical ontologist can remain unimpressed by Godlovitch's arguments, which mistakenly offer observations about the social history of music making as a constraint on clear-headed ontologizing, Dodd holds. He suggests (2007a: 36) 'that the practice of musicians embodies a commitment to instrumentalism does not entail that this doctrine is correct.' If the performer uses replacement technology to produce a version of the *Hammerklavier* that is sonically indistinguishable from that of an accurate performance on the piano, we might think she 'cheats' in that she does not display the skill needed to elicit the work from a piano in the standard manner, but that is a judgment of the performer, not of the authenticity of the performance that is produced. Similarly, qualities that implicate the means of performance, such as that of being virtuosic, belong to the performer or performance, not to the work as such. And works are not unusual or original in terms of their use of instruments. Rather, it is the composers of such works and their compositional acts that display such characteristics. Meanwhile, properties that genuinely do belong to the work by virtue of its timbral qualities, such as some expressive properties for instance, do not depend on the means by which those timbral qualities are produced. And if, nevertheless, audiences no longer hear the same gestural or expressive qualities in the sound of the Perfect Timbral Synthesizer, that is 'caused by a failure of imagination on their part: a failure to hear the sounds *as if* made by' (2007a: 45) the ordinarily expected instrument.

I hope it is clear by now that Dodd awards himself an invincible position. If the relevant properties cannot be heard, they must belong not to the work but to the composer, the performer, the social history of music making, the performance tradition, or whatever. And if they can be heard, so that they belong to the work, it must be that their being heard does not presuppose anything about the sound's provenance. Moreover, we cannot appeal to what composers intend, musicians expect, and listeners experience when objecting to timbral sonicism, because Dodd offers an error theory, according to which composers, musicians, and listeners are liable to be wrong in their beliefs about the relevant matters. When composers intend to require performers to use the specified instruments, they are in error. Performers who think they can establish standards of authentic performance in terms of the musical skills involved in using the specified instruments are also mistaken, as are listeners who, through a failure of imagination, feel that something is lacking in the rendition given by the Perfect Timbral Synthesizer. Dodd's stance makes his position unfalsifiable. And because of his opening assumption, that the onus of proof is not on him but on his opponents, timbral sonicism is guaranteed to triumph.

The perfect timbral synthesizer

The issue is not whether the rendition by the Perfect Timbral Synthesizer provides epistemic access to how an authentic performance would sound. It does. Nor is it about whether we might counterfactually entertain the thought that what issues from the Perfect Timbral Synthesizer is the sound of some performance. We might do so and, in a world without pianists who can play the *Hammerklavier*, could fruitfully use the Perfect Timbral Synthesizer as a prop in such an imaginative game. Instead, the debate is over whether the Perfect Timbral Synthesizer provides a fully complete and faithful performance of the *Hammerklavier*. Dodd thinks it does. It preserves all the properties constitutive of the work, he insists. I disagree.

Here are my intuitions on the Perfect Timbral Synthesizer's rendition: I am reluctant to regard the result as a performance, because the actions characteristic of performing the *Hammerklavier*, over nearly two hundred years, do not take place. Moreover, the sounding produced by the Perfect Timbral Synthesizer is deficient in its representation of Beethoven's sonata; it lacks some of the features that are constitutive of Beethoven's work. One of these is the virtuosity of the last movement. Unlike Dodd, I see no reason to think that virtuosity belongs exclusively to the performer or the performance, as opposed to the work. It is a characteristic of the work that it is technically demanding of the pianist who would perform it (Mark 1980). In addition, the human warmth of performance is missing from the electronically generated sounding and this affects expressive and other features that belong to the work. To quote myself (Davies 2003: 114):

> For the accomplished player, the instrument is experienced as an extension of the body, as continuous with it. Just as a walking stick projects its user's boundary, because the ground is felt at its tip, so the musical instrument extends the boundaries of the person who plays it. And this expansion is emotional and personal, as well as physical, to the extent that the instrument provides the player with new means for expressing her ideas, personality, and passions. This nexus of corporeal embodiment, action, and expression is melded indissolubly with the music that is sounded, which in its turn implicates the human body and organic processes through the ebb and flow of its pulse and rhythm, of its gestures and sighs, of its tensions and resolutions.

The person who listens as the Perfect Timbral Synthesizer outputs the *Hammerklavier* will not hear in it the gestural and expressive actions that properly belong to it if she remains aware throughout that the Perfect Timbral Synthesizer generates its sounds according to some program the authoring, installation, and execution of which involves something other than real-time piano playing.

Timbral sonicism tested

It is instructive to note how profound and tenacious are the tendencies Dodd diagnoses as error-prone.

The question of whether listeners perceive 'pure' sounds or their sources has been widely debated over the past decade by musicologists and psychologists, and the evidence is widely interpreted as supporting the second view (see Dibben 2001). For a start, our tendency to process sounds in terms of their sources carries over to the musical case. Eric Clarke observes (2005: 74): 'since sounds in the everyday world specify (among other things) the motional characteristics of their sources, it is inevitable that musical sounds will also specify movements and gestures—both the real movements and gestures involved in actually producing music...and also the fictional movements and gestures of the virtual environment which they conjure up.'[11]

Composer-musicians think in terms of the instruments they play when they create music. The spatial layouts of instruments as diverse as Afghanistan's dutâr, the African thumb piano, and the blues guitar condition the music created by performer-composers, suggesting that musical cognition may involve thinking in terms of movement, of how the hands engage the instrument, not only of sound.[12] Pascal Bujold (2005) explains that his learning to play music from Argentina, Morocco, and West Africa depended on his imitating the 'dancing' movements with which native musicians engage their instruments. Not surprisingly, when musicians merely imagine playing, the relevant motor regions of the brain are stimulated (Zatorre and Halpern 2005).

---

[11] See also Bregman (1990: 469).
[12] See Blacking (1961), Baily (1977, 1985), Iyer (1998, 2002), Nelson (2002), Cross (2007).

The connection between music and movement is no less significant for the listener. The sight of musicians playing contributes to the audience's recognition and experience of music's expressive qualities (Davidson 1993, Vines et al. 2005). Albert Bregman (1990: 483–4) notes that when we listen to a sound, we experience it not in terms of the qualities of the sounds we are sensing but in terms of the physical properties of the source. As well, music stirs its audience. Many cultures do not have separate words for music and dance and the idea of a passive audience not actively engaged with the music is unfamiliar to most cultures (Arom 1991, Cross 2007). Music has the power to entrain even passive listeners—that is, to synchronize their breathing, pulse, and movements such as foot-tapping—which is why it is used to accompany work and to induce group solidarity.[13] Meanwhile, neurological scans show that, even in passive listening, music stimulates the parts of the brain that are involved in motor activation and vocal sound production.[14] The broad, operational account of music offered by Ian Cross (2007; also Cross and Morley 2009)—as embodying, entraining, and transposably intentionalizing time in sound and action—nicely expresses the interpenetration of music by human movement and action. So, timbre or color is to be regarded as a property of instruments or the voice and, along with all aspects of the instrument's sound, is conceived in terms of action and gesture, specifically those involved in getting the sound from the instrument and those elicited from the listener, but also in terms of qualities of expressive movement inherent to the music itself.

These data indicate that it is not merely the accident of association that leads us to think of sounds in terms of their sources. Indeed, wider consideration of the evolutionary function of our senses suggests that, rather than being concerned primarily with what impinges directly on the ears, and then with what causes this only by association, their adaptive function is to provide knowledge of those sources. Our senses evolved to provide us with information about the world that is relevant to our survival. To do so effectively, they must tell us the nature of distant causes through providing sensory awareness of their proximal effects. Accordingly, we generally experience not the qualities of the sound we are sensing but the physical properties of its source. In other words, we register changes in the sound as changes in the cause of the sound. For example, if a percussionist strikes his instrument with decreasing force, rather than following the subtle, complex acoustic changes that occur, we hear the change in the force with which the instrument is struck.[15]

All this suggests that Dodd's claim that timbre is a property solely of a sound, rather than of a voice or a played instrument, is as weird as saying that color is solely a property of light, rather than of the object from which the light is reflected. If our senses evolved

---

[13] See McNeil (1995), Benzon (2001), London (2004), Higgins (2006, 2012), Cross (2007), Cross and Morley (2009).
[14] See Janata and Grafton (2003), Koelsch and Siebel (2005), Koelsch et al. (2006).
[15] See Bregman (1990), and for further discussion along the same lines, Gibson (1968), Vanderveer (1979), Clarke (1985, 2005), Handel (1989), Shove and Repp (1995), Windsor (2000).

to provide us with information relevant to our survival and accommodation to our environment, as seems likely, it is predictable they tell us of the nature of distant causes just as and through providing awareness of proximal effects. As James Gibson, who was an advocate of this 'ecological' account of perception, noted (1968: 87, 89): 'the sound of rubbing, rolling, and brushing, for example, are distinctive acoustically and are distinguished phenomenally.... The sounds made by various tools are specific to the mechanical action of the tool, as in sawing, pounding, filing, and chopping.' Accordingly, listeners tend to identify everyday sounds in terms of the objects or events that cause them (Vanderveer 1979; see also Windsor 2000).

I suppose Dodd will dismiss such considerations as illegitimately substituting study of the psychology of the experience of music for ontological analysis, as he does also in rejecting the sociological claims made by Godlovitch. Yet these data are surely relevant to how we should assess his assertion that the burden of proof lies exclusively with his opponent. The intuition that musical works are sound-events is certainly widespread, but not that they are *pure* sound-events. Rather, the standard intuition is that they are the outcome of specific kinds of actions that engage or impinge upon particular kinds of sound-generators. Dodd can deal with this reality only by arguing that composers, musicians, and many listeners are systematically mistaken about what they experience when they appreciate musical works for what they are. What is deeply intuitive to Dodd is not deeply intuitive to others, however. It is simply not true, I think, that everyone (except those 'encumbered by the developments in analytical aesthetics') will accept that a performance of a Schubert song on an appropriately programmed Perfect Timbral Synthesizer, indistinguishable to the ears from a performance by a vocalist accompanied by a piano but not involving either, would be 'a no less satisfactory presentation of the piece' (Dodd 2007a: 27). When we call into doubt Dodd's claim that timbral sonicism is the default position that wins unless it is defeated, his subsequent arguments seem to beg the ontological question.

I believe also that Dodd is mistaken in thinking that the issues of musical ontology should or could be quarantined from the sociological and psychological concerns he dismisses as solely epistemological, as I now explain.

We are capable of distinguishing fine shades of timbral difference and we sometimes value those differences. A Stradivarius has a different tone and sounds better than a cheap violin, though both sound unmistakably like violins. A Steinway grand piano is similarly different in tone from a mass-produced upright that is, nevertheless, unquestionably a piano. However, a performance of a violin concerto is not inauthentic as a result of being played on a mass-produced violin, not a Stradivarius, and a piano sonata is not performed less faithfully on an upright piano than on a Steinway grand. In addition, composers have often matched their music to the distinctive timbral and other sonic features of individual performers. Mozart wrote the Queen of the Night's music to highlight the coloratura abilities and tessitura of Josepha Hofer. Béla Bartók wrote for the violinist Joseph Szigeti, who played with a distinctive, metallic tone. Despite this, we allow that any sufficiently skilled soprano or violinist can perform

Mozart's or Bartók's music in a fully authentic fashion, though the result does not faithfully reproduce the timbral specificity that these composers had in mind. In other words, we regard the relevant pieces as for the soprano and the violin, not solely for Hofer or Szigeti. These observations invite the question: given that timbre counts among the work's identifying features, why does it count only so much and not more, despite the composer's more detailed timbral conception of the music and our capacity to discriminate relevant timbral subtleties?[16]

It seems to me that there are two fairly obvious answers to this question, neither of which can be congenial to the timbral sonicist. The first notes that works are almost always specified at the level of instrument-types (bass viol, snaredrum, clarinet, serpent, sackbut), without regard to individual (usually subtle) differences between instances of any given type. This is because works of the kind in question are supposed and acknowledged to be for multiple performances, with different performances involving different musicians and orchestras. So, once again, reference to the means of performance is implicated in the musical work's identity, not sound qualities alone.

The second answer goes further. The level of timbral detail that is work-constitutive depends on social conventions adopted within the relevant musical tradition of work creation and presentation. In other words, the standard might have been set higher, and probably would have been if there had been less regularity among musical instruments and a greater valuing of idiosyncratic instruments. Or it could have been set lower, with considerable discretion allowed to performers in the choice of the work's instrumentation without consequent loss in the faithfulness of their performances. Indeed, this seems to be the case in jazz. For classical music, the eventual standardization of orchestras and instruments (across broad limits) allowed the best of both worlds: highly portable and repeatable works that are, nevertheless, rich in timbral qualities that make a significant expressive and structural contribution to the work's interest. Within contrasting socio-historical practices or musical traditions, the situation could be very different, however. For example, as purely electronic works show, there could be works in which timbre is significant but the instrumental means for performance are replaced by automated mechanisms for playback.

Lessons for the ontology of music

Dodd dismisses the human factor as irrelevant, as if he is dealing with the ontology of a natural kind. He writes of music as if it possesses a universal and unchanging essence. That is, he writes as if what we believe about musical works, how we respond to them, and how our social practices and histories incorporate them are irrelevant to the kind of things they are, just as a ruby is what it is even if humans believe it to be the frozen blood of the gods.

---

[16] Note that the instrumentalist also faces the same troublesome query. I have suggested (Davies 2001a: 66–8) that Levinson, who defends the view that the use of the indicated performance-means is needed for a performance to be fully faithful to the work, fails to address this issue

That approach may be appropriate for rubies but is not appropriate for musical works and other socially contextualized items identified as human creations.

A timbral sonicist might cleave to the idea that the metaphysics of sound is independent of the ways people experience it and conceive of what they experience, but that commits him to arguing for an error theory according to which composers are mistaken in thinking the use of the instruments they indicate is mandated, performers are mistaken in assuming that authenticity requires meeting the challenge of the music by using the relevant instruments in the expected fashion, and listeners are unacceptably hidebound if they are made uneasy on learning that the sounds of a voice are synthesized electronically, without passing through a human throat. Where the focus falls on music, I find it hard to believe that an error theory and serious conceptual revisionism is likely to be plausible.

Because musical works are human creations, the sociology and psychology of music—what composers intend, what musicians do, and what listeners prefer, along with the interpersonal arrangements that emerge from or are based on such intentions, actions, and preferences—are relevant to an account of the character of the musical works that are made. Consideration of such matters is not, as Dodd suggests, a turning away from metaphysics. It is, instead, the adoption of a metaphysics that is appropriately informed by relevant data from social and musical history, as Dodd's abstract metaphysics in the formalist mode is not.

The second answer given above to the question asking why timbre counts only so much and not more indicated that there is a degree of cultural flexibility to our characterization of musical works. In turn, this implies the possibility that the ontological nature of musical works is mutable, being responsive to changes in the socio-musical environment.

The history of Western classical music and its associated practices clearly indicate that the ontological character of musical works is flexible in the way just suggested. In the past, when orchestras and instruments were not uniform and works were adapted for local circumstances, the conventions of performance did not treat all of a composer's indications or intentions as regards the means of performance as among her work's identifying features. Vocal music and songs did have to be sung for a fully faithful rendition, but the performers could and often did substitute what they had in the way of instrumental resources for the instrumentation the composer intended and preferred. (Also, they had much more editorial discretion than was allowed later.) However desirable it was from an aesthetic point of view to meet the composer's wishes as regards the performance-means, a performance was not less faithful to the work if these were bypassed. Not surprisingly, under such circumstances composers were less liable to invest their works with instrument-specific timbral effects, except where the instruments were very widespread and similar, as was true for the lute in the fifteenth century and the violin in the seventeenth. Performances of music were replete with timbral effects, of course, but most of these were attributable to the performer as part of his individual interpretation, not to the composer as part of her work's identifying features. Beginning in the eighteenth century, the performer's discretion in the selection and use of performance-means gradually diminished, following the publication of scores, the regularization of the orchestra, and moves toward professional, public performance. By the nineteenth century, the practice of Western classical music's performance suggested that the work's instrumentation, and hence its color, was mandated by its composer. In other words, changes in musical practice and reception over time shifted timbral effects from the sphere of the performer's interpretative freedom to the sphere of the work's constitutive properties, and this was achieved via an equivalent change in the status of the composer's indication of the work's performance-means, from recommendations for best interpretative practice to work-identifying directions.

In acknowledgement of this, I reject not only pure sonicism and timbral sonicism but also thoroughgoing instrumentalism. There have been periods or genres in which instrumental color was more a feature of the performance than a constituent of the work performed. This was typically the case when convention and the default circumstances made it impossible for composers to require what performance-means could be employed in realizing their works. And in addition, technology has allowed for the creation of purely electronic works issued on discs. Such works are for playback, not performance, which means that instrumentalism is not an appropriate ontological model for them.[17] So, instrumentalism fails if it is presented as a timeless or overarching theory.

Musical works come in a variety of ontological types. I have argued that works for live performance, works for studio performance, and works for playback (such as purely electronic compositions that are not for performance) should be distinguished.[18] And among those for performance, works can be variously 'thick' or 'thin' with constitutive properties. A work with mandated, detailed instrumentation will be thicker than one designated as for performance on any instruments, even if the latter's sound-structural profile is otherwise identical to the former's. (Even if a group performs the second work with the instruments specified for the first, with the result that their performance is sonically indistinguishable from a rendition of the first, timbral features belonging to the first work in its performance are, in the performance of the second, attributable only to the interpretation offered, not to the piece.) The ontological analysis of the nature of musical works must respect this diversity. To do so, account must be taken of how the circumstances and practices of the time of the work's creation are relevant to its nature. Rarefied, monolithic theories, like Dodd's timbral sonicism, traduce the rich variety in music and its works.

---

[17] Dodd's timbral sonicism would apply more readily to compositions generated not by sampling 'real' sounds but instead by purely electronic means. We approach such works as timbrally inflected sound structures without considering or being fully aware usually of the procedures that affect the timbral and other qualities of the sounds. But Dodd intends his theory specifically to characterize traditional works, such as the *Hammerklavier*, that were intended for performance on acoustic instruments.

[18] For critical discussion of my attempt in Davies (2001a) to separate live from studio performances, see Kania (2006).

Conclusion

I have argued that timbre, or vocal and instrumental color, often contributes to the identity of a musical work much as a painting's colors usually contribute to its identity. These conclusions are predictable if we assume that the evolutionary purpose of our senses is to furnish information about what is in the world, and that the relevant aural capacities are generalized in the musical case to identifying and cataloguing the elements that make up the world of the musical work. To achieve their evolutionary function, our senses go beyond light and sound waves that impinge immediately on our bodies to represent their sources or bearers, and our phenomenological awareness is more often of these distant causes than of their local effects. This is also relevant to how we should conceive of the sound of music and, where appropriate, the works made up of these sounds. We hear through musical sounds and timbres to the voices and musical instruments from which they issue and to the manner in which these are used. So integral is this to our way of hearing music (and all other sounds) that the use of the appropriate instrumental forces (as against simulations of these made without input from vocalists or musicians) is usually required for music's authentic rendition. This final conclusion counts against the model of musical works proposed by ontological formalists. Unless we are deeply and systematically mistaken, musical works are not merely 'colorless' sound sequences. Nor are they colored merely in that their sounds are as of the specified instruments. In other words, the means of performance, as well as the sounds produced, are implicated among the identity conditions of musical works.

12

Versions of Musical Works and Literary Translations

The composition of a musical piece can fall short of the work's completion. In 1821, Schubert sketched an E-major symphony he did not finish. The following year, he abandoned another symphony after writing two movements and outlining its scherzo. We call it the 'Unfinished.' Mahler notated much of his Tenth Symphony in short score, but only the first movement was fully orchestrated before his death. A less often remarked fact is that a work's composition can overshoot its completion. It is the description apt for these cases that is the topic of this chapter. But before I get to that, it is useful to describe some of the signs that show a work to be finished.

What signifies the completion of a musical work?

There are a number of indicators that a musical work is complete. (1) The composer declares that it is so. In a letter to his father dated 10 April 1784, Mozart writes of his piano concerto in G, K. 453: 'I have finished today another new concerto for Fräulein Ployer.'[1] (2) Or the composer marks the score or a catalogue. In the case of K. 453, Mozart entered the opening theme into the thematic catalogue he had started in February 1784.[2] (3) Or the score is copied for performance. Along with other manuscripts, that of K. 453 was dispatched to Mozart's father in Salzburg on 15 May 1784. Mozart wrote: 'I am not particular about the symphony, but I do ask you to have the four concertos copied at home, for the Salzburg copyists are as little to be trusted as the Viennese.' (4) Or the work receives a public performance designated as its premier. K. 453 was played publicly for the first time with Fräulein Ployer as the soloist on June 13, 1784 (Deutsch 1966: 225). (5) Or an authorized version of the score is printed and sold. The published score of K. 453 was advertised for sale in Vienna in August and September of 1785 (Deutsch 1966: 249–52).

Published in K. Stock (ed.), *Philosophers on Music: Experience, Meaning and Work*. Oxford: Oxford University Press (2007): 79–92.

[1] Translations of Mozart's letters are by Emily Anderson.
[2] Bach penned the letters 'S. D. G.' in the margins of his scores, which translates as 'solely to the glory of God.' At the end of his scores, Haydn wrote: 'Fine. Laus Deo.' Other composers have signed and dated their scores.

None of these signs of a work's completion is necessary. The unsigned but finalized manuscript of many an unperformed and unpublished symphony has languished in its composer's bottom drawer. Also, because they are temporally spread, the combination of these markers can leave the precise moment of completion somewhat uncertain. Writing to his father on 12 June 1784, Mozart observes of the autograph score of his piano concerto in D, K. 451, that there is 'something missing' in the solo passage in C in the Andante. He continues: 'I will supply the deficiency as soon as possible and send it with the cadenzas.' Yet the concerto was 'finished' about three months earlier, on 22 March 1784, and premiered with Mozart as soloist on 31 March at a subscription concert. It was fairly common for Mozart not to write out the detail of the soloist's part if he was its player. He would later record the part in full for the concerto's publication.

Nevertheless, if all these signs are in place, we can have a high level of confidence that the work is finished. (Cases in which an unfinished work bears all these markers are conceivable but, in practice, more or less non-existent.)

Versions by the composer

As I indicated at the outset, the process of composition sometimes outlives the work's completion. In other words, the signs of completion, including public premier and publication, are plainly in place, and the composer designates that the work is finished, yet he later changes it in ways that should affect its identity. As I discuss below when considering (self-authored) transcriptions, sometimes the result is a new, derivative work. My concern, though, is with the case in which the composer's post-completion efforts result in a change or addition to the finished work, not in a new one. I call the result a *version*.

Here are some examples: Bruckner revised and altered his early symphonies after their first publication. For instance, in 1891 he recomposed his First Symphony of 1866.[3] Published editions and manuscripts of Chopin's works differ, and not only as a result of editorial error. Chopin was responsible for most of the variants. This has led some musicologists to claim that Chopin did not share our modern concept of musical works as completed, fixed, re-identifiable individuals. I disagree (see Davies 2001a: 92–7, 119–23). Whereas composers of earlier eras quickly moved on to new pieces even if they frequently inserted into these material borrowed from prior works written by themselves or others, Chopin and his contemporaries became more reluctant to relinquish control of their compositions, even after publication. I do not interpret this as showing that the work concept had yet to take shape. Instead, I see it as reflecting a pragmatic concern within a tough but unregulated market, both to do

---

[3] To complicate matters, the status of many editions of Bruckner's symphonies is controversial. Other composers and editors mangled the early editions and the twentieth-century scholarly editions of Robert Haas and Leopold Nowak by no means agree. My comments do not rely on these uncertainties, however.

what was necessary to cater to the taste of the purchasing public and to exploit any work for all that could be wrung from it.[4]

Hardheaded pragmatism can be seen also to lie behind the creation of work versions in other situations. Mozart had a great success with *Don Giovanni* in the provincial center of Prague, but when he took it to Vienna the court singers expected him to add numbers tailored for them, which he did. Throughout the nineteenth century, composers who exported their operas to Paris had to conform to the French passion for ballet by inserting dances. When Stravinsky lost access to royalties for *Firebird* and *Petrushka*, following the revolution in Russia, he re-scored them and had the new versions published in Europe and America. The alterations are modest—the notations of certain rhythms are simplified and there is a reduction in the numbers of flutes and such like. As was plainly intended, the changes did not depart so far from the originals that they counted as new pieces, but they did make it more likely that the new incarnations would be played and that the revenue could again go to the composer. In all these cases, what resulted were *versions* of old works, not new ones.

By contrast, consider Stravinsky's composition of *Les Noces*. With the sound structure more or less intact, he struggled with the orchestration. He scored the piece for a large orchestra and, again, for mechanical pianos, before settling on the instrumentation that is now familiar, which uses percussion and four pianos played live. On the account presented here, the work does not have three versions because the various changes antedated the work's completion. Instead, it had several drafts. They were phases in its initial composition, not alterations made after its finalization. More generally, it is not unusual for a composer to tinker with the work during rehearsals or after its premier, as it is prepared for publication. Though the completion date is not always clear-cut, these changes usually concern the work's finalization. Authors' versions, if there are any, come after that point.

As I use the term, a version is produced by the work's composer if he changes elements that should be constitutive of the work's identity after the piece's completion, and where the alterations intentionally and moderately alter identity-relevant features of the original but without resulting in the production of a new but derivative work. Drafts are like versions, except they are made *prior* to the work's completion.[5] Multiple versions of the same musical work can coexist. Though the final version sometimes has a special authority because it indicates the composer's definitive thoughts about the work, this is by no means always the case. For instance, the opera composers who

---

[4] The same phenomenon is evident with new music that is posted on the Internet and frequently remixed. Composers of such pieces seem to have a robust idea (the standard one) of what a work is and of when it gets released to the community, but they take advantage of the chance to play around with it after 'completion.'

[5] Where one studies the psychology or history of the work's creation, drafts may be more interesting than versions, but versions are more *philosophically* intriguing, which is why I focus on them. The production of succeeding drafts is a predictable part of the piece's development and completion. By contrast, versions are ontologically provocative, since, with them, the identity of the work apparently survives alteration in the kinds of features we would normally think of as work-constitutive.

adapted their works for Paris productions often found the process distasteful even if pragmatically desirable. The order in which versions are produced implies nothing on its own about their aesthetic importance.

The introduction of work versions to our musical ontology is messy, but so what? It respects a lack of neatness shown by composers themselves in the labeling and dissemination of their music. And, apart from the discomfort that untidiness among our classifications can bring, this ontological profligacy is supportable. All that is required is that the performers (analysts, historians) make clear that they are dealing with the version published in Paris, or the version of 1863, or the version for Prague as against the one for Vienna, or whatever. In other words, even if works with multiple versions are equivocal, we can usually individuate their versions clearly enough.

Versions by others

A version of a work can be produced by a person other than its composer. This happens, for example, when an unfinished piece is completed by a third party. Deryck Cooke produced a performing version of Mahler's Tenth Symphony. Each of the many composers who continued the last, unfinished fugue of Bach's *Art of the Fugue* produced a different version of the work. Mozart's Requiem exists only in a version finished by three of his pupils. For these cases, there is no definitive, finalized composition. There is the piece left unfinished by the composer and one or more versions indicating a way of completing it.

Versions of a work are also produced by music editors if the composer's text, or extant copies of it, are ambiguous or conflicting. If the editor chooses between several possibilities—for instance, she decides that the C in measure 40 should be sharpened, though the sharp is indicated in only some sources for the work and is not mandated by the performance practice or conventions—the result is a version.

Work versions versus performance interpretations

Work versions should be distinguished from performance interpretations. Because the prescriptions addressed to the work's performers underdetermine the detail of the performance, the players must go beyond what is work-determinative in rendering the work. There are many ways of doing this while remaining faithful to the piece. The differences that result mark distinctions in the interpretations the work receives.[6] When a composer interprets his own piece in performance, the outcome is an interpretation, not a new work version.

---

[6] This is not to say that interpretation comes into the picture as something added only after faithfulness has been achieved. Interpretation is not reserved solely for the 'gap' between the work and the concrete detail of its performance. It reaches all the way down, as it were.

The production of a work version requires changes in features that are usually constitutive for pieces of the kind in question. By contrast, accurate interpretations respect what is work constitutive. They vary qualities, features, or levels of detail that are not identity determining for the work. For instance, it may be prescribed that the performer decorates the melody when it is repeated, but the detail of that decoration might be left open and the player's choices add to her performance interpretation. Though the work includes decoration, no particular set is mandated and many choices (even if they are not all equally tasteful or effective) can be consistent with respecting the work's identity. And even where the interpretation deliberately deviates from what the composer instructs, the acts involved are ones of performance, not composition.

Where one draws the line between work versions and work interpretations is likely to depend on the level of detail at which works of the relevant kind are specified. In other words, it depends on the work's ontological character. If the work is 'thin,' wide variety among its instances is likely to be a function of its interpretation, not of its re-composition into versions. If the work is very 'thick,' significant differences between its instances, where they are not accidental, may be indicative of versions.

Interpretations within some performance traditions share important characteristics with work versions, however. I have in mind cases in which interpretations attain an autonomous standing, with the expectation that they are to be repeated and preserved, and in this resemble work versions. Also, where the piece being interpreted is onto-logically thin, its interpretation involves creative decisions of the kind that composers make and these decisions post-date the work's completion, which again makes them similar to work versions. The result can be called an *interpretation version*. It is not a work version, as I have characterized that notion, because it aims to establish a repeatable way of performing the source work, not to recompose that work.

Interpretation versions are common and well known, but let me introduce an out of the way example: in the Balinese gamelan gong kebyar tradition, *Teruna Jaya* is a piece that has existed in its modern form for more than fifty years. Though much is common between renditions of the work by different ensembles, there is also considerable variety. It is expected both that different performance groups will create their own interpretation and that each performance group will stick closely to the interpretation it establishes as its own.[7] Because these interpretations are worked out, are preserved and repeated, and are associated with particular groups, they are paradigms of interpretation versions. They do not involve post-completion changes to features that the tradition treats as work-constitutive, but neither are they as ephemeral as interpretations that are specific to a single performance.

A more familiar example of an interpretation version is the rock 'cover.' Because rock songs are typically rather spare as regards their work-identifying elements,

---

[7] Over the years, a group's interpretation can evolve and alter along with wider aspects of the prevailing style, but these alterations are more gradual and less self-conscious than is the creation of the initial interpretation.

re-recordings can remain faithful while differing in many respects from the original.[8] Joe Cocker's account of 'With a Little Help from my Friends' differs considerably from the Beatles', but is not thereby unfaithful as a performance, I hold. As a recording, the cover attains a status in its own right as a repeatable individual—not only can it be re-played, it can be performed again and again by Cocker or by his emulators— so it is a version, not a one-time-only interpretation. Because the cover does not involve the re-composition of work-constitutive elements of the original, despite differing in many respects from the Beatles' source, it qualifies as an interpretation version, however, not as a work version.[9]

For reasons that have been already acknowledged, interpretation versions can be like work versions in many respects and the terminologies I have specified are not clearly observed in ordinary discourse about music. Nevertheless, it is worthwhile to mark their differences. We expect completed works to receive differing interpretations and we regard interpretational variety and creativity as consistent with faithfulness to the work being performed, so long as its work-constitutive elements are preserved. Also, where works are thin, we appreciate that interpreters are creative after the manner of composers. As well, there is nothing surprising about the fact that interpretations can achieve standing in their own right as repeatable, persevering entities. By contrast with all this, it is disconcerting to have to accept that a work's identity can survive alteration to its work-constitutive features following its authorization as a completed piece, and to allow that a single work can exist in multiple incarnations. These latter characteristics are the hallmarks of what I have called work versions, as opposed to interpretation versions.

Composers' versions versus transcriptions

Just as work versions should be distinguished on the one side from performance interpretations and interpretation versions, so, on the other, they must be separated from derivative yet distinct new works, a prominent example being transcriptions. Where a medium-specific piece is adapted to a new medium, as when a nineteenth-century symphony is rewritten for the piano, the result is a distinct work, I claim (Davies 2003: ch. 3). Usually the transcription postdates the original, but it can anticipate it if, for example, the composer creates a symphonic work on the piano.

---

[8] I defend this account of rock's ontology in Davies (2001a). Gracyk (1996) takes the different view that the works in rock are electronic compositions that are presented via recordings and, hence, that are not for performance (see also Fisher 1998). In his theory, the cover is a new but derivative piece, not a new performance of the same song, as I maintain.

[9] In Davies (2001a: 180–1), I suggest that Benny Goodman's band arrangement of George Gershwin's *Fascinating Rhythm* and Glenn Miller's rendering of Joe Garland's *In the Mood* qualify as independent but derivative works, because they achieved the status of autonomous, repeatable versions preserved via recordings and notations. It is no less plausible to regard them as interpretation versions, as I imply here, however. Unlike transcriptions, which are discussed in the next section, these adaptations generate performances that are faithful to the original, ontologically thin, sources.

The first outing of *The Rite of Spring* came when Stravinsky and Debussy played the composer's transcription for two pianos.

Work versions involve changes to work-constitutive properties. Their creation can include alterations to pieces' orchestrations. As mentioned above, Stravinsky reduced the number of wind players in later versions of *Firebird* and *Petrushka*. These modifications did not depart from the *medium* in which the original was written, however. For these, the medium is the symphony orchestra, but such an orchestra can be treated flexibly as regards its forces; in particular, with regard to the number of woodwind, brass, and percussion lines. When he created new work versions of these early ballets, Stravinsky lightly reworked them in the same medium. Transcriptions also involve changes to work-constitutive instrumentations.[10] I regard transcriptions as new works, not as new work versions, however, because they involve changes in instrumentation that alter the work's medium and its medium-specific contents. When one instrumental medium is replaced by a significantly different one, the work's contents must be adapted accordingly. Among other matters, this usually involves changes to the piece's notes or their relative dispositions, and imposes different technical requirements and constraints on the piece's new performers. When a work's features are filtered though a new medium, the impact is usually sufficiently radical that a new piece results.

A musician might begin to compose, using a finished work as her source. If she carries the process of re-composition far enough, she writes a new piece. The new work is influenced by the original and perhaps audible traces of this inspiration remain detectable in quotations or allusions. In a different scenario, the composer does not carry the process very far and she conceives of herself as revising the source rather than going beyond it. The product is what I have called a work version. The practice of transcription lies between these extremes.[11] The audible relation with the original is preserved, as is the sound-structural outline and much else, yet the change in instrumental medium distances the transcription from its model, with the result that a new work is produced.

At what point does the process of composition leave the original work behind? When do alterations to the original cross the border between a work version and an entirely new, albeit derivative, piece? There is no simple answer, of course. And as long as we are all clear about the degree of arbitrariness involved, perhaps we can say what we like. Nevertheless, my intuition is that transcriptions usually achieve a degree of independence from their sources that versions do not. This is intended and reflects differences in what typically motivates the act of reconstruction in the first place. Work

---

[10] If the instrumentation of a piece is not work-determinative, varying its orchestration would result in an interpretation, not a transcription. Many musical pieces—folk songs, Bach's *Art of Fugue*, most pop songs, much music composed prior to the standardization of the orchestra—do not have work-determinative instrumentations.

[11] On the border between transcriptions and entirely new pieces is the 'fantasia after' and 'homage to.' Sometimes these are labeled as transcriptions, an example being Percy Grainger's 'transcription' of Tchaikovsky's 'Waltz of the Flowers.'

versions re-compose their sources, but in a deliberately restrained way, so that they do not threaten to count as new pieces. Also relevant is this: if we were to count transcriptions as work versions, not as new works, there would be the implication that the composer of the transcription is a co-author of the work. We would have, not Liszt's transcription of Beethoven's Fifth, but Beethoven's Fifth as composed by Liszt. When one composer completes another's work, the final result should be credited to both. When one composer transcribes another's piece, she deserves acknowledgment as the *transcription*'s author, but not as the co-author of (a version of) the *original*.[12]

Versions in other artforms

Much of what I have written about work versions in music could be applied to works produced in other artforms. The novelist can rewrite her already published book. The movie can be re-released as the director's cut, the modified-for-TV print, and the DVD supplement, which might include deleted scenes and an alternative ending. The artist can add to a previously completed oil painting and the sculptor can cut bits from a marble statue that was designated as finished long before.

These last cases provoke the following thoughts: it is common to distinguish artforms with works that must be singular from those in which multiple instances of the work are possible. Handmade sculptures, drawings, and paintings are singular; prints, cast statues, novels, plays, songs, movies, and musical works are potentially multiple. Some philosophers, Gregory Currie (1988) being one, reject this division, however. They regard all artworks as potentially multiple. A doppelganger of *Mona Lisa* would instance the same work as Leonardo's painting, provided it was accurate enough. Does the earlier observation—that oil paintings and marble sculptures can exist in more than one version—show that ontological multiplists are right?

Handmade paintings and sculptures can be made in sets. An artist might paint more or less identical copies of a single scene, and sell one to the palace, one to the church, and so on. We might regard these paintings as presenting different *versions* of the same subject matter, but there is no reason to treat the members of the set as versions of a single, generic painting. Members of the set can be identified as discrete but related works. When it was said earlier that there can be more than one version of an oil painting, the relevant example was not this but a different one, which I now describe. The artist completes a work but returns (much later, let us assume) to the same canvas or statue and takes to it again with brush or chisel. In doing so, he does not obliterate the original, though he does alter it in ways that should be relevant to its identity. He adds an angel or two in the sky, trims fat from the statue's thighs, or whatever.

---

[12] Sometimes transcribers deserve and get equal billing with the composer of the original, as Ravel does for his orchestral transcription of Mussorgsky's *Pictures at an Exhibition*, which was written for the piano. This equal acknowledgment is justified by the level of creativity and originality displayed by Ravel, but we do not identify him as co-author of the work.

As a result, the work exists through time in more than one version, and to that extent it appears to be multiple.

I deny that this counts against the commonsense view that handmade paintings and sculptures are singular, however. The multiple versions of plays and novels are numerically distinct and coexistent. This is possible because they are types or kinds indicated as such by an artist. By contrast, the painter in oils or the sculptor in marble can create a version only by laboring directly and concretely on the original work and its material. The new version supplants the earlier one; in other words, such works exist in only one version at a given time. The work preserves its identity through the process of change, but this does not make it a universal or type. Instead, it might be compared to a person, who can be stooped and gray *now* yet be the same as the child who *formerly* was blond and upright. Oil paintings and hewn statues can have successive versions, but unlike plays and novels, they cannot have coexistent versions (and instances), which is what would be required if they were to be multiple in the relevant sense. Rather than deducing from the possibility of their having versions that paintings and sculptures are all potentially multiple, it is more sensible to observe that the ontological differences between singular and multiple works dictate a corresponding difference in what is involved in creating versions of them.

Translations in literature and poetry

Here is a new issue. What is the status of *translations* of literary works to a language other than that in which they are written? Are translations equivalent to work versions or to transcriptions? Is a translation a variant that instances the original work or is it a distinct but derivative piece?

If we ask a person if she has read *War and Peace*, she is likely to answer 'yes' if she has read an English translation. It would be odd if she replied: 'no, only the translation.'[13] But it would be hasty to conclude from this that the translation thereby counts as an English-language version of Tolstoy's novel. It is likely that the respondent interprets the question as asking if she is familiar with Tolstoy's work *via its translation*, not as asking if she accepts their co-identity.

People turn to a translation usually because they do not read the language of the original and, therefore, for the case of *War and Peace*, cannot access Tolstoy's work as he wrote it. In the past, musical transcriptions were the same. Before there were radios, recordings, or affordable subscription concerts, piano transcriptions provided the main route to many orchestral works because households frequently possessed a piano and a competent pianist. It would have been natural in those times to claim acquaintance with Beethoven's Fifth on the basis only of Liszt's transcription. Nowadays we are liable to insist that a person does not really know Beethoven's Fifth until she hears the

---

[13] That answer might be more likely, though, if the question had been 'Have you read Voiynah ee meer?' supposing the person to understand this as the Russian title.

work as it was written for orchestra. A person's claim to have read Tolstoy's work by reading a translation might seem natural, then, only because the original remains comparatively inaccessible to most native speakers of English.[14] But in that case, it could be that the translation is best regarded as a distinct piece, which is the way Liszt's transcription should be considered.

Notwithstanding these observations, there are good reasons for thinking of the translation as a work version. It is intended and represented as a variant of the original, not as a new though derivative piece. And this is plausible, to the extent that it is possible to achieve a high degree of accuracy (as regards content and general mood) in converting one language to another. Admittedly, it can be difficult for a foreigner to appreciate the nuances and associations of a story in translation, but that problem may be *cultural* rather than *linguistic*. A foreigner who could read the work in its original language might miss exactly the same features through a lack of sensitivity to the conventions and values of the culture in which the story finds its home. If the work is the story, and if the story survives its translation, the translation is best regarded as a version, not as an autonomous work.

Though I stand by it, this conclusion should be viewed warily. The more resistant to translation are linguistic and semantically relevant features of the work, the nearer translation approaches the case of musical transcription; that is, to being an autonomous though related work. An example might be that of translating from a tone language (such as Mandarin) to a non-tone language (such as English). The relevance of pitch to meaning may be exploited in the original to present artistically relevant possibilities that cannot survive in translation. A different, more obvious case is that of poetry or rhyming verse. It is notoriously difficult to reproduce in another language the subtle semantic content and ease of expression of something written in rhyming iambic pentameter while respecting the same formal constraint.

The nearer language comes to being merely a vehicle for meaning, so that the content of the story is 'transparent' to the language in which it is written, the nearer translations approach work versions so long as the translator aims successfully to produce a literal rendering of the original. But the more the language of writing becomes a medium that draws attention to itself and, prism-like, modulates, filters, and inflects the message expressed through it—or alternatively, the freer and more 'creative' the translator tries to be—the more translations are analogous to musical transcription. In this latter case, translations must function like transcriptions, either

---

[14] Compare the role of literary translations with that played by mass reproductions of singular or limited edition paintings and sculptures. Reproductions can range from photographs to duplicates done in the same medium as the original. We are liable to regard these as standing in for the original but not as work versions. Perhaps this is because they are often less than fully faithful to the original. If we had a matter replicator that could reproduce physical objects down to the molecular level, we might be inclined to accept clones of the originals as work-*equivalents*. They are not *work versions*, because they preserve rather than modify work-identifying features. And neither are they genuine instances, if the works in question necessarily are singular or limited in number.

because they lose the original's interplay between medium and content or because they reproduce an appropriate effect via the different resources and possibilities of the alternate language. In other words, where the treatment of the language of the original is such that a translation cannot convey what is required simply by telling the same story under similar formal constraints, the translation might better be seen as a new but derivative piece than as a version of the original. But where the audience is not multilingual, the translation then provides a useful substitute, if not a work version.

13

Profundity in Instrumental Music

According to Peter Kivy (1990: ch. 10), to be profound music would have to be about a profound subject that is treated in an exemplary way or in some way adequate to its subject matter. Though he allows that music expresses emotion, Kivy denies that it is profound in virtue of doing so. This is because it is not *about* the emotions it expresses. Indeed, instrumental music is not usually about anything, though some works, such as J. S. Bach's contrapuntal compositions, are about the possibilities of musical materials and are thereby about music itself. Bach's treatment of his musical ideas is exemplary, but his subject matter, the potential of musical materials, is not worthy of great concern and does not go to the moral heart of human life. Accordingly, while Bach's music is of abiding interest and of importance to many people, it does not qualify as profound. Kivy's intuition is that some music is profound and Bach's should qualify if any does, but his intuition gives way under the pressure of his own analysis.

I share Kivy's intuition. Unlike him, I would be inclined to reject the analysis of profundity, rather than to abandon the intuition that some music is profound. His account of profundity is vulnerable in its insistence on what I will call the 'aboutness' criterion. Kivy (1997: ch. 6) seems to require for aboutness both reference and predication. This makes the expression of profundity essentially propositional, so it is not surprising that instrumental music fails to make the grade. But surely this sets too restrictive a standard? (It will exclude, as well as music and painting, all but the most explicitly didactive literature.) I agree with Kivy that profound things should draw our attention to important matters or truths, but they might do so by revealing, depicting, exhibiting, pointing to, or exposing those matters or truths, instead of by stating or describing them. There are ways of conveying ideas other than by asserting them. These ways might show rather than say how things are (Davies 1999a).

If the analysis of profundity is made more plausible by being weakened in the manner suggested, it is immediately easier to see both how instrumental music might qualify as profound and how its expressive powers could feature as elements in its profundity. Be that as it may, most of Kivy's commentators have accepted the outline of his theory and have replied by arguing that instrumental music can satisfy it.[1] They

---

First published in *British Journal of Aesthetics*, 42 (2002): 343–56. For Kivy's response, see Kivy (2003).

[1] Some of Kivy's critics simply change the topic. Ridley (1995b) argues that music can be *profoundly* so-and-so. Kivy (1997) agrees that this adverbial sense applies when music is *very* so-and-so—that is, when it

adopt one (or both) of two strategies. The first argues that music is profound in terms of a direct connection it makes to extra-musical matters of importance in the world, usually via emotions it expresses. The second locates music's profundity more squarely with the manner of treatment of purely musical elements of content and form, as Kivy does in his initial discussion of Bach's supreme craftsmanship. Unlike Kivy, the proponents of this line suggest there are indirect ties between music's autonomous character and matters of human importance that are sufficient to vouch for music's profundity.

Jerrold Levinson (1992) advocates the most compelling version of the first response to Kivy's analysis. He begins by arguing, as I have done above, that Kivy's account of the 'aboutness' criterion is inappropriately restrictive. He avers that it is reasonable to regard music as about the emotions expressed in it since composers intend it to be about them, a third party can make a reference to an emotion via an illustrative use of the music's expressiveness, listeners expect music to be expressive and take it to be designed to be such, and music's expressiveness often is salient and central to its character. Beyond the ways in which music can be profound that are considered by Kivy, Levinson recommends as worth considering (1992: 59): '(1) it explores the emotional or psychic realm in a more insightful or eye-opening way than most music; (2) it epitomizes or alludes to more interesting or complex extra-musical modes of growth and development than most music, and gives us a vicarious experience of such modes; (3) it strikes us as touching, in some fashion or other, on the most fundamental and pressing aspects of human existence—e.g. death, fate, the inexorability of time, the space between aspiration and attainment.' (See also Levinson 1996a: ch. 2.)

Kivy responds (1997) as follows: it is not true that composers generally intend that their works have the expressive properties they do; expressiveness is an unintended epiphenomenon accompanying musical features that are intentionally chosen to be as they are for reasons other than their expressiveness. Only with the Romantics does one get music that includes expressive properties as part of the work's structural plan, Kivy says. For my part, I find these claims not to be credible. I think that many composers are fully aware of their music's expressiveness and that they do not separate its expressive from its structural character, so that they might intend the one by intending the other. But let us not dwell on these points, nor on Kivy's reaffirmation of a restricted, quasi-linguistic approach to the 'aboutness' criterion, since he is prepared to concede, if only for the sake of the argument, that music may be about the emotions it expresses. He allows the point because he has a yet more telling objection to follow. Even if it is

possesses whatever qualities it has to a marked degree—but denies that this deals with the adjectival sense that is at issue. He was writing not about profoundly contrapuntal music but about contrapuntally profound music. Reimer (1995) notes that the subjective experience of music can be profound, which is to say that music (along with other factors) sometimes occasions an intense or deeply moving response. It is clear from his examples that Reimer has in mind experiences of transport or transcendence that are fuelled by music, and that his concern, unlike Kivy's, is not with intersubjective properties or the value of music as such.

about the emotions and they are of considerable importance, music is not capable of conveying more than dull banalities about them. In effect, it fails the final necessary condition for profundity, namely, that its subject matter be treated in a way adequate to its significance. We might learn from the exposition of the first movement of Mozart's Symphony No. 40 that the experience of happiness could naturally follow one of unhappiness but where is the profundity in that? And if the first movement of Beethoven's Symphony No. 5 refers us to growth, and we speculate on the growth of the cosmos since the Big Bang, our thoughts on that subject are unlikely to be profound. And even if they are, the profundity surely attaches to the thoughts rather than to the music.

I confess I am sympathetic to these final objections of Kivy's. I do not deny that instrumental music can be expressive or that we might come to new beliefs and understandings as a result of contemplating or being moved by its expressiveness, and I allow (1994a: chs 5, 6) that music occupies a central place in the lives of some people as a result of its expressive power or associations, but I share with Kivy the view that music is not profound as a result of revealing deep truths or ideas about emotions or their place in human life.[2] One cannot articulate the lessons taught about life by music's expressive progress without being made painfully aware of their prosaic nature. And if, perchance, one's thoughts are profound, this profundity is occasioned by the music without being attributable to it, because the content of those thoughts inevitably goes beyond anything conveyed unequivocally by the music.

At this point it is common for the defender of music's expressive profundity to invoke the idea that music presents emotions too subtle and individual to be named. As a result, the truths conveyed by music are ineffable and are all the more important for not being expressible in language.[3] I will not pursue here my objections to such claims. I think (Chapter 1 and Davies 1994a) that, typically, instrumental music expresses only a limited range of the most general emotions by presenting the dynamic profiles of their normal behavioral expressions. Music is very detailed, however, in the particular means by which it generates these emotion-characteristics. They are embodied in complex, highly specific musical sequences. The sadness expressed in Mozart's and Tchaikovsky's music differ in the note sequences that realize them. Yet there need be no corresponding, phenomenal difference in the kind or quality of sadness in the two cases. Specificity in the *means* or *manner* of expression is not necessarily matched by specificity in the emotion expressed (Chapters 7 and 8 and Davies 1999a). I suspect that the temptation to talk of music's ineffability is stoked by the mistaken assumption that differences in notes must map onto indescribably subtle differences in emotional

---

[2] McAdoo (1992) accuses Kivy of denying a connection between human experience and musical expressiveness. I think he is mistaken. Kivy holds that music expresses emotions and that these are of the ordinary, human kind. What he denies is that, in expressing them, it says anything profound about them.

[3] One who heads in this direction is Herzog (1995), but the path is already well trodden by Langer (1942) and the like.

content. In any event, I agree with Kivy that our reports of what is conveyed by music's expressiveness tend to the banal because what is communicated lacks depth and detail, not because it is profound but otherwise inarticulable.

I think the second line of argument fares better than the first against Kivy's approach (though there is nothing against combining the two, as Levinson does). This second approach, recall, hopes to cash talk of musical profundity in terms, first, of what is achieved in the treatment of the piece's contents and form, and second, of some indirect connection between these musical events, processes, features, or whatever and matters that are significant in the human realm. Several philosophers locate a crucial source of music's value not in its direct connection with the extra-musical but rather in its abstractness and independence from the real world. Malcolm Budd (1995: ch. 4) thinks that much of the value of music lies in the treatment of its abstract form, which resembles social and dramatic processes, such as dialogue, conflict, and resolution. Though abstract, it can be 'about' other abstractions, such as similarity and difference, the unification of diverse materials, the harmonious reconciliation of multiplicity within a unity, and so on. In a similar vein, David A. White suggests that a musical work is profound when it is unified, both in its parts and as a whole. He writes (1992: 32–3): 'concepts such as unity, whole and part, identity and difference are essential elements in the articulation of profundity precisely because these concepts are necessary to any account that purports to describe reality.... The work is, of course, not intended to be a sort of musical metaphysics. But if introducing concepts of wide generality can help account for certain prominent features in the experience and organization of the work, then this account articulates profundity by showing how the work can be approached as a simulacrum of reality.' R. A. Sharpe (1991) observes that music provides a paradigm of order in an uncertain world, and can have a dialogic character. Alan H. Goldman (1992; see also 1995) claims that music creates an alternative world of pure tones in ideal space. As such, it allows for 'the purest meeting of minds.' He continues (1992: 43): 'music itself represents the purest kind of Hegelian overcoming of matter by mind, of objectivity by subjectivity.... Thus, music is not only another world. It is a world that can be completely satisfying and fully revealing of the creative power of other minds. Its peculiar value lies in the purity of its revelation of the human spirit.' And though he criticizes Budd and finds more to value in music's expressiveness than the contribution this makes to the piece's formal development and coherence, Levinson stresses the importance of the mutual interaction and dependence between form and content, both at the local and the global level. 'What one finds intrinsically rewarding in the experience a good piece of music offers, and what perhaps most importantly determines its artistic value, is its very particular *wedding* of its form and content.... Above all, however, one enjoys and finds intrinsically rewarding the *fusion* of how it goes and what it conveys, the precise way in which what it conveys is embodied in and carried by how it goes' (Levinson 1998: 100).

Proponents of this second approach agree with one of Kivy's desiderata for an account of musical profundity: they look to the specifics of the music. Too few of those who find the meaning to life, the universe, and everything in Beethoven's late quartets get round to mentioning anything distinctive to the quartets' musical contents and form, yet these are supposed to be the source of the insights achieved. By contrast, both Levinson and White provide painstaking discussion of particular works to back up their views. That is on the plus side. On the negative is a general vagueness about the manner of music's contribution to our understanding of the metaphysical notions that are mentioned. In other words, we are back to the earlier complaint that, even if music can direct our focus to humanly important notions, it is not clear that it can clarify our understanding of them as such. What exactly does the music convey about sameness and difference or about unity that is profound? The connection between what is in the music and philosophical speculation on the nature of identity, say, seems too attenuated to allow that the music directs and accounts for that speculation, even when it is inspired by listening to the music and is profound. Alternatively, if one replies that one learned from the music that a movement with themes thus and so, a structure and development of this distinctive kind, etc. can unify apparently contrasting musical ideas into a satisfyingly complete manifold, then one has not answered the problem that floored Kivy in the first place, which was to reveal how the materials of music can touch on matters worthy of great concern and that go to the heart of human life.

Profundity in chess

I have a third take on music's profundity that avoids some of the obvious problems with the first two. Like other philosophers in this area, I will present my case through examples. Unfortunately, no examples strictly entail the theory they are supposed to illustrate. Kivy is likely to agree with his opponents on a list of the most plausible candidates for musical profundity, but not with claims for the actual success of these candidates in achieving profundity. As a result, argument by example, unless it is handled very carefully, is bound to beg the question. Nevertheless, views about the nature of music and what it can do are unconvincing in the absence of model cases. How, then, is one to advance the discussion? I do so by beginning with examples that have nothing to do with instrumental music, yet which come from a realm that is no less self-contained and detached from real-world concerns.

In 1956 in the Rosenwald Chess Tournament, Donald Byrne came up against the thirteen-year-old Bobbie Fischer. Fischer had played badly so far in the tournament, while Byrne was more experienced and probably expected to win. Byrne played white and, after his seventeenth move, appeared to have an overwhelming advantage. One of Fischer's unprotected knights was under attack and his queen was threatened by a bishop. The queen could not both defend itself and guard the endangered knight (see Figure 13.1).

Fischer's response must have jolted Byrne. He retreated his white bishop to a square (K3/e6) where it too could be taken. Byrne captured the queen. In another seven moves, Fischer had removed a rook and both bishops of his opponent. Instead of

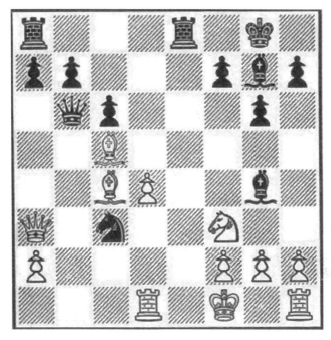

Figure 13.1 Black (Fischer) to play. Rosenwald Tournament, 1956.

resigning, as is customary, Byrne gave Fischer the satisfaction of completing the game with checkmate at move forty-one. In post-game analysis, Fischer was able to demonstrate that all of white's replies to his seventeenth move were losing ones.

Fischer's coup was a masterpiece of tactical calculation. He saw his way through all the complications to clearly winning positions in each variation. But in chess, genius in strategy is no less important than tactical brilliance. It was strategic judgment and skill that were displayed by Raoul Capablanca when he faced Frank J. Marshall in 1918. The opening was the Spanish game (or Ruy Lopez), the most used and analyzed in grandmaster chess. As black, Marshall introduced an innovation on move eight. He had nursed and prepared the novelty for years, holding it back in order to spring it on Capablanca in revenge for the humiliating drubbing he received from the Cuban in an exhibition series they played in 1909.

Marshall gambitted a pawn, for the loss of which he would obtain positional pressure and attacking impetus. If he took the pawn, Capablanca would have to counter over the board moves and combinations analyzed at length and leisure by his opponent. And if he declined it, Marshall would be no less well prepared for what eventuated, would have gained ground, and would have scored a major psychological victory. Capablanca understood the situation. He said after the game that he realized the attack would be 'terrific' if he accepted the gambit pawn, which he did. He defended superbly against the storm that followed and by move twenty-five had neutralized black's pressure.

He preserved his material advantage and with it obtained a winning endgame. Marshall resigned on move thirty-eight.

The Marshall gambit, as it is now called, remains playable to this day. Though it is not guaranteed to produce a sustainable advantage, neither has it been refuted. Unlike Fischer, Capablanca did not see his way through to a forced win, though footnotes show he set tactical traps that Marshall was able to sidestep. But Capablanca did show deep judgment and sustained calculative ability in out-thinking his opponent on that day and he did all this under the pressure of the occasion and under the fixed time constraints of competition games. His play was a masterpiece of strategy, I claim.

Chess fails Kivy's conditions for profundity. It is not obviously *about* anything and certainly is not about anything that goes to the moral heart of human life. Of course, some will claim that chess is about struggle, conflict, mortality, and the rest. But either the connection between chess and such perennially important themes is too tendentious or chess fails to say anything meaningful about these topics even if it brings them to mind. I think Kivy would be bound to hold that chess fails his analysis, just as instrumental music does. In particular, neither Fischer's move nor Capablanca's strategic play could be profound on Kivy's account. Yet I maintain that these abstract, intellectual achievements are profound in their way. And I would say the same of some complex mathematical proofs, for instance, though their profundity may be harder for most of us to appreciate because we lack the background skills to follow what was done.

How should the account of profundity be modified to accommodate examples of these kinds? It is true that chess moves are not about the powers of pieces, the possibilities of the position, or the end of beating the opponent. They presuppose such things but do not refer to them. In Kivy's terms, they are not *about* anything, not even their own rules and materials. But I have already indicated that Kivy's 'aboutness' criterion, which requires reference to a subject of abiding human importance and predication of something insightful about it, sets an inappropriate standard. It is sufficient that profundity is *shown* or *displayed* in an activity or judgment. Profundity might be revealed or exhibited in the manner of doing something, such as playing chess or proving a theorem, without being enunciated self-consciously or requiring linguistic expression. According to standard dictionary meanings, the profound has great depth and, in human activity, demonstrates great knowledge or insight. Fischer's tactical move and Capablanca's strategic play surely reveal these qualities in graphic form. These players penetrated further into the positions than their expert opponents and their play was farsighted. The skills displayed were not merely those of the master craftsperson, which are algorithmic even if they have been honed to perfection. Chess of this kind, play that is exceptional even by the standards of the best grandmasters, relies on imagination, originality, and a deep (though not necessarily articulable) understanding of the principles and potentialities of the game as well of the particular position.

Yet is Kivy not correct to insist that the profound must take some matter of human importance as its topic? Yes and no. It should connect with such a subject, certainly, but it need not take anything as its topic. If poetry is sometimes profound and pushpin never is, this is not because poetry sometimes takes significant matters as its subject whereas pushpin is about nothing as such. Rather, it is because poetry, like chess and music, has the potential to engage the mind and spirit more fully and intensely than pushpin, whatever, if any, topic it addresses. In Kivy's terms, chess is not itself a subject of human importance, but the games just described illustrate to a jaw-dropping degree the inexhaustible fecundity, flexibility, insight, vitality, subtlety, complexity, and analytical far-reachingness of which the human mind is capable. That is something on which to marvel. And because of the wider evolutionary consequences of our intellectual and imaginative capacities, that demonstration is of significance even where those who display such capacities are not also trying to say anything about the competence they bring to our attention.[4] Understanding our own human natures is of considerable importance, and those natures are revealed sometimes in the way chess is played, for instance.[5] Indeed, the separation of the realm of chess from the practical, real world might have the consequence of making more salient the cognitive potentials manifested in chess, just because those manifestations are abstracted from the practical situations and consequences with which they are ordinarily meshed. Kivy is correct to think that the profound goes beyond what is merely skilled or intense, but he underestimates the variety of ways in which what is of human significance and value can be exhibited.

Musical profundity

Obviously, I mean to claim that purely instrumental music can be profound in something like the way that chess can be. Like chess, instrumental music is valued for itself, not merely as a means to other things, and it creates its own, autonomous world. Of course, the mental powers needed to compose great music are not all the same as those that suit a player for chess (although Philidor is one person who achieved eminence in both areas). In music, being able to unify the whole economically, and being clear and elegant, are much more relevant than is calculative power, say.[6] The crucial similarity, though, is this: in creating the very greatest music, composers display to an extraordinary degree many of the general cognitive capacities seen also in

---

[4] What is profound is the play, not the player. There is no reason to think that Fischer or Capablanca could discourse interestingly on human cognitive abilities or that they had thoughts on this subject that they were trying to communicate.

[5] As I quoted earlier, Goldman thinks that music involves a communion of minds in that it can reveal the transcendence of Hegelian spirit over matter. My claim is much less metaphysical. We see particular, very great minds at work, doing what ordinary people cannot, and this makes us aware of the extent of our—that is, humankind's—creative and cognitive capacities.

[6] For an exchange on the aesthetics of chess, see P. N. Humble (1993, 1995), Ravilous (1994).

196 MUSICAL UNDERSTANDINGS

outstanding chess, namely, originality, far-sightedness, imagination, fertility, plasticity, refinement, intuitive mastery of complex detail, and so on. And as in chess, they cannot rely merely on following rules or statistical norms to see them through to success.

I now offer some examples that I regard as revealing musical profundity in a manner similar to those taken from chess.

The first movement of Béla Bartók's *Music for Strings, Percussion, and Celesta* is a fugue. The subject begins on the note A. Subsequent entries are always at the interval of the fifth; at E, B, F-sharp, etc. for the ascending entries, and at D, G, C, and so on for the descending ones. As students of music theory are taught, there is a circle of fifths. Successive fifths cycle back eventually to the starting pitch and the return begins when the tritone is reached and passed. Bartók's fugue mimics the theory books. It climaxes at measures 56–7 when both the ascending and descending entries converge on the note that lies a tritone from the opening A, E-flat. At that moment, the dense, harmonically complex texture dissolves into the stark clarity of octave unisons, played fortissimo. The cycle is reversed in measures 58–77, which involve inversion of the subject, stretto entries, and compression to the point of structural collapse. The fugue theme, having now returned to its opening note of A, is presented simultaneously in its original and inverted forms through measures 78–81, and fragments of its beginning, again in original and inverted forms, echo each other through measures 82–85. These fragments end variously on F-natural and C-sharp. How can the circle be completed, with a resolution on A? Bartók achieves this in the final three measures. He presents what was the second phrase (first presented at measure two) of the fugue subject, stated simultaneously in its original and inverted forms. This motive follows naturally from the fragments that precede it, since these were based on the first phrase of the fugue theme, and it achieves closure because instead of being left hanging, it proceeds to the A that is its natural conclusion.

Here is the miracle. The closing three measures not only draw the movement to its close, they recapitulate and thereby summarize the whole movement's structure. The two voices move in contrary motion from A, settle simultaneously on E-flat, the tritone, and then reverse the process until they converge in unison on the final A (see Figure 13.2).

For another case, take the first movement of Beethoven's Third Symphony, *Eroica*. At 691 measures, it was of unprecedented length. The coda (beginning at 553) was also

Figure 13.2 Béla Bartók, *Music for Strings, Percussion, and Celesta*. First Movement, ending.

Figure 13.3 Beethoven. Third Symphony. First Movement, bars 3–8.

far more extended than was standard. It rivals the (unrepeated) exposition. Moreover, the final sixty-four measures hammer with hardly any relief on tonic and dominant chords. To understand why the movement has these relative dimensions and why it ends in triumph and apotheosis rather than in banal monotony, it is necessary to go back to the unexpected C-sharp in the fifth measure of the opening theme (see Figure 13.3). This note sets in motion a dramatic progress that inevitably requires distortion of the expected proportions. However, Beethoven does not abandon the guiding principles of first movement sonata form, but instead, he plays on tensions generated between that underlying formal pattern and the substance of his musical ideas.

The theme's C-sharp is melodically unexpected, because it blocks the symmetrical continuation that is anticipated. It 'shuts down' the theme by excluding the four-measure second phrase that would normally balance the first. It is also tonally ambiguous, though in the opening statement the tonic key is immediately restored and affirmed. When the theme returns at measure 15, the C-sharp is absent but so too is the second phrase, and this is again the case at 37, where the C-sharp is notated enharmonically as D-flat, passing to C. With the recapitulation (398), the theme returns with the notated C-sharp, but here it again functions as a D-flat in a chromatic progression from E-flat to C. That C heralds a modulation to F, followed quickly by one to D-flat, with the theme's opening arpeggio sounded in both tonalities. In other words, the tonal instability implicit in the theme's C-sharp is brought into prominence at the beginning of the recapitulation, just when one would expect a stable tonic key. Meanwhile, the balancing second phrase is still withheld, so the melodic uncertainty of the opening is recapitulated along with the theme. The coda begins with a celebration of tonal chaos: successive major chords on E-flat, D-flat, and C (555–60), which descent recalls the theme's first appearance in the recapitulation (at 398–407; see also 42–3). The theme's opening arpeggio is treated sequentially (564–77), which recalls similar passages in the development (at 178–87 and 338–60) but with this important difference: the tonal stability at 565–72 makes it easy to hear what follows the repeated first phrase as an answering second. At last, melodic closure is near to being achieved, but in the key of C, not the tonic E-flat. That oversight is corrected when the theme achieves its final, triumphant version (see Figure 13.4). Not only is a second, melodically and tonally unambiguous, phrase supplied, but also an inverted variant provides a counterpoint. Meanwhile, the key could not be more firmly anchored in the tonic, where it remains until the end.

Now we can see why Beethoven's coda is so extended. The first subject in sonata form usually is melodically complete and tonally unambiguous. Whatever vicissitudes

Figure 13.4 Beethoven. Third Symphony. First Movement, bars 631–638.

it undergoes in the development, its recapitulation represents a return to order. The coda need not be long, since the thematic and tonal closure it emphasizes has already been achieved. By contrast, Beethoven's first subject is melodically incomplete and tonally unstable. At some times he stresses the incompleteness, at others the instability. Given what happens earlier, these tensions cannot suddenly disappear with the arrival of the recapitulation. No precedent for doing so is established in the preceding development. Indeed, the tonal instability associated in the development with sequential treatments of the theme's opening permeates the recapitulation, which is less secure than is common as a result. The movement's melodic and tonal tensions are finally resolved in the coda, and even at that late stage, this is done gradually. The fully articulated theme does not appear strongly in the tonic key until some seventy measures after the close of the recapitulation. The coda must be so massive, then, because it must achieve all the reconciliations and reaffirmations that would normally take place in the recapitulation. As I suggested at the outset, the coda (and with it, the movement as a whole) is prolonged as a consequence of the unexpected C-sharp played by the cellos in measure 7.

By way of conclusion and summary, let me compare my examples with Kivy's. Bach was a pedagogue, and the *Well-tempered Clavier*, the French Suites, the suites for unaccompanied violin and cello, *Art of Fugue*, and like works, are studies in compositional and instrumental technique. In consequence, they are about the kinds for which they serve as paradigms. They are about the nature of the fugue and the suite, and about all the musical methods and styles they encompass. The composition of music, though, does not typically take in this ambitious sweep. Nevertheless, a fair amount is self-conscious in being about the potentials of the specific musical ideas and fragments of which it is comprised. This is true not only of Bach's contrapuntal pieces, taken in their particularity as individual works, but also of the first movement of Bartók's *Music for Strings, Percussion, and Celesta*. Its closing makes a quite deliberate reference to the structural principles on which the unfolding of the movement is based. Most music, by contrast, does its thing without referring either to what that thing is or to wider musical types and styles. This is true of Beethoven's *Eroica*. Within the piece, there is a working out of a balance between the nature of the materials and the exigencies of the form, but without self-reference. The composer might be unaware of the bases on which he makes his choices, relying on his intuitions and taste to select what will succeed, or he might be fully aware of and deliberately engineer the underlying relationships and processes that generate the effects he is after (see Chapter 7). Beethoven probably belonged to the latter camp, given the care he lavished on his creations and the long periods of gestation and experiment that led up to them. But that does not mean he set about establishing internal connections that his audience is supposed to appreciate as referring one part of the work or movement to others. While my Bartók example might be 'about' its own form, the same could not be claimed for the first movement of Beethoven's *Eroica*.

This does not matter, though. I claim that Bach's music is profound in displaying the depths and extent of his creative genius, and through that, showing more generally the elasticity, fertility, creativity, vision, and so on of the human mind. So, even Bach's contrapuntal music, in being about the potential of its own materials, is not about what makes it profound, which is what it reveals about its composer and, thereby, about the extraordinary capacities of human beings. The same is true of Bartók's music and of Beethoven's. Neither is it about what it reveals regarding the mental capacities and potentials needed for its creation, but as I have suggested earlier, music's greatest masterpieces are profound in terms of what they show, whether or not this involves reference and an equivalent to predication.

My central thesis is that some music is profound as some chess play is, namely, for what it exemplifies and thereby reveals about the human mind. So far I have stressed the cognitive and formal aspects of this, which is natural in drawing the parallel with chess. But music has far greater powers, for instance in its expressiveness. Earlier I argued that music does not convey important truths about the emotions, but now it is time to incorporate its expressiveness into a wider story about its profundity. Music's expressiveness can contribute to and shape its formal character and in that way may display the cognitive capacities I stressed earlier. More than this, the greatest masterpieces can be revealing of human powers for representing, understanding, controlling, balancing, and reflecting on the emotions, and thereby exhibit the affective dimension of our nature, as well as our more purely cognitive side.

References

Adelmann, Pamela K., and Zajonc, R. B. (1989). Facial Efference and the Experience of Emotion. *Annual Review of Psychology*, 40: 249–80.

Alperson, Philip. (1980). 'Musical Time' and Music as an 'Art of Time.' *Journal of Aesthetics and Art Criticism*, 38: 407–17.

——. (1987). Introduction. In P. Alperson (ed.), *What is Music? An Introduction to the Philosophy of Music*. University Park: Pennsylvania State University Press.

Apel, Willi. (ed.). (1966). *Harvard Dictionary of Music*. Cambridge, MA: Harvard University Press.

Arom, Simha. (1991). *African Polyphony and Polyrhythm*. Cambridge: Cambridge University Press.

——. (1997). Le 'Syndrome' du Pentatonisme Africain. *Musicae Scientiae*, 1: 139–63.

Bach, Kent. (2001). You Don't Say? *Synthese*, 128: 15–44.

Baily, John. (1977). Movement Patterns in Playing the Herati Dutâr. In J. Blacking (ed.), *The Anthropology of the Body*. London: Academic Press, 275–330.

——. (1985). Music Structure and Human Movement. In P. Howell, I. Cross, and R. West (eds), *Musical Structure and Cognition*. London: Academic Press, 237–58.

Balkwill, Laura-Lee. (2006). Perceptions of Emotion in Music across Cultures. Emotional Geographies: The Second International and Interdisciplinary Conference, May, Queen's University, Kingston, Canada.

Balkwill, Laura-Lee, and Thompson, William Forde. (1999). A Cross-Cultural Investigation of the Perception of Emotion in Music: Psychophysical and Cultural Cues. *Music Perception*, 17: 43–64.

Balkwill, Laura-Lee, Thompson, William Forde, and Matsunaga, Rie. (2004). Recognition of Emotion in Japanese, Western, and Hindustani Music by Japanese Listeners. *Japanese Psychological Research*, 46: 337–49.

Barsalou, Lawrence. W. (1992). *Cognitive Psychology: An Overview for Cognitive Scientists*. Hillsdale: Erlbaum Associates.

Bartlett, Dale L. (1996). Physiological Responses to Music and Sound Stimuli. In D. A. Hodges (ed.), *Handbook of Music Psychology*, 2nd edn. San Antonio: Institute for Music Research Press, 343–85.

Benamou, Marc. (2003). Comparing Musical Affect: Java and the West. *The World of Music*, 45: 57–76.

Benzon, William. (2001). *Beethoven's Anvil: Music in Mind and Culture*. New York: Basic Books.

Bigand, Emmanuel. (1990). Abstraction of Two Forms of Underlying Structure in a Tonal Melody. *Psychology of Music*, 18: 45–59.

Bird, John. (1976). *Percy Grainger*. London: Paul Elek.

Blacking, John. (1961). Patterns of Nsenga *Kalimba* Music. *African Music*, 2 (4): 26–43.

Bregman, Albert S. (1990). *Auditory Scene Analysis: The Perceptual Organization of Sound*. Cambridge, MA: MIT Press.

Brennan, Teresa. (2004). *The Transmission of Affect*. Ithaca: Cornell University Press.

Brophy, Brigid. (1974). *The Snow Ball*. London: Allison & Busby. First published in 1964.
Brown, Lee B. (2000). Phonography, Repetition and Spontaneity. *Philosophy and Literature*, 24: 111–25.
Bruner, Gordon C. (1990). Music, Mood, and Marketing. *Journal of Marketing*, 54 (4): 94–104.
Budd, Malcolm. (1985). Understanding Music. *Proceedings of the Aristotelian Society*, Supp. Vol. 59: 233–48.
——. (1995). *Values of Art*. London: Penguin Press.
——. (2008). *Aesthetic Essays*. Oxford: Oxford University Press.
——. (2009). Response to Christopher Peacocke's 'The Perception of Music: Sources of Significance.' *British Journal of Aesthetics*, 49: 289–92.
Bujold, Pascal. (2005). Towards a 'Dancing Analysis' of Rhythms from Other Musical Cultures. *Conference: Music and Dance Performance: Cross-cultural Approaches*. SOAS, 12–15 April.
Bunt, Leslie, and Pavlicevic, Mercédès. (2001). Music and Emotion: Perspectives from Music Therapy. In P. N. Juslin and J. A. Sloboda (eds), *Music and Emotion: Theory and Research*. Oxford: Oxford University Press, 181–201.
Capurso, A. A., Fisichelli, V. R., Gilman, L., Gutheil, E. A., Wright, J. T., and Paperte, F. (eds) (1952). *Music and your Emotions: A Practical Guide to Music Selections Associated with Desired Emotional Responses*. New York: Liveright.
Carlson, John G., and Hatfield, Elaine. (1992). *Psychology of Emotion*. Fort Worth: Harcourt, Brace, Jovanovitch.
Carroll, Noël. (1990). *The Philosophy of Horror or Paradoxes of the Heart*. New York: Routledge.
——. (1997). Art, Narrative, and Emotion. In M. Hjort and S. Laver (eds), *Emotion and the Arts*. Oxford: Oxford University Press, 190–211.
Cavell, Stanley. (1977). Music Discomposed. In S. Cavell (ed.), *Must We Mean What We Say?* Cambridge: Cambridge University Press, 180–212.
Clarke, Eric F. (1985). Structure and Expression in Rhythmic Performance. In P. Howell, I. Cross, and R. West (eds), *Musical Structure and Cognition*. London: Academic Press, 209–36.
——. (2005). *Ways of Listening: An Ecological Approach to the Perception of Musical Meaning*. New York: Oxford University Press.
Cochrane, Tom. (2010). A Simulation Theory of Musical Expressivity. *Australasian Journal of Philosophy*, 88: 191–207.
Cogan, Robert, and Escot, Pozzi. (1976). *Sonic Design: The Nature of Sound and Music*. Englewood Cliffs: Prentice-Hall.
Coker, Wilson. (1972). *Music and Meaning*. New York: Free Press.
Conard, Nicholas J. (2005). An Overview of the Patterns of Behavioural Change in Africa and Eurasia during the Middle and Late Pleistocene. In F. d'Errico and L. Blackwell (eds), *From Tools to Symbols: From Early Hominids to Humans*. Johannesburg: Witwatersrand University Press, 294–332.
Conard, Nicholas J., Malina, Maria, and Münzel, Susanne C. (2009). New Flutes Document the Earliest Musical Tradition in Southwestern Germany. *Nature*, 460: 737–40.
Cone, Edward T. (1974). *The Composer's Voice*. Berkeley: University of California Press.
Cook, Nicholas. (1987a). *A Guide to Musical Analysis*. Oxford: Oxford University Press.
——. (1987b). Musical Form and the Listener. *Journal of Aesthetics and Art Criticism*, 46: 23–9.
——. (1990). *Music, Imagination, and Culture*. Oxford: Clarendon Press.

Coplan, Amy. (2004). Empathic Engagement with Narrative Fictions. *Journal of Aesthetics and Art Criticism*, 62: 141–52.
——. (2006). Catching Characters' Emotions: Emotional Contagion Responses to Narrative Fiction Film. *Film Studies: An International Review*, 8, Summer: 26–38.
Cramer, Alfred. (2002). Schoenberg's *Klangfarbenmelodie*: A Principle of Early Atonal Harmony. *Music Theory Spectrum*, 24: 1–34.
Critchley, Macdonald. (1977). Ecstatic and Synaesthetic Experiences During Musical Perception. In M. Critchley and R. A. Henson (eds), *Music and the Brain: Studies in the Neurology of Music*. London: William Heinemann Medical Books, 217–32.
Cross, Ian. (2007). Music and Cognitive Evolution. In R. I. M. Dunbar and L. Barrett (eds), *Oxford Handbook of Evolutionary Psychology*. Oxford: Oxford University Press, 649–67.
Cross, Ian, and Morley, Iain. (2009). Music in Evolution: Theories, Definitions and the Nature of the Evidence. In S. Malloch and C. Trevarthen (eds), *Communicative Musicality: Narratives of Expressive Gesture and Being Human*. Oxford: Oxford University Press, 61–82.
Cumming, Naomi. (1993). Music Analysis and the Perceiver: A Perspective from Functionalist Philosophy. *Current Musicology*, 54: 38–53.
Currie, Gregory. (1988). *An Ontology of Art*. London: Macmillan.
Cytowic, Richard E. (1989). *Synesthesia: A Union of the Senses*. New York: Springer-Verlag.
——. (1993). *The Man Who Tasted Shapes: A Bizarre Medical Mystery Offers Revolutionary Insights into Emotions, Reasoning, and Consciousness*. New York: G. P. Putnam's Sons.
Dahlhaus, Carl. (1973). Das 'Verstehen' von Musik und die Sprache der musikalischen Analyse [Musical 'Understanding' and the Language of Musical Analysis]. In P. Faltin and H.-P. Reinecke (eds), *Musik und Verstehen*, Cologne: Arno Volk, 37–47.
Darrow, Alice-Ann, Haack, Paul, and Kuribayashi, Fumio. (1987). Descriptors and Preferences for Eastern and Western Musics by Japanese and American Nonmusic Majors. *Journal of Research in Music Education*, 35 (4): 237–48.
Darwin, Charles. (1998). *The Expression of Emotion in Man and Animals*. London: Harper Collins. First published 1889.
Davidson, Jane W. (1993). Visual Perception of Performance Manner in the Movements of Solo Musicians. *Psychology of Music*, 21: 103–12.
Davies, John Booth. (1979). Memory for Melodies and Tonal Sequences: A Theoretical Note. *British Journal of Psychology*, 70: 205–10.
Davies, Stephen. (1994a). *Musical Meaning and Expression*. Ithaca: Cornell University Press.
——. (1994b). Kivy on Auditors' Emotions. *Journal of Aesthetics and Art Criticism*, 52: 235–6.
——. (1999a). Response to Robert Stecker. *British Journal of Aesthetics*, 39: 282–7.
——. (1999b). Review of Levinson's *Music in the Moment*. *Philosophical Quarterly*, 49: 403–5.
——. (1999c). Rock versus Classical Music. *Journal of Aesthetics and Art Criticism*, 57: 193–204.
——. (2001a). *Musical Works and Performances: A Philosophical Exploration*. Oxford: Clarendon Press.
——. (2001b). Interpretation. In S. Sadie (ed.), *New Grove Dictionary of Music*, 2nd edn. London: Macmillan, Vol. 12: 497–9.
——. (2003). *Themes in the Philosophy of Music*. Oxford: Oxford University Press.
——. (2006). Balinese *Legong*: Revival or Decline? *Asian Theatre Journal*, 23: 314–41.
——. (2007). *Philosophical Perspectives on Art*. Oxford: Oxford University Press.
——. (2009). Responding Emotionally to Fictions. *Journal of Aesthetics and Art Criticism*, 67: 269–84.

——. (2010). Why Art is not a Spandrel. *British Journal of Aesthetics*, 50: 333–41.

DeBellis, Mark. (1991). Conceptions of Musical Structure. *Midwest Studies in Philosophy*, 16: 378–93.

——. (1995). *Music and Conceptualization*. Cambridge: Cambridge University Press.

——. (1999a). The Paradox of Musical Analysis. *Journal of Music Theory*, 43: 83–99.

——. (1999b). What is Musical Intuition? Tonal Theory as Cognitive Science. *Philosophical Psychology*, 12: 471–501.

——. (2002). Musical Analysis as Articulation. *Journal of Aesthetics and Art Criticism*, 60: 119–35.

——. (2003). Schenkerian Analysis and the Intelligent Listener. *Monist*, 86: 579–607.

——. (2005). Conceptual and Nonconceptual Modes of Music Perception. *Postgraduate Journal of Aesthetics*, 2: 45–61.

Decety, Jean, and Hodges, Sara D. (2006). The Social Neuroscience of Empathy. In P. A. M. Van Lange (ed.), *Bridging Social Psychology: Benefits of Transdisciplinary Approaches*. Mahwah: Erlbaum, 103–9.

Decety, Jean, and Jackson, Philip L. (2004). The Functional Architecture of Human Empathy. *Behavioral and Cognitive Neuroscience Reviews*, 3: 71–100.

Dempster, Douglas. (1991). Review of Kivy's *Music Alone*. *Journal of Aesthetics and Art Criticism*, 49: 381–3.

Dempster, Douglas, and Brown, Matthew. (1990). Evaluating Musical Analyses and Theories: Five Perspectives. *Journal of Music Theory*, 34: 247–79.

Dennett, Daniel C. (1987). *The Intentional Stance*. Cambridge, MA: MIT Press.

DeNora, Tia. (2000). *Music in Everyday Life*. Cambridge: Cambridge University Press.

Deutsch, Diana. (1999). The Processing of Pitch Combinations. In D. Deutsch (ed.), *The Psychology of Music*, 2nd edn. San Diego: Academic Press, 349–411.

Deutsch, Otto Erich (ed.). (1966). *Mozart: A Documentary Biography*, trans. E. Blom, P. Branscombe, and J. Noble, 2nd edn. London: Adam & Charles Black.

Dibben, Nicola. (2001). What Do We Hear When We Hear Music? Music Perception and Musical Material. *Musicae Scientiae*, 5: 161–94.

Dodd, Julian. (2007a). Sounds, Instruments and Works of Music. In K. Stock (ed.), *Philosophers on Music: Experience, Meaning and Work*. Oxford: Oxford University Press, 23–51.

——. (2007b). *Works of Music: An Essay in Ontology*. Oxford: Oxford University Press.

——. (2010). Confessions of an Unrepentant Timbral Sonicist. *British Journal of Aesthetics*, 50: 33–52.

Dowling, W. Jay. (1972). Recognition of Melodic Transformations: Inversion, Retrograde, and Retrograde Inversion. *Perception and Psychophysics*, 12: 417–21.

Dowling, W. Jay, and Harwood, Dane L. (1986). *Music Cognition*. New York: Academic Press.

Dreyfus, Hubert L., and Dreyfus, Stuart E. (1986). *Mind over Machine: The Power of Human Intuition and Expertise in the Era of the Computer*. New York: Harper & Row.

Ekman, Paul. (1972). Universals and Cultural Differences in Facial Expression of Emotion. In J. R. Cole (ed.), *Nebraska Symposium on Motivation*. Lincoln: University of Nebraska Press, Vol. 19, 207–83.

——. (1980). Biological and Cultural Contributions to Body and Facial Movements in the Expression of the Emotions. In A. O. Rorty (ed.), *Explaining Emotions*. Los Angeles: University of California Press, 73–101.

——. (1992). An Argument for Basic Emotions. *Cognition and Emotion*, 6: 169–200.

Elfenbein, Hilary Anger, and Ambady, Nalini. (2002). On the Universality and Cultural Specificity of Emotion Recognition: A Meta-analysis. *Psychological Bulletin*, 128: 203–35.

Ellis, Nick C. (ed.). (1994). *Implicit and Explicit Learning of Language*. London: Academic Press.

Evans, Paul, and Schubert, Emery. (2008). Relationships between Expressed and Felt Emotions in Music. *Musicae Scientiae*, 12: 75–99.

Feagin, Susan. (1996). *Reading with Feeling: The Aesthetics of Appreciation*. Ithaca: Cornell University Press.

Ferguson, Donald. (1960). *Music as Metaphor: The Elements of Expression*. Minneapolis: University of Minnesota Press.

Fernald, Anne. (1992). Meaningful Melodies in Mothers' Speech to Infants. In H. Papousek, U. Jurgens, and M. Papousek (eds), *Nonverbal Vocal Communication: Comparative and Developmental Aspects*. Cambridge: Cambridge University Press, 262–82.

Fisher, John A. (1994). The New Guinea Drone Beetle vs. the Teutonic Symphony Orchestra: Discerning Music Cross-Culturally. Unpublished.

——. (1998). Rock 'n' Recording: The Ontological Complexity of Rock Music. In P. Alperson (ed.), *Musical Worlds: New Directions in the Philosophy of Music*, University Park: Pennsylvania State University Press, 109–23.

Francès, Robert. (1988). *The Perception of Music*, trans. W. J. Dowling. Hillsdale: Lawrence Erlbaum Associates.

Franklin, Nancy, and Tversky, Barbara. (1990). Searching Imagined Environments. *Journal of Experimental Psychology: General*, 119: 63–76.

Franks, Jeffery J., and Bransford, John D. (1971). Abstraction of Visual Patterns. *Journal of Experimental Psychology*, 90: 65–74.

French, Robert M., and Cleeremans, Axel. (eds). (2002). *Implicit Learning and Consciousness: An Empirical, Philosophical and Computational Consensus in the Making*. Hove: Psychology Press.

Fritz, Thomas, Jentschke, Sebastian, Gosselin, Nathalie, Sammler, Daniela, Peretz, Isabelle, Turner, Robert, Friederici, Angela D., and Koelsch, Stefan. (2009). Universal Recognition of Three Basic Emotions in Music. *Current Biology*, 19: 573–6.

Gabrielsson, Alf. (2002). Emotion Perceived and Emotion Felt: Same or Different? *Musicae Scientiae*, Special number (2001–02): 123–47.

——. (2003). Music Performance Research at the Millennium. *Psychology of Music*, 31: 221–72.

Gaut, Berys, and Livingston, Paisley (eds). (2003). *The Creation of Art: New Essays in Philosophical Aesthetics*. Cambridge: Cambridge University Press.

Gibson, James J. (1968). *The Senses Considered as Perceptual Systems*. London: George Allen & Unwin.

Gjerdingen, Robert O. (1993). 'Smooth' Rhythms as Probes of Entrainment. *Music Perception*, 10: 503–8.

Godlovitch, Stan. (1990). Artists, Programs, and Performance. *Australasian Journal of Philosophy*, 68: 301–12.

——. (1998). *Musical Performance: A Philosophical Study*. London: Routledge.

Goldie, Peter. (2000). *The Emotions: A Philosophical Exploration*. Oxford: Clarendon Press.

Goldman, Alan H. (1992). The Value of Music. *Journal of Aesthetics and Art Criticism*, 50: 35–44.

——. (1995). *Aesthetic Value*. Boulder: Westview Press.

Goodman, Nelson. (1968). *Languages of Art*. New York: Bobbs-Merrill.

Gracyk, Theodore A. (1996). *Rhythm and Noise: An Aesthetics of Rock Music*. Durham: Duke University Press.

——. (1999). Valuing and Evaluating Popular Music. *Journal of Aesthetics and Art Criticism*, 57: 205–20.

——. (2001). Music's Worldly Uses, or How I learned to Stop Worrying and to Love Led Zeppelin. In A. Neill and A. Ridley (eds), *Arguing about Art*, 2nd edn. London: Routledge, 135–47.

Grammer, Karl, Keki, Viktoria, Striebel, Beate, Atzmüller, Michaela, and Fink, Bernhard. (2003). Bodies in Motion: A Window to the Soul. In E. Voland and K. Grammer (eds), *Evolutionary Aesthetics*. Berlin: Springer Verlag, 295–323.

Grant, James. (2010). The Dispensability of Metaphor. *British Journal of Aesthetics*, 50: 255–72.

Green, Lucy. (1988). *Music on Deaf Ears*. Manchester: Manchester University Press.

Gregory, Andrew H., and Varney, Nicholas. (1996). Cross-cultural Comparisons in the Affective Response to Music. *Psychology of Music*, 24: 47–52.

Griffiths, Paul. (1997). *What Emotions Really Are*. Chicago: University of Chicago Press.

Hamilton, Andy. (2007). *Aesthetics and Music*. London: Continuum.

Handel, Stephen. (1989). *Listening: An Introduction to the Perception of Auditory Events*. Cambridge, MA: MIT Press.

——. (1995). Timbre Perception and Auditory Object Identification. In B. J. Moore (ed.), *Hearing (Handbook of Perception and Cognition)*, 2nd edn. Orlando: Academic Press, 425–61.

Hatfield, Elaine, Cacioppo, John T., and Rapson, Richard L. (1994). *Emotional Contagion*. New York: Cambridge University Press.

Herzog, Patricia. (1995). Music Criticism and Musical Meaning. *Journal of Aesthetics and Art Criticism*, 53: 299–312.

Hicks, Michael. (1991). Serialism and Comprehensibility: A Guide for the Teacher. *Journal of Aesthetic Education*, 25 (4): 75–85.

Higgins, Kathleen Marie. (1997). Musical Idiosyncracy and Perspectival Listening. In J. Robinson (ed.), *Music and Meaning*. Ithaca: Cornell University Press, 83–102.

——. (2006). The Cognitive and Appreciative Impact of Musical Universals. *Revue Internationale de Philosophie*, 60: 487–503.

——. (2012). *As Human as They Sound: The Limits and Potentials of Musical Universality*. Chicago: University of Chicago Press.

Hoshino, Etsuko. (1996). The Feeling of Musical Mode and Its Emotional Character in a Melody. *Psychology of Music*, 24: 29–46.

Humble, P. N. (1993). Chess as an Artform. *British Journal of Aesthetics*, 33: 59–66.

——. (1995). The Aesthetics of Chess: A Reply to Ravilous. *British Journal of Aesthetics*, 35: 390–4.

Humphrey, N. K. (1976). The Social Function of Intellect. In P. P. G. Bateson and R. A. Hinde (eds), *Growing Points in Ethology*. Cambridge: Cambridge University Press, 303–17.

Huovinen, Erkki. (2008). Levels and Kinds of Listeners' Musical Understanding. *British Journal of Aesthetics*, 48: 315–37.

Huron, David. (2001). What is a Musical Feature? Forte's Analysis of Brahms's Opus 51, No. 1, Revisited. *Music Theory Online*, 7 (4).

Irvin, Sherri. (2003). *Work and Object: The Artist's Sanction in Contemporary Art*. Doctoral dissertation, Princeton University.

Iyer, Vijay S. (1998). *Microstructures of Feel, Macrostructures of Sound: Embodied Cognition in West African and African-American Musics*. Doctoral dissertation, University of California.

——. (2002). Embodied Mind, Situated Cognition, and Expressive Microtiming in African-American Music. *Music Perception*, 19: 387–414.

Jakobson, Roman. (1971). *Selected Writings*. The Hague: Mouton, Vol. 3.

Janata, Petr, and Grafton, Scott T. (2003). Swinging in the Brain: Shared Neural Substrates for Behaviors Related to Sequencing and Music. *Nature Neuroscience*, 6: 682–7.

Johnson, Mark, and Lakoff, George. (2003). *Metaphors We Live By*. Chicago: University of Chicago Press.

Judkins, Jennifer. (1997). The Aesthetics of Silence in Live Musical Performance. *Journal of Aesthetic Education*, 31 (3): 39–53.

Juslin, Patrik N. (2001). Communicating Emotion in Music Performance: A Review and Theoretical Framework. In P. N. Juslin and J. A. Sloboda (eds), *Music and Emotion: Theory and Research*. Oxford: Oxford University Press, 309–37.

Juslin, Patrik N., and Laukka, Petri. (2003). Communication of Emotion in Vocal Expression and Music Performance: Different Channels, Same Code? *Psychological Bulletin*, 129, 770–814.

Juslin, Patrik N., and Sloboda, John A. (eds). (2010). *Oxford Handbook of Music and Emotion: Theory, Research, Applications*. Oxford: Oxford University Press.

Juslin, Patrik N., and Västfjäll, Daniel. (2008a). Emotional Responses to Music: The Need to Consider Underlying Mechanisms. *Behavioural and Brain Sciences*, 31: 559–75.

Juslin, Patrik N., and Västfjäll, Daniel. (2008b). All Emotions are not Created Equal: Reaching beyond the Traditional Disputes. *Behavioral and Brain Sciences*, 31: 600–12.

Justus, Timothy, and Hutsler, Jeffrey J. (2005). Fundamental Issues in the Evolutionary Psychology of Music: Assessing Innateness and Domain Specificity. *Music Perception*, 23: 1–27.

Kania, Andrew. (2006). Making Tracks: The Ontology of Rock Music. *Journal of Aesthetics and Art Criticism*, 64: 401–14.

Karl, Gregory, and Robinson, Jenefer. (1995a). Levinson on Hope in *The Hebrides*. *Journal of Aesthetics and Art Criticism*, 53: 195–9.

Karl, Gregory, and Robinson, Jenefer. (1995b). Shostakovitch's Tenth Symphony and the Musical Expression of Cognitively Complex Emotions. *Journal of Aesthetic and Art Criticism*, 53: 401–15.

Keil, Frank C. (1994). The Birth and Nurturance of Concepts by Domains: The Origins of Concepts of Living Things. In L. A. Hirschfield and S. A. Gelman (eds), *Mapping the Mind: Domain Specificity in Cognition and Culture*. Cambridge: Cambridge University Press, 234–54.

Kenny, Anthony. (1963). *Action, Emotion, and Will*. London: Routledge & Kegan Paul.

Kerman, Joseph. (1985). *Musicology*. London: Fontana.

Kieran, Matthew. (1996). Incoherence and Musical Appreciation. *Journal of Aesthetic Education*, 30 (1): 39–49.

Kivy, Peter. (1987). How Music Moves. In P. Alperson (ed.), *What Is Music? An Introduction to the Philosophy of Music*. New York: Haven, 149–63.

——. (1988a). Orchestrating Platonism. In T. Anderberg, T. Nilstun, and I. Persson (eds), *Aesthetic Distinction*. Sweden: Lund University Press, 42–55.

——. (1988b). *Osmin's Rage: Philosophical Reflections on Opera*. Princeton: Princeton University Press.

——. (1989). *Sound Sentiment*. Philadelphia: Temple University Press.

——. (1990). *Music Alone: Philosophical Reflection on the Purely Musical Experience*. Ithaca: Cornell University Press.

——. (1992). Review of Cook's *Music, Imagination, and Culture*. *Journal of Aesthetics and Art Criticism*, 50: 76–9.

——. (1993). Auditor's Emotions: Contention, Concession and Compromise. *Journal of Aesthetics and Art Criticism*, 51: 1–12.

——. (1994). Armistice, But No Surrender: Davies on Kivy. *Journal of Aesthetics and Art Criticism*, 52: 236–7.

——. (1997). *Philosophies of Arts: An Essay in Differences*. New York: Cambridge University Press.

——. (1999). Feeling the Musical Emotions. *British Journal of Aesthetics*, 39: 1–13.

——. (2001). Music in Memory and *Music in the Moment*. In P. Kivy (ed.), *New Essays on Musical Understanding*. Oxford: Oxford University Press, 183–217.

——. (2003). Another Go at Musical Profundity: Stephen Davies and the Game of Chess. *British Journal of Aesthetics*, 43, 401–11.

——. (2006). Critical Study: *Deeper than Emotion*. *British Journal of Aesthetics*, 46: 287–311.

Koelsch, Stefan, and Siebel, Walter A. (2005). Towards a Neural Basis of Music Perception. *Trends in Cognitive Sciences*, 9: 578–84.

Koelsch, Stefan, Fritz, Thomas, Cramon, D. Yves v., Müller, Karsten, and Friederici, Angela D. (2006). Investigating Emotion with Music: An fMRI Study. *Human Brain Mapping*, 27: 239–50.

Krumhansl, Carol L. (1995). Music Psychology and Music Theory: Problems and Prospects. *Music Theory Spectrum*, 17: 53–80.

——. (1997). An Exploratory Study of Musical Emotions and Psychophysiology. *Canadian Journal of Experimental Psychology*, 51: 336–52.

——. (2002). Music: A Link Between Cognition and Emotion. *Current Directions in Psychological Research*, 11 (2): 45–50.

Krumhansl, Carol L., Sandell, Gregory J., and Sergeant, Desmond C. (1987). Tone Hierarchies and Mirror Forms in Serial Music. *Music Perception*, 5: 31–78.

Krumhansl, Carol L., Louhivuori, Jukka, Toiviainen, Pekka, Järvinen, Topi, and Eerola, Tuomas. (1999). Melodic Expectation in Finnish Spiritual Folk Hymns: Convergence of Statistical, Behavioural, and Computational Approaches. *Music Perception*, 17: 151–95.

Krumhansl, Carol L., Toivanen, Pekka, Eerola, Tuomas, Toivianen, Petri, Järvinen, Topi, and Louhivuori, Jukka. (2000). Cross-cultural Music Cognition: Cognitive Methodology Applied to North Sami Yoiks. *Cognition*, 76: 13–58.

Kurth, Ernst. (1991). *Ernst Kurth: Selected Writings*, ed. and trans. by L. A. Rothfarb. Cambridge: Cambridge University Press.

Lamarque, Peter. (1981). How Can We Fear and Pity Fictions? *British Journal of Aesthetics*, 21: 291–304.

——. (1996). *Fictional Points of View*. Ithaca: Cornell University Press.

Lamb, Roger. (1987). Objectless Emotions. *Philosophy and Phenomenological Research*, 48: 107–17.

Lamont, Alexandra, and Dibben, Nicola. (2001). Motivic Structure and the Perception of Similarity. *Music Perception*, 18: 245–74.

Langer, Susanne K. (1942). *Philosophy in a New Key*. Cambridge, MA: Harvard University Press.

Lazarus, Richard S. (1991). *Emotion and Adaptation*. New York: Oxford University Press.

Le Doux, Joseph. (1996). *The Emotional Brain*. New York: Simon and Schuster.

Lerdahl, Fred, and Jackendoff, Ray. (1983). *A Generative Theory of Tonal Music*. Cambridge, MA: MIT Press.
Levinson, Jerrold. (1990). *Music, Art, and Metaphysics*. Ithaca: Cornell University Press.
——. (1992). Musical Profundity Misplaced. *Journal of Aesthetics and Art Criticism*, 50: 58–60.
——. (1996a). *The Pleasures of Aesthetics*. Ithaca: Cornell University Press.
——. (1996b). Review of DeBellis's *Music and Conceptualization*. *Music Perception*, 14: 86–93.
——. (1997). *Music in the Moment*. Ithaca: Cornell University Press.
——. (1998). Evaluating Music. In P. Alperson (ed.), *Musical Worlds: New Directions in the Philosophy of Music*. University Park: Pennsylvania State University Press, 93–107.
——. (1999). Reply to Commentaries on *Music in the Moment*. *Music Perception*, 16: 485–94.
——. (2002). Sound, Gesture, Spatial Imagination, and the Expression of Emotion in Music. *European Review of Philosophy*, 5: 137–50.
——. (2006). Musical Expressiveness as Hearability-as-expression. In M. Kieran (ed.), *Contemporary Debates in Aesthetics and the Philosophy of Art*. Oxford: Blackwell, 192–204.
Levinson, Jerrold, and Alperson, Philip. (1991). What Is a Temporal Art? *Midwest Studies in Philosophy*, 16: 439–50.
London, Justin. (2004). *Hearing in Time*. Oxford: Oxford University Press.
Lyons, William. (1980). *Emotions*. Cambridge: Cambridge University Press.
McAdams, Stephen, and Matzkin, Daniel. (2001). Similarity, Invariance, and Musical Variation. *Annals of the New York Academy of Sciences*, 93: 62–76.
McAdoo, Nick. (1992). Can Art Ever Be Just About Itself? *Journal of Aesthetics and Art Criticism*, 50: 131–7.
——. (1997). Hearing Musical Works in their Entirety. *British Journal of Aesthetics*, 37: 66–74.
McDermott, Josh, and Hauser, Marc D. (2005). The Origins of Music: Innateness, Uniqueness, and Evolution. *Music Perception*, 23: 29–59.
McKay, Cory. (2002). *Emotion and Music: Inherent Responses and the Importance of Empirical Cross-cultural Research*. Course Paper, McGill University, Canada.
McNeil, William H. (1995). *Keeping Together in Time: Dance and Drill in Musical History*. Cambridge, MA: Harvard University Press.
Maconie, Robin. (2002). *The Second Sense*. Lanham: Scarecrow Press.
Madell, Geoffrey. (2002). *Philosophy, Music and Emotion*. Edinburgh: Edinburgh University Press.
Mark, Thomas Carson. (1980). On Works of Virtuosity. *Journal of Philosophy*, 77: 28–45.
——. (1981). Philosophy of Piano Playing: Reflections on the Concept of Performance. *Philosophy and Phenomenological Research*, 41: 299–324.
Marks, Lawrence E., Hammeal, Robin J., Bornstein, Marc H., and Smith, Linda B. (1987). Perceiving Similarity and Comprehending Metaphor. *Monographs of the Society for Research in Child Development*, Serial No. 215, (52): 1–102.
Matravers, Derek. (1998). *Art and Emotion*. Oxford: Clarendon Press.
Merriam, Alan P. (1964). *The Anthropology of Music*. Chicago: Northwestern University Press.
Meyer, Jürgen. (1978). *Acoustics and the Performance of Music*, trans. J. Bowsher and S. Westphal. Frankfurt am Main: Verlag Das Musikinstrument.
Meyer, Leonard B. (1956). *Emotion and Meaning in Music*. Chicago: University of Chicago Press.
——. (1961). On Rehearing Music. *Journal of the American Musicological Society*, 14: 257–67.
——. (1967). *Music, the Arts, and Ideas*. Chicago: University of Chicago Press.

Milinski, Manfred. (2003). Perfumes. In E. Voland and K. Grammer (eds), *Evolutionary Aesthetics*. Berlin: Springer Verlag, 325–39.

Milliman, Ronald E. (1982). Using Background Music to Affect the Behavior of Supermarket Shoppers. *Journal of Marketing*, 46 (3): 86–91.

——. (1986). The Influence of Background Music on the Behavior of Restaurant Patrons. *Journal of Consumer Research*, 13 (2): 286–9.

Narmour, Eugene. (1990). *The Analysis and Cognition of Basic Melodic Structures*. Chicago: Chicago University Press.

——. (1991). The Top-down and Bottom-up Systems of Musical Implication. *Music Perception*, 9: 1–26.

——. (1992). *The Analysis and Cognition of Melodic Complexity*. Chicago: University of Chicago Press.

Nattiez, Jean-Jacques. (1990). *Music and Discourse*, trans. C. Abbate. Princeton: Princeton University Press.

Neill, Alex. (1993). Fiction and the Emotions. *American Philosophical Quarterly*, 30: 1–13.

Nelson, Simon J. (2002). *Melodic Improvisation on a Twelve-bar Blues Model: An Investigation of Physical and Historical Aspects, and their Contribution to Performance*. Doctoral dissertation, City University of London.

Neubauer, John. (1986). *The Emancipation of Music from Language: Departure from Mimesis in Eighteenth-century Aesthetics*. New Haven: Yale University Press.

Neumann, Roland, and Strack, Fritz. (2000). 'Mood Contagion': the Automatic Transfer of Mood between Persons. *Journal of Personality and Social Psychology*, 79: 211–23.

North, Adrian C., and Hargreaves, David J. (1997). Music and Consumer Behaviour. In D. J. Hargreaves and A. C. North (eds), *The Social Psychology of Music*. Oxford: Oxford University Press, 268–89.

Nöth, Winfried. (1990). *Handbook of Semiotics*. Bloomington: Indiana University Press.

Nussbaum, Charles O. (2007). *The Musical Representation: Meaning, Ontology, and Emotion*. Cambridge, MA: MIT Press.

Patel, Aniruddh D. (2008a). *Music, Language and the Brain*. Oxford: Oxford University Press.

——. (2008b). A Neurobiological Strategy for Exploring Links between Emotion Recognition in Music and Speech. *Behavioral and Brain Sciences*, 31: 589–90.

Peacocke, Christopher. (2009a). The Perception of Music: Sources of Significance. *British Journal of Aesthetics*, 49: 257–75.

——. (2009b). Experience Metaphorically-As in Music Perception: Clarifications and Commitments. *British Journal of Aesthetics*, 49: 299–306.

Peretz, Isabelle, and Zatorre, Robert J. (2005). Brain Organization for Music Processing. *Annual Review of Psychology*, 56: 89–114.

Perrett, Roy W. (1999). Musical Unity and Sentential Unity. *British Journal of Aesthetics*, 39: 97–111.

Pinker, Steven. (1998). *How the Mind Works*. London: Penguin Books.

Plantinga, Carl. (1999). The Scene of Empathy and the Human Face on Film. In C. Plantinga and G. M. Smith (eds), *Passionate Views: Film, Cognition, and Emotion*. Baltimore: John Hopkins University Press, 239–55.

Platel, Herve, Price, Cathy, Baron, Jean-Claude, Wise, Richard, Lambert, Jany, Frackowiak, Richard S. J., Lechevalier, Bernard, and Eustache, Francis. (1997). The Structural Components of Music Perception: A Functional Anatomical Study. *Brain*, 120: 229–43.

Platel, Herve, Eustache, Francis, and Baron, Jean-Claude. (2004). The Cerebral Localization of Musical Perception and Musical Memory. In F. Clifford Rose (ed.), *Neurology of the Arts*. London: Imperial College Press, 175–90.

Plutchik, Robert. (1980). A General Psychoevolutionary Theory of Emotions. In R. Plutchik and H. Kellerman (eds), *Emotion: Theory, Research, and Experience*. Vol 1. Theories of emotion. New York: Academic Press, 3–33.

Price, Kingsley. (1992). Review of Kivy's *Music Alone*, *Philosophy of Music Education Newsletter*, 4 (1): 11–20.

Prinz, Jesse J. (2004). *Gut Reactions: A Perceptual Theory of Emotion*. Oxford: Oxford University Press.

Provine, Robert R. (1996). Laughter. *American Scientist*, 84 (January–February): 38–45.

Putman, Daniel A. (1989). Some Distinctions on the Role of Metaphor in Music. *Journal of Aesthetic Education*, 23 (2): 103–6.

Radford, Colin. (1975). How Can We Be Moved by the Fate of Anna Karenina? *Proceedings of the Aristotelian Society*, Supp. Vol. 49: 67–80.

——. (1989). Emotions and Music: A Reply to the Cognitivists. *Journal of Aesthetics and Art Criticism*, 47: 69–76.

——. (1991). Muddy Waters. *Journal of Aesthetics and Art Criticism*, 49: 247–52.

Raffman, Diana. (1993). *Language, Music, and Mind*. Cambridge, MA: MIT Press.

Ravilous, C. P. (1994). The Aesthetics of Chess and the Chess Problem. *British Journal of Aesthetics*, 34: 285–90.

Reeves, Byron, and Nass, Clifford. (1996). *The Media Equation: How People Treat Computers, Television, and News Media Like Real People and Places*. Cambridge: Cambridge University Press.

Reimer, Bennett. (1995). The Experience of Profundity in Music. *Journal of Aesthetic Education*, 29 (4): 1–21.

Repp, Bruno H. (1998). Variations on a Theme by Chopin: Relations Between Perception and Production of Timing in Music. *Journal of Experimental Psychology*, 24: 791–811.

——. (1999). Individual Differences in the Expressive Shaping of a Musical Phrase: The Opening of Chopin's Etude in E Major. In S. W. Yi (ed.), *Music, Mind, and Science*. Seoul: Seoul National University Press, 239–70.

——. (2000). The Timing Implications of Musical Structures. In D. Greer (ed.), *Musicology and Sister Disciplines*. Oxford: Oxford University Press, 60–70.

Reti, Rudolph. (1961). *The Thematic Process in Music*. London: Faber & Faber. First published 1951.

Ridley, Aaron. (1992). Review of Cook's *Music, Imagination, and Culture*. *British Journal of Aesthetics*, 32: 91–3.

——. (1995a). *Music, Value and the Passions*. Ithaca: Cornell University Press.

——. (1995b). Profundity in Music. In A. Neill and A. Ridley (eds), *Arguing About Art: Contemporary Philosophical Debates*. New York: McGraw-Hill, 260–70.

——. (1997). Review of DeBellis's *Music and Conceptualization*. *British Journal of Aesthetics*, 37: 187–9.

——. (2004). *The Philosophy of Music: Theme and Variations*. Edinburgh: Edinburgh University Press.

Risset, Jean-Claude, and Wessel, David L. (1999). Exploration of Timbre by Analysis and Synthesis. In D. Deutsch (ed.), *The Psychology of Music*, 2nd edn. San Diego: Academic Press, 113–69.

Robinson, Jenefer. (1998). The Expression and Arousal of Emotion in Music. In P. Alperson (ed.), *Musical Worlds: New Directions in the Philosophy of Music*. University Park: Pennsylvania State University Press, 13–22.

——. (2005). *Deeper than Reason: Emotion and Its Role in Literature, Music, and Art*. Oxford: Clarendon Press.

——. (2008). Do all Musical Emotions have the Music Itself as their Intentional Object? *Behavioral and Brain Sciences*, 31: 592–3.

Rosch, E. (1975). Cognitive Representations of Semantic Categories. *Journal of Experimental Psychology: General*, 104: 192–233.

Ross, Stephanie. (1985). Chance, Constraint, and Creativity: the Awfulness of Modern Music. *Journal of Aesthetic Education*, 19 (3): 21–35.

Rothstein, Pia, Malach, Rafael, Hadar, Ure, Graif, Moshe, and Hendler, Talma. (2001). Feeling of Features: Different Sensitivity to Emotion in High-order Visual Cortex and Amygdala. *Neuron*, 32: 747–57.

Schachter, Stanley, and Singer, Jerome E. (1962). Cognitive, Social, and Physiological Determinants of Emotional States. *Psychological Review*, 69: 379–99.

Schellenberg, E. Glenn. (1996). Expectancy in Melody: Tests of the Implication-realization Model. *Cognition*, 58: 75–125.

——. (1997). Simplifying the Implication-realization Model of Melodic Expectancy. *Music Perception*, 14: 295–318.

Schenker, Heinrich. (1925–30). *Das Meisterwerk in der Musik*. 3 Vols. Munich: Drei Masken Verlag.

Schmuckler, Mark A. (1999). Testing Models of Melodic Contour Similarity. *Music Perception*, 16: 295–326.

Schulkind, Matthew D., Posner, Rachel J., and Rubin, David C. (2003). Musical Features that Facilitate Melody Identification: How Do You Know It's 'Your' Song when They Finally Play It? *Music Perception*, 21: 217–49.

Scruton, Roger. (1974). *Art and Imagination*. London: Methuen.

——. (1983). Understanding Music. In R. Scruton (ed.), *The Aesthetic Understanding*. London: Methuen, 77–100.

——. (1987). Analytical Philosophy and the Meaning of Music. *Journal of Aesthetics and Art Criticism*, 46: 169–76.

——. (1997). *The Aesthetics of Music*. Oxford: Clarendon Press.

——. (2004). Musical Movement: A Reply to Budd. *British Journal of Aesthetics*, 44: 184–7.

Sharpe, R. A. (1982). Review of Kivy's *The Corded Shell*. *British Journal of Aesthetics*, 22: 81–2.

——. (1991). Review of Kivy's *Music Alone*. *British Journal of Aesthetics*, 31: 276–7.

——. (1993). What is the Object of Musical Analysis? *Music Review*, 54: 63–72.

——. (2000). *Music and Humanism: An Essay in the Aesthetics of Music*. Oxford: Oxford University Press.

——. (2004). *Philosophy of Music: An Introduction*. Chesham: Acumen.

Shatin, Leo. (1970). Alteration of Mood via Music: A Study of the Vectoring Effect. *Journal of Psychology*, 75: 81–6.

Shove, Patrick, and Repp, Bruno H. (1995). Musical Motion and Performance: Theoretical and Empirical. In J. Rink (ed.), *The Practice of Performance: Studies in Musical Interpretation*. Cambridge: Cambridge University Press, 55–83.

Simpson, Elisabeth A., Oliver, William T., and Fragaszy, Dorothy. (2008). Super-expressive Voices: Music to my Ears? *Behavioral and Brain Sciences*, 31: 596–7.

Small, Christopher. (1998). *Musicking: The Meanings of Performing and Listening*. Hanover: Wesleyan University Press.

Snowdon, Paul F. (2009). Peacocke on Musical Experience and Hearing Metaphorically-As. *British Journal of Aesthetics*, 49: 277–81.

Solomon, Robert C. (1976). *The Passions*. Garden City: Anchor.

——. (2003). Thoughts and Feelings: What is a 'Cognitive Theory' of the Emotions and does it Neglect Affectivity. In *Not Passion's Slave: Emotions and Choice*. Oxford: Oxford University Press, 178–94.

Solso, Robert L. (2003). *The Psychology of Art and the Evolution of the Conscious Brain*. Cambridge, MA: MIT Press.

Solso, Robert L., and McCarthy, Judith E. (1981). Prototype Formation for Faces: A Case of Pseudomemory. *British Journal of Psychology*, 72: 499–503.

Stecker, Robert. (1997). *Artworks: Definition, Meaning, Value*. University Park: Pennsylvania State University Press.

——. (1999). Davies on the Musical Expression of Emotion. *British Journal of Aesthetics*, 39: 273–81.

Steinbeis, Nikolaus, and Koelsch, Stefan. (2009). Understanding the Intentions behind Man-Made Products Elicits Neural Activity in Areas Dedicated to Mental State Attribution. *Cerebral Cortex*, 19 (March): 619–23.

Sunberg, Johan. (1977). The Acoustics of the Singing Voice. *Scientific American*, 236: 82–91.

Tanner, Michael. (1985). Understanding Music. *Proceedings of the Aristotelian Society*, Supp. Vol. 59: 215–32.

Tarr, Michael J., and Bülthoff, Heinrich H. (1998). Image-based Object Recognition in Man, Monkey and Machine. *Cognition*, 67: 1–20.

Thom, Paul. (1993). *For an Audience: A Philosophy of the Performing Arts*. Philadelphia: Temple University Press.

Thompson, William Forde, and Balkwill, Laura-Lee. (2010). Cross-cultural Similarities. In P. N. Juslin and John Sloboda (eds), *Oxford Handbook of Music and Emotion: Theory, Research, Applications*. Oxford: Oxford University Press, 755–88.

Thornhill Randy, and Gangestad, Steven W. (2003). Do Women have Evolved Adaptation for Extra-Pair Copulation? In E. Voland and K. Grammer (eds), *Evolutionary Aesthetics*. Berlin: Springer Verlag, 342–60.

Tilghman, Benjamin R. (1984). *But Is It Art?* Oxford: Blackwell.

Trainor, Laurel J., and Trehub, Sandra E. (1994). Key Membership and Implied Harmony in Western Tonal Music: Developmental Perspectives. *Perception and Psychophysics*, 56: 125–32.

Trehub, Sandra E. (2000). Human Processing Predispositions and Musical Universals. In N. L. Wallin, B. Merjker, and S. Brown (eds), *The Origins of Music*. Cambridge, MA: MIT Press, 427–48.

——. (2003). The Developmental Origins of Musicality. *Nature Neuroscience*, 6: 669–73.

Trehub, Sandra E., Thorpe, Leigh A., and Trainor, Laurel J. (1990). Infants' Perception of Good and Bad Melodies. *Psychomusicology*, 9: 5–19.

Trehub, Sandra E., Unyk, Anna M. and Trainor, Laurel J. (1993a). Adults Identify Infant-directed Music across Cultures. *Infant Behavior and Development*, 16(2): 193–211.

Trehub, Sandra E., Unyk, Anna M., and Trainor, Laurel J. (1993b). Maternal Singing in Cross-cultural Perspective. *Infant Behavior and Development*, 16 (3): 285–95.

Trivedi, Saam. (2003a). The Funerary Sadness of Mahler's Music. In M. Kieran and D. McIver Lopes (eds), *Imagination, Philosophy, and the Arts*. London: Routledge, 259–71.

———. (2003b). Review of Davies's *Themes in the Philosophy of Music*, *Journal of Aesthetic Education*, 37 (3): 108–12.

———. (2008). Metaphors and Musical Expressiveness. In K. Stock and K. Thomson-Jones (eds), *New Waves in Aesthetics*. New York: Palgrave Macmillan, 41–57.

Troeger, Richard. (2003). *Playing Bach on the Keyboard: A Practical Guide*. Pompton Plains: Amadeus Press.

Unyk, Anna M., Trehub, Sandra E. Trainor, Laurel J., and Schellenberg, E. Glenn. (1992). Lullabies and Simplicity: A Cross-cultural Perspective. *Psychology of Music*, 20: 15–28.

Vanderveer, N. J. (1979). Ecological Acoustics: Human Perception of Environmental Sounds. *Dissertation Abstracts International*, 40: 4543B.

Vines, Bradley W., Krumhansl, Carol L., Wanderly, Marcelo M., Dalca, Ioana M., and Levitin, Daniel J. (2005). Dimensions of Emotion in Expressive Musical Performance. *Annals of the New York Academy of Sciences*, 1060: 462–66.

Walker, Robert. (1996). Open Peer Commentary: Can We Understand the Music of Another Culture? *Psychology of Music*, 24: 103–30.

Walton, Kendall L. (1970). Categories of Art. *Philosophical Review*, 79: 334–67.

———. (1988). What is Abstract about the Art of Music? *Journal of Aesthetics and Art Criticism*, 46: 351–64.

———. (1990). *Mimesis as Make-Believe: On the Foundations of the Representational Arts*. Cambridge, MA: Harvard University Press.

———. (1997). Spelunking, Simulation, and Slime: On Being Moved by Fiction. In M. Hjort and S. Laver (eds), *Emotion and the Arts*. Oxford: Oxford University Press, 37–49.

Webster, William E. (1974). A Theory of the Compositional Work of Music. *Journal of Aesthetics and Art Criticism*, 33: 59–66.

Welker, Robert L. (1982). Abstraction of Themes from Melodic Variations. *Journal of Experimental Psychology: Human Perception and Performance*, 8: 435–47.

Wheeler, Ladd. (1966). Toward a Theory of Behavioral Contagion. *Psychological Review*, 73: 179–92.

White, David A. (1992). Toward a Theory of Profundity in Music. *Journal of Aesthetics and Art Criticism*, 50: 23–34.

Wilson, J. P. R. (1972). *Emotion and Object*. Cambridge: Cambridge University Press.

Windsor, W. Luke. (2000). Through and Around the Acousmatic: The Interpretation of Electroacoustic Sounds. In S. Emmerson (ed.), *Music, Electronic Media and Culture*. Aldershot: Ashgate, 7–25.

Wiseman, Ari, and Zilczer, Judith. (eds). (2005). *Visual Music: Synaesthesia in Art and Music since 1900*. London: Thames & Hudson.

Wittgenstein, Ludwig. (1967). *Philosophical Investigations*, trans. G. E. M. Anscombe. Oxford: Blackwell.

Wolterstorff, Nicholas. (1975). Toward an Ontology of Artworks. *Noûs*, 9: 115–42.

Worth, Sarah E. (2000). Understanding the Objects of Music. *Journal of Aesthetic Education*, 34 (1): 102–7.

Wright, Anthony A., Riviera, Jacquelyne J., Hulse, Stewart H., Shyan, Melissa, and Neiworth, Julie J. (2000). Music Perception and Octave Generalization in Rhesus Monkeys. *Journal of Experimental Psychology: General*, 129: 291–307.

Zangwill, Nick. (2007). Music, Metaphor, and Emotion. *Journal of Aesthetics and Art Criticism*, 65: 391–400.

Zatorre, Robert J. and Halpern, Andrea R. (2005). Mental Concerts: Musical Imagery and Auditory Cortex. *Neuron*, 47: 9–12.

Zbikowski, Lawrence M. (2002). *Conceptualizing Music: Cognitive Structure, Theory, and Analysis*. Oxford: Oxford University Press.

Zeki, Semir. (1999). Art and the Brain. *Journal of Consciousness Studies: Art and the Brain*, 6: 76–96.

Zemach, Eddy M. (2002). The Role of Meaning in Music. *British Journal of Aesthetics*, 42: 169–78.

Zentner, Marcel R., and Kagan, Jerome. (1996). Perception of Music by Infants. *Nature*, 383: 29.

Index

Adelmann, Pamela K. 62 n. 19
'affect program' emotions 16, 34–5, 37–9, 60–1
Aldrich, Putnam 107
Alperson, Philip 72, 152 n. 3
Ambady, Nalini 35 n. 1
analysis of music 4, 120–6
   and testability of analytic hypotheses 125–6
   understanding afforded by 78–9, 81, 124
   see also hearability of musical relationships
Apel, Willi 66, 152
appearance emotionalism 2, 8–17, 19–20, 26–7, 31–2, 37–8, 57, 68
   see also emotion characteristics in appearances
Arom, Simha 155, 171
arousal theory of musical expressiveness 47, 54 n. 9, 67
artworks
   singular versus multiple 184–5
   versions of 184–5
   see also works of music
Astaire, Fred 118
authenticity in performance 4, 69, 106–9, 131–2, 176
   see also interpretation in performance

Bach, Johann Sebastian 66, 92 n. 7, 177 n. 2, 188–9, 199
Bach, Kent 26 n. 12
   Art of Fugue 95, 122, 153, 164, 180, 183 n. 10, 198
   Brandenburg Concerto No. 5 107
   Musical Offering 156
   Violin Concerto in E 164
   Well-tempered Clavier 82, 164, 198
Bacharach, Burt
   'Raindrops keep falling on my Head' 158
Baily, John 170 n. 12
Balinese dance and music 89, 136–7, 181
Balkwill, Laura-Lee 36, 40 n. 9, 42, 44, 45
Barber, Samuel
   Adagio 44
Barsalou, Lawrence. W. 157
Bartlett, Dale L. 57
Bartók, Béla 6, 172–3
   Divertimento 115
   Music for Strings, Percussion, and Celesta 196, 198–9
Beaumarchais, Pierre de 147
Beethoven, Ludwig van 6, 66, 99, 131, 192
   Fidelio 141–2

Leonore Overture No. 3 115
Piano Sonata No. 29, 'Hammerklavier' 168–70, 175 n. 17
Symphony No. 3, 'Eroica' 1, 14, 130, 196–9
Symphony No. 5 91, 184–5, 190
Symphony No. 6 112
Symphony No. 9 121, 123, 154
Benamou, Marc 42
Benucci, Francesco 142–3
Benzon, William 171 n. 13
Berg, Alban
   Lulu 122
Bigand, Emmanuel 156
Bird, John 90
Blacking, John 170 n. 12
Boulez, Pierre 115
Brahms, Johannes 83
Bransford, John D. 157 n. 12
Bregman, Albert S. 156, 158, 162, 170 n. 11, 171
Brennan, Teresa 62
Brophy, Brigid 146 n. 5
Brown, Lee B. 136 n. 4
Brown, Matthew 124–6
Bruckner, Anton
   Symphony No. 1 178
Bruner, Gordon C. 63 n.
Budd, Malcolm 9, 23 n. 5, 25 ns 10, 11, 72, 101 n. 16, 191
   on whether music is described metaphorically 27–9, 35 n. 3
Bujold, Pascal 170
Bülthoff, Heinrich H. 151 n. 1
Bunt, Leslie 63 n.
Byrne, Donald 192–3

Cacioppo, John T. 15, 56, 61–2
Cage, John
   4′33″ 89 n. 2, 164
Capablanca, Raoul 193–4, 195 n. 4
Capurso, A. A. 63 n.
Carlson, John G. 59 n.
Carroll, Noël 50
Cavell, Stanley 79, 93 n. 10
chess 6, 192–5
Chopin, Frédéric 131, 178
Clarke, Eric F. 154 n. 8, 170, 171 n. 15
Clarke, Jeremiah 110
Cleeremans, Axel 117 n. 35
Cochrane, Tom 64 n. 26
Cocker, Joe 182

Cogan, Robert 161 n. 1
cognitive theory of the emotions 2, 15–17, 47–51, 54–6
Coker, Wilson 72, 74, 76
color
  in music 6, 160–3, 165, 171–3, 176
  in visual art 5, 163–4, 176
  see also ontology of musical works
composer's understanding of music 127–8
composing 4, 122–3, 126–7, 199
  and Mozart 142, 144–7, 150
  as involving expression of emotion 13, 19
Conard, Nicholas J. 167 n. 10
concatenationism 3, 78, 81, 96–9, 120
Cone, Edward T. 141–2
Cook, Nicholas 96 n., 124, 153
Cooke, Deryck 180
Coplan, Amy 57, 61 n. 17
Cramer, Alfred 165
Critchley, Macdonald 161 n. 2
critical interpretation of music; *see* interpretation by critics
Cross, Ian 170 n. 12, 171
cross-cultural studies of music's expressiveness; *see* expression of emotion in music
Cumming, Naomi 125
Currie, Gregory 184
Cytowic, Richard E. 161 n. 2

Dahlhaus, Carl 75
Darrow, Alice-Ann 43–4
Darwin, Charles 49
Davidson, Jane W. 171
Davies, John Booth 156
DeBellis, Mark 3, 100–1, 103–4, 120, 121 ns 37, 38, 125
Debussy, Claude 183
Decety, Jean 61 n. 17
Delius, Frederick 90
Dempster, Douglas 104 n. 21, 124–6
Dennett, Daniel C. 31
DeNora, Tia 19
Derain, André 163
Deutsch, Diana 156
Deutsch, Otto Erich 145, 177
Dibben, Nicola 158, 170
Dodd, Julian 160 n.
  on timbral sonicism 168–75
Dowling, W. Jay 153, 155–6, 158, 161 n. 1
Dreyfus, Hubert L. 118
Dreyfus, Stuart E. 118
Dufay, Guillaume
  Missa l'homme armé 122

Ekman, Paul 16, 34, 61
Elfenbein, Hilary Anger 35 n. 1

Ellis, Nick C. 117 n. 34
emotional contagion
  house décor-to-person 57, 62
  music-to-listener 2, 15, 43, 47, 56–60, 62–5, 69
    attentional versus non-attentional 3, 52–3, 56–7, 60, 63–4, 138
    as counterexample to cognitive theory of the emotions 2, 15–16, 48–9, 51–2, 55–6
    denied as an effect of listening 15–16, 54
    as involving objectless response 15, 51–2, 55–6
    as non-rational 51–2, 55–6
  person-to-person 15, 47–8, 56–7, 61–2, 65
  weather-to-person 58
emotional response to music
  mirroring response; *see* emotional contagion
emotion characteristics in appearances
  of dogs 26, 57
  of music 2, 10–11, 26–7, 37–8, 68
  of people 1, 10–12, 25, 38
  of trees 2, 10, 20
  see also appearance emotionalism
Escot, Pozzi 161 n. 1
Evans, Paul 54 n. 10
expression of composer's emotions in music 13, 19, 23, 58, 66–7
  see also expression theory
expression of emotion in music 165
  as involving association 7, 44
  as limited in the range of emotions presented 11, 13–14, 35, 37
  as literal 2, 8, 11–12, 23, 25, 33, 35–6, 63, 68
  as metaphoric 1, 12, 21–2, 31–2, 35
  as not physiognomic 9, 37
  as objective 11, 23, 33, 68
  as response-dependent 8–10, 32–3, 76–7
  as sui generis 24–5
  cross-cultural studies of 2, 36, 41–6
  see also appearance emotionalism; arousal theory of musical expressiveness; expression of composer's emotions in music; hypothetical emotionalism; metaphoric descriptions of music; prosodic theory of musical expressiveness
expression theory 66–7
  see also expression of composer's emotions in music

face inversion effect 152
Farinelli 136
Feagin, Susan 50
Ferguson, Donald 22 n. 2
Fernald, Anne 41
Fischer, Bobbie 192–4, 195 n. 4
Fisher, John A. 162 n., 182 n. 8
formalism
  see ontology of musical works

Fragaszy, Dorothy 64 n. 25
Francès, Robert 165
Franklin, Nancy 29 n. 21
Franks, Jeffery J. 157 n. 12
French, Robert M. 117 n. 35
Fritz, Thomas 42–4
functional music 53, 138

Gabrieli, Giovanni 90
Gabrielsson, Alf 11, 15, 35 n. 2, 54 n. 10
Gangestad, Steven W. 62 n. 20
Garland, Joe 182 n. 9
Gaut, Berys 127 n.
Gershwin, George 182 n. 9
Gibson, James J. 157, 171 n. 15, 172
Gjerdingen, Robert O. 152 n. 5
Godlovitch, Stan 93 n. 9, 106 n., 110 n. 28, 167–8, 172
Goldie, Peter 50, 61 n. 17
Goldman, Alan H. 80, 97, 191, 195 n. 5
Goodman, Benny 182 n. 9
Goodman, Nelson 12, 22
Gracyk, Theodore A. 94 n., 106 n., 182 n. 8
Grainger, Percy 164, 183 n. 11
Grammer, Karl 64 n. 23
Grant, James 27 n. 16
Green, Lucy 72
Gregory, Andrew H. 43–5
Grieg, Edvard 90
Griffiths, Paul 50 n., 59 n.
Gurney, Edmund 96

Halpern, Andrea R. 170
Hamilton, Andy 164 n. 6
Handel, Stephen 161 n. 1, 171 n. 15
Hargreaves, David J. 63 n.
Harwood, Dane L. 155–6, 158, 161 n. 1
Hatfield, Elaine 15, 56, 59 n., 60–2
Hauser, Marc D. 40, 44
Haydn, Franz Joseph 95, 131, 145–6, 177 n. 2
  Symphony No. 94, 'Surprise' 37
hearability of musical relationships 4, 121–6, 153–4, 199
  see also analysis of music
Hendrix, Jimi 91, 154
Herzog, Patricia 190 n. 3
Hicks, Michael 91 n.
Higgins, Kathleen Marie 83, 95 n., 139, 161 n. 2, 171 n. 13
  on musical universals 29 n. 20, 36, 155
Hindemith, Paul
  Ludus Tonalis 153
historically informed performance; *see* authenticity in performance
Hodges, Sara D. 61 n. 17
homonymy 2, 29, 35
Honegger, Arthur 165 n.

Hoshino, Etsuko 44–5
Humble, P. N. 195 n. 6
Humphrey, N. K. 154
Huovinen, Erkki 105 n. 23
Huron, David 158
Hutsler, Jeffrey J. 40
hypothetical emotionalism 1, 16–19, 24, 54–5, 58, 68, 80
hypothetical persona in music; *see* hypothetical emotionalism

ineffability of musical meaning
  see meaning in music
infant-directed speech
  see Motherese
interpretation by critics 4
interpretation in performance 4, 108, 110–15
  as creative 69, 109–10, 180
  by composers of own works 4–5, 111, 128, 180
  compared with descriptive interpretations 115–16
  instrumentation as aspect of 6, 175
  see also authenticity in performance; interpretation versions
interpretation versions 181–2
  see also interpretation in performance; works of music
Irvin, Sherri 164 n. 5
Iyer, Vijay S. 170 n. 12

Jackendoff, Ray 121 n. 37, 124–5, 156
Jackson, Philip L. 61 n. 17
Jakobson, Roman 72
jazz 5, 132
Johnson, Mark 29 n. 21
Josquin des Prez
  Missa Hercules Dux Ferrarie 122
Judkins, Jennifer 89 n. 2
Juslin, Patrik N. 9, 26 ns 13, 14, 31, 35 ns 1, 2, 39, 51–2
  on music-to-listener emotional contagion 63, 64 n. 25
  see also prosodic theory of musical expressiveness
Justus, Timothy 40

Kagan, Jerome 40 n. 9
Kania, Andrew 175 n. 18
Karl, Gregory 17, 105 n. 22
Keil, Frank C. 154
Kennedy, Gary Neill 164
Kenny, Anthony 48
Kerman, Joseph 119–20
Kieran, Matthew 91 n.
Kivy, Peter 31, 53 n., 58, 71, 93 n. 9, 96 n., 97 n., 101 n. 16, 104 ns 20, 21, 105 n. 22, 129, 140

Kivy, Peter (cont.)
  as formalist about music ontology 164
  denying sad music makes people feel sad
    15–16, 54
  on analysis of music 121–3, 125
  on profundity in music 188–92, 194–5, 198
know-how 116–18
Koelsch, Stefan 31, 64 n. 25, 171 n. 14
Krumhansl, Carol L. 35 n. 2, 42, 44, 54 n. 10,
    57, 153 n.
Kurth, Ernst 76

Lakoff, George 29 n. 21
Lamarque, Peter 50
Lamb, Roger 50
Lamont, Alexandra 158
Langer, Susanne K. 9, 130, 190 n. 3
Laukka, Petri 26 n. 13, 31, 35 n. 1, 39, 64 n. 25
Lazarus, Richard S. 50 n.
Le Doux, Joseph. 50 n.
Lennon, John 126
Leonardo 184
Lerdahl, Fred 121 n. 37, 124–5, 156
Levinson, Jerrold 3, 80, 101 n. 16, 110 n. 26–7,
    116, 129, 132, 152 n. 3, 166, 167 n. 9
  on concatenationism 78, 81, 96–9, 120
  on hypothetical emotionalism 17–18, 24 n. 8,
    54, 68
  on ontology of musical works 93 n. 9, 165,
    173 n.
  on profundity in music 189, 191–2
  on understanding music 77–8, 81
listener's understanding of music 3, 8, 19, 73–8,
    88–96, 114, 129, 171
  as historically relativized 5, 68, 93, 131–2
  does not require ear training 3, 92, 100–5
  does not require technical knowledge 92–3,
    95, 100–5, 130
  goes beyond moment-to-moment
    listening 3, 78, 81, 96–9
  see also meaning in music; re-hearing music
Liszt, Franz 6, 184–6
literary translations 111–12
  compared to musical transcriptions and
    versions 185–7
  see also transcriptions; works of music
Livingston, Paisley 127 n.
London, Justin 171 n. 13
lullabies 41
Lyons, William 48, 50

McAdams, Stephen 158
McAdoo, Nick 97 n., 190 n. 2
McCarthy, Judith E. 157 n. 12
McCartney, Paul 126
McDermott, Josh 40, 44
Machaut, Guillaume de

'My end is my beginning' 152
McKay, Cory 45 n.
McKeown-Green, Jonathan 154 n. 9
McNeil, William H. 171 n. 13
Maconie, Robin 102 n., 152, n. 4, 158
Madell, Geoffrey 16, 53 n.
Mahler, Gustav 5, 92 n. 7, 95, 108
  Symphony No. 1 154
  Symphony No. 5 14, 51
  Symphony No. 10 177, 180
Mark, Thomas Carson 93 n. 9, 111, 169
Marks, Lawrence E. 161 n. 2
Marshall, Frank J. 193–4
Matravers, Derek 10
Matzkin, Daniel 158
meaning in music
  as contrasted with linguistic meaning 37,
    71–4
  contingent association as 51, 82
  experiential formal meaning 3, 75–81, 97–105
  formal meaning 3, 72–5, 87, 99
  ineffability of 5, 14, 77–8, 99–101, 129–31, 190
  meaning-for-the-subject 3, 81–3, 139
  meaning-for-us 3, 83–7
  see also analysis of music;
melodies, recognition of 3, 8, 89, 91–2, 95–9,
    104, 129–30
  in inversion or retrograde 5, 152–4, 196
  when transformed 154–9
Mendelssohn, Felix 130, 165 n.
Merriam, Alan P. 161 n. 2
Messiaen, Olivier 161 n. 2
metaphoric descriptions of music 11, 32
  musical animation as metaphoric 30–1
  musical expressiveness as metaphoric 12, 21,
    27, 31–2, 36
    denial of this view 25–7, 36, 63
  musical spatial descriptions as metaphoric
    27–30
    denial of this view 31–3, 63
Meyer, Jürgen 161 n. 1
Meyer, Leonard B. 72–3, 76, 92 n. 6, 136 n. 3,
    156
Milinski, Manfred 62 n. 20
Milliman, Ronald E. 63 n.
mirroring response to music's expressiveness; see
    musical contagion
moment-to-moment music appreciation
    see concatenationism
Monet, Claude 163
Monteux, Pierre 105
moods 16, 49–50, 63
Morley, Iain 171
Motherese 41
movement in music 10
Mozart, Wolfgang Amadeus 5, 66, 76, 122, 131,
    152, 172–3

INDEX 219

Abduction from the Seraglio 141–2, 144
Così fan tutte 6, 140–50
Don Giovanni 140, 142, 144–50, 179
Idomeneo 144–5
Piano Concerto K. 451 178
Piano Concerto K. 453 177
Requiem 180
Symphony No. 40 190
Symphony No. 41, 'Jupiter' 95
The Impressario 140, 143
The Marriage of Figaro 140, 142, 143 n., 144–50
musical universals; *see* universals in music
Mussorgsky, Modest 184 n.

Narmour, Eugene 124–5, 156, 157 n. 10
Nass, Clifford 31
Nattiez, Jean-Jacques 72
Neill, Alex 50
Nelson, Simon J. 170 n. 12
neonates and music 40
Neubauer, John 9
Neumann, Roland 64 n. 25
Nono, Luigi 90
North, Adrian C. 63 n.
notation of music 4, 93–4, 167–8
   as work prescriptions 69, 106, 180
   interpretation of 106–7
   underdetermine details of performances 69, 112, 180–1
Nöth, Winfried 72
Nussbaum, Charles O. 31

Oliver, William T. 64 n. 25
ontology of musical works 175–6, 178, 181
   as (sometimes) requiring use of the specified instruments 6, 166, 174–5
   formalism 93 n. 9, 164
      denial of this view 165–6, 175–6
   timbral sonicism 160, 166, 168–9
      denial of this view 167, 169–75
   see also artworks; transcriptions; works of music

Patel, Aniruddh D. 29, 40, 64 n. 25
Pavlicevic, Mercédès 63 n.
Peacocke, Christopher 22–3
Peirce, C. S. 72
Peretz, Isabelle 157 n. 13
performance 112–13, 167, 170
   as modeled on quotation 4, 66–7, 111
   as modeled on translation 111–12
   as practical know-how 4, 68, 70, 118–20
   expressiveness in 3
      as involving feeling or simulated feeling 66–7, 70
      as playing the notes 68–9
      subtleties controlled by performer 69–70

interpretation always involved in 4–5, 110–13
live versus recording 115, 137–8
   see also authenticity in performance; interpretation in performance; know-how
performer's understanding of music 4, 68–70, 105–20
Perrett, Roy W. 97 n.
personal identity and music 5, 80, 134–6
Philidor, François-André Danican 195
Pinker, Steven 151 n. 1
Plantinga, Carl 57
Platel, Herve 157 n. 13
pleasure in enjoyment of music 5, 84, 95, 132–5
   see also value of music
Plutchik, Robert 50 n.
polysemy 2, 26, 29–33, 35–6
Ponte, Lorenzo da 145, 147
Presley, Elvis 91
Price, Kingsley 104 n. 21
Prinz, Jesse J. 59 n.
profundity in music 6, 188–92, 195–9
prosodic theory of musical expressiveness 9, 26, 39–40
Provine, Robert R. 48
Puccini, Giacomo
   La Bohème 49
Purcell, Henry 110
Putman, Daniel A. 22 n. 2

Radford, Colin 50, 53 n., 54
Raffman, Diana 99–100, 124
Rapson, Richard L. 15, 56, 61–2
Ravel, Maurice 184 n.
Ravilous, C. P. 195 n. 6
Reeves, Byron 31
Reger, Max 82
re-hearing music 5, 94 136–7
Reimer, Bennett 189 n.
Repp, Bruno H. 109, 171 n. 15
Reti, Rudolph 121, 123
Ridley, Aaron 24 n. 8, 80 n. 2, 88 n. 1, 96 n., 101 n. 17, 188 n. 1
Risset, Jean-Claude 161 n. 1
Robinson, Jenefer 17–18, 24 n. 8, 52 n. 6, 54, 105 n. 22
   on music-to-listener emotional contagion 56–60
rock music 5, 132
Rodgers, Richard
   'Climb Ev'ry Mountain' 154, 156
Rogers, Ginger 118
Rosch, E. 157
Ross, Stephanie 93 n. 10
Rothstein, Pia 152

Schachter, Stanley 59–60
Schellenberg, E. Glenn 44, 155–6

Schenker, Heinrich 121, 123–5
Schmuckler, Mark A. 158
Schoenberg, Arnold 82, 122, 153, 165–6
Schubert, Emery 54 n. 10
Schubert, Franz 167, 172, 177
Schulkind, Matthew D. 157 n. 13, 159
Scriabin, Alexander 161 n. 2
Scruton, Roger 18, 25 n. 11, 33, 75–6, 79, 92 n. 7, 130
  as formalist about music ontology 93 n. 9, 164
  on analysis of music 121–3, 125
  on musical expressiveness as metaphoric 12, 21, 25 n. 10, 27, 35 n. 3
  on musical spatial terms as metaphoric 27–8, 30–1
Seurat, Georges 163
Shaffer, Peter 146 n. 6
Sharpe, R. A. 25 n. 11, 92 n. 7, 93 n. 10, 95 n., 96 n., 104 n. 21, 124, 134–5, 191
Shatin, Leo 63 n.
Shostakovitch, Dmitri
  Twenty-four Preludes and Fugues, Op. 87 153
Shove, Patrick 171 n. 15
Siebel, Walter A. 171 n. 14
Simpson, Elisabeth A. 64 n. 25
Singer, Jerome E. 59
Sloboda, John A. 35 n. 2
Small, Christopher 76
Snowdon, Paul F. 23 n. 5
Solomon, Robert C. 48, 49 n., 50
Solso, Robert L. 152, 157 n. 12
Stecker, Robert 12, 26 n. 15, 132, 134
Steinbeis, Nikolaus 31
Stockhausen, Karlheinz
  Grüppen für drei Orchester 90
Strack, Fritz 64 n. 25
Strauss, Richard 82
Stravinsky, Igor
  Firebird 179, 183
  Jeu de Cartes 89
  Les Noces 179
  Petrushka 179, 183
  The Rite of Spring 183
Sunberg, Johan 162

Tanner, Michael 91 n., 101 n. 16
Tarr, Michael J. 151 n. 1
Tchaikovsky, Piotr 90, 183 n. 11, 190
Thom, Paul 106 n., 110 n. 28
Thompson, William Forde 36, 40 n. 9, 42, 44–5
Thornhill Randy 62 n. 20
Tilghman, Benjamin R. 25 n. 11
timbral sonicism; *see* ontology of musical works
timbre
  see color
Tolstoy, Leo 185–6
Trainor, Laurel J. 40 n. 9

transcriptions 6, 83, 127, 164–6, 178, 182–7
  see also ontology of musical works; works of music
translations
  see literary translations
Trehub, Sandra E. 40 n. 9, 41, 153 n.
Trivedi, Saam 21, 31, 35 n. 3
Troeger, Richard 107
Tversky, Barbara 29 n. 21

understanding music; *see* analysis of music; composer's understanding of music; composing; listener's understanding of music; meaning in music; performance; performer's understanding of music; profundity in music
unfinished musical works 177
  see also ontology of musical works
universals in music 29, 36, 40–2, 155
Unyk, Anna M. 41

value of music 71, 79–80, 85–7, 95 n. 12, 105, 113, 132, 134, 139, 191, 195
  see also pleasure in enjoyment of music; profundity in music
Vanderveer, N. J. 171 n. 15, 172
Van Gogh, Vincent 163
Varèse, Edgard 165
Varney, Nicholas 43–5
Västfjäll, Daniel 26 n. 13, 31, 51–2, 63, 64 n. 25
Vines, Bradley W. 171
Vivaldi, Antonio
  The Four Seasons, 'Spring' 43–4

Wagner, Richard 82, 157
Walker, Robert 36 n.
Walton, Kendall L. 24 n. 8, 50, 68, 166
Webern, Anton 115, 165
  Symphony, Op. 21 153
Webster, William E. 164
Welker, Robert L. 157 n. 12
Wessel, David L. 161 n. 1
Wheeler, Ladd 61 n. 17
White, David A. 191–2
Wilson, J. P. R. 51 n. 5
Windsor, W. Luke 171 n. 15, 172
Wiseman, Ari 161 n. 2
Wittgenstein, Ludwig 25 n. 11, 54, 98
Wolterstorff, Nicholas 165
works of music
  completion of 177–8
  drafts of 179
  unfinished 177
  versions of 6, 178–81
    compared to interpretation versions 181–2
    compared to literary translations 185–7
    compared to transcriptions 182–4
  see also ontology of musical works

Worth, Sarah E. 54
Wright, Anthony A. 153 n.

Zajonc, R. B. 62 n. 19
Zangwill, Nick 21, 25 n. 10, 27, 30–1, 33, 35 n. 3
Zatorre, Robert J. 157 n. 13, 170

Zbikowski, Lawrence M. 157
Zeki, Semir 163 n.
Zemach, Eddy M. 92 n. 7
Zentner, Marcel R. 40 n. 9
Zilczer, Judith 161 n. 2